*Music, Authorship, and the Book
in the First Century of Print*

The publisher gratefully acknowledges the generous support
of the Music Endowment Fund of the
University of California Press Foundation.

Music, Authorship, and the Book in the First Century of Print

KATE VAN ORDEN

University of California Press

BERKELEY   LOS ANGELES   LONDON

University of California Press, one of the most distinguished university presses in the United States, enriches lives around the world by advancing scholarship in the humanities, social sciences, and natural sciences. Its activities are supported by the UC Press Foundation and by philanthropic contributions from individuals and institutions. For more information, visit www.ucpress.edu.

University of California Press
Berkeley and Los Angeles, California

University of California Press, Ltd.
London, England

Library of Congress Cataloging-in-Publication Data

van Orden, Kate.
    Music, authorship, and the book in the first century of print /
Kate van Orden.
        pages cm
    Includes bibliographical references and index.
    ISBN 978-0-520-27650-5 (hardback)
    1. Music printing—History—16th century.   2. Music publishing—
History—16th century.   3. Music—16th century—History and
criticism.   I. Title.
    ML112.V36 2013
    070.5'79409031—dc23

                                                        2013035478

23   22   21   20   19   18   17   16   15   14
10   9   8   7   6   5   4   3   2   1

To Howard and Martha, for everything

Contents

List of Illustrations   ix
Acknowledgments   xi

INTRODUCTION   1
What Is an Author?   3
Partbooks, Choirbooks, and Beyond   6
The Cultures of Print   12
From Mass to Chanson   15

1. THE WORLD OF BOOKS   19
Anthologies and Anonyms   19
The Names of Authors   22

2. MUSIC BOOKS AND THEIR AUTHORS   30
Editors and Craftsmen   30
Choirbooks, Masses, and Fame   42
The Real Stories behind Single-Composer Choirbooks   55

3. AUTHORS OF LYRIC   69
The Parisian Chanson and Composers as "Autheurs"   74
The Lyric Economy at Mid-Century   84

4. THE BOOK OF POETRY BECOMES A BOOK OF MUSIC   103
Settings of Ronsard's Poetry, 1550–1570   109
Les Amours de P. de Ronsard Mises en Musique   115
A Culture of Music Books   129
Books, *Bibliothèques,* and Bibliographies   135

5. RESISTING THE PRESS: PERFORMANCE   143

Notes   159
Select Bibliography   207
Index   233

Illustrations

FIGURES

1. A choirbook and a single partbook compared. 8
2. Title page, *Sixiesme livre contenant xxvij. Chansons nouvelles.* 22
3. Title page, *Liber quindecim missarum.* 32
4. Title page, *Frottole intabulate da sonare organi.* 35
5. Title page, *Canzoni, sonetti, strambotti et frottole libro quarto.* 36
6. Title page of superius partbook, *Misse Josquin.* 43
7. One of several versions of the printer's mark "Fama" used by Ottaviano Scotto. 45
8. Carpentras, "Lamentations," in the manuscript version prepared by the composer for presentation to Pope Clement VII. 52–53
9. Title page of Giovanni Pierluigi da Palestrina, *Missarum liber primus.* 59
10. *Le recueil de chansons nouvelles.* 97
11. Frontispiece, *Les Amours de P. de Ronsard, Vandomois, nouvellement augmentées par lui, & commentées par Marc Antoine de Muret.* 106
12. Costeley at the age of thirty-nine. From the beautifully printed and grandly titled *Musique de Guillaume Costeley, organiste ordinaire et vallet de chambre, du treschrestien et tresinvincible roy de France, Charles IX.* 117
13. Anthoine de Bertrand, *Premier livre des Amours de P. de Ronsard.* 134

MUSIC EXAMPLES

1. Claudin de Sermisy, "Jouyssance vous donneray."   80–81
2. French musical settings of "Laissez la verde couleur"
   (Mellin de Saint-Gelais).   96
3. Pierre Certon, "J'espere et crains," measures 1–9.   112
4. Fabrice Marin Caietain, "Air pour chanter tous sonets."   154–156

Acknowledgments

> No one who cooks, cooks alone. Even at her most solitary, a cook in the kitchen is surrounded by generations of cooks past, the advice and menus of cooks present, the wisdom of cookbook writers.
>
> —LAURIE COLWIN, *Home Cooking: A Writer in the Kitchen* (New York: Harper, 2000), p. ix

Authoring a book is not a solitary endeavor, and given the theme of collaboration threaded throughout this one, it gives me special pleasure to thank the people who helped create it. Many of the intellectual inspirations for this study are cited in the notes and bibliography; here let me acknowledge as well the more ephemeral encounters in classrooms, at conferences, and in private exchanges that likewise leave their impression on these pages. In 1994–1995, I was fortunate enough to participate in two pivotal seminars that set the stage for my future research, one taught by Martha Feldman at the Newberry Library in Chicago, and the second by Roger Chartier at the University of Chicago; both Feldman and Chartier subsequently contributed key articles to the collection I edited in 2000, *Music and the Cultures of Print*, and I thank them and all the authors of that volume for their field-defining essays.

Beginning in 2000, several academic generations of students at the University of California, Berkeley threw themselves into seminars on music and book history that allowed me to workshop the research presented here with tough, smart crowds that considerably improved my thinking. Numerous colleagues likewise rose to the challenge of conference sessions designed to investigate issues central to my research, and I hope this book repays their enthusiasm. I thank Jane Bernstein, Anthony Newcomb, and Jessie Ann Owens, for agreeing to speak on the session "Print Culture in the Renaissance" at the Sixty-Ninth Annual Meeting of the American Musicological Society in Houston, Texas in 2003; Elizabeth Eva Leach, Emma Dillon, Jane Alden, Henri Vanhulst, and Iain Fenlon, for agreeing to speak at the session "Music and the History of the Book in Manuscript and Print" at the Thirtieth Annual Conference on Medieval and Renaissance Music, Tours, France in 2005; and Kerry McCarthy, Jane

Alden, and Michael Markham for speaking at the session "Authors and Authority in the Renaissance" at the Seventy-First Annual Meeting of the American Musicological Society in Washington D.C. In addition to colloquium invitations on several campuses, I thank Cécile Alduy for drawing me into the session "French Poetry: Rethinking the Sixteenth-Century Canon" at the Annual Meeting of the Renaissance Society of America in San Francisco in 2006; Iain Fenlon and Richard Wistreich for the invitation to participate in the Round Table "Imparare, leggere, comprare musica nell'Europa del Rinascimento," at the Thirteenth Annual Colloquio del "Saggiatore Musicale" in Bologna in 2009; and Paolo Cecchi for the opportunity to keynote the "Saggiatore" Giornata internazionale di studi, "Il compositore come autore e la musica tra testo e performance nell'Europa della prima età moderna" in Bologna in 2013. Thomas Kelly and the Early Music Study Group at Harvard University read and workshopped my introduction in the fall of 2012. The intellectual energy of these gatherings has sustained this project from start to finish.

Initial stages of research began with a Studium Fellowship from the Centre National de la Recherche Scientifique to work under the direction of Philippe Vendrix at the Centre d'Études Supérieures de la Renaissance, Tours, France, from 2003 to 2005, which provided crucial access to original source materials and landed me in a phenomenal team of scholars with parallel interests at a formative point in my project. Subsequent research and writing were supported by a President's Research Fellowship in the Humanities from the University of California Office of the President in 2006–2007, a Gladys Krieble Delmas Foundation Fellowship for Research in Venice and the Veneto in 2008, a Humanities Research Fellowship from the University of California, Berkeley, and research grants from the Committee on Research at Berkeley.

This book owes much to the encouragement and advice of its first readers, who reviewed some or all of it in drafts: Jane A. Bernstein, Stanley Boorman, Paolo Cecchi, Richard Freedman, Timothy Hampton, Franco Piperno, Julie Wachowski, and a very helpful anonymous reader for UC Press. For insightful conversations and assistance with specific matters over the last years, thanks are owed to Jeanice Brooks, Philippe Canguilhem, Tim Carter, David Crook, Marc Desmet, Frank Dobbins, Martha Feldman, Iain Fenlon, Susan Filter, John Griffiths, Laurent Guillo, Daniel Heartz, Anthony Newcomb, Tommy Tristram, Richard Wistreich, and my dear friend and colleague Davitt Moroney, whose golden touch with old books never ceases to amaze and enlighten. Nicholas Manjoine improved my translations from French and provided boundless friendship at every stage of the process.

And Peter Koch gave me tutorials in the art of fine printing at his press in Berkeley, California.

Paolo Cecchi, Esther Criscuola de Laix, Scott Edwards, and Giordano Mastrocola assisted in procuring photographs, and special gratitude goes out to the photo service at the Vatican for filling an emergency order, as well as to Richard Šípek at the National Museum in Prague. Leon Chisholm and Margaret Jones provided research assistance, including nights and weekends.

Finally, my deepest thanks go to the keepers of the books I have studied, especially John Roberts and John Shepard at the Jean Gray Hargrove Music Library at the University of California, Berkeley; the librarians at the Bibliothèque nationale de France, the British Library, the Österreichische Nationalbibliothek in Vienna, and the Bayerische Staatsbibliothek in Munich; Marco Materassi and his assistant, Michele Magnobosco, at the Accademia filarmonica di Verona; and Alfredo Vitolo at the Museo internazionale e Biblioteca della musica in Bologna. Their profound appreciation for book history and the histories of their collections enriched this study at every turn.

Introduction

> I recall a certain great man saying that now Josquin is dead he is
> writing more compositions than when he was still alive.
>
> GEORG FORSTER, preface to the *Selectissimarum*
> *mutetarum . . . tomus primus* (Nuremberg, 1540)[1]

We can laugh with Georg Forster at his joke about Josquin des Prez, who
by 1540 had been dead for almost twenty years. Josquin was enjoying a
personal Renaissance in those years, with German printers such as Hans
Ott, Johann Petreius, Georg Rhau, and Melchior Kriesstein issuing his
music as quickly as possible.[2] Forster, who put out the *Selectissimarum*
mutetarum motet anthology in Nuremberg right in the midst of this Josquin craze, pointedly refused to play along and deliberately excluded Josquin from his collection, explaining in his preface that he was not going to
print works of doubtful authenticity just to keep up with the Joneses. We
can nod knowingly, modern editors of Josquin can appreciate Forster's integrity, and any of us who love Josquin's music (or the music attributed to
him) will catch a little zing of the frisson that comes from knowing that—
like us—early moderns recognized Josquin as a composer of greatness.

But how, exactly, did Josquin come to loom so large that he had to be
cited even in books that did not include his music? How did he become
such an authoritative figure? And can we assume that the motivations of
early moderns so closely mirrored our own? On the face of it, it may seem
self-evident that Josquin's music—excellent as it is—was prized by musicians and that, with the establishment of commercial music printing in
the North around 1535, it was considered prime repertoire for publication.
Judging from Forster's remark, Josquin's name sold music, and just as I am
hoping to hook you into reading on and purchasing this book by beginning with Josquin (JOSQUIN!), the easy argument would run that money-
hungry printers, eager for a quick sale, printed as much of Josquin's music
as they could find and occasionally also falsified their attributions, "dis-
covering" new pieces by the master that they anticipated being received
with great joy by an avid (paying) public. "Josquin" guaranteed printers

returns on their outlay for paper and labor or at least helped them hedge their investments.

True as this may be, the career of this paper "Josquin," the author, merits scrutiny.[3] His appearance in print coincides almost exactly with the beginnings of music printing itself, for Ottaviano Petrucci devoted his very first print of Masses to the works of Josquin.[4] With this book, Petrucci might even be said to have invented Josquin's authorship, for eventually becoming an author would depend on entering into print. By the seventeenth century, authors were defined as writers of printed books, and in this sense "Josquin" was arguably the first author of a music book.[5] The case of the 1502 *Misse Josquin* is even more dramatic when considered against the surviving corpus of manuscripts that preceded it, for it apparently issued into a world of music books made up of anthologies and miscellanies. By contrast, Petrucci's *Misse Josquin* of 1502 included only music by Josquin, whose name likewise figures in its title. In short, the *Misse Josquin* is the only surviving music book of its time—manuscript or print—that contains the works of a single composer.[6] Anticipated solely by the extraordinary manuscripts compiled in the fourteenth century by Guillaume de Machaut (ca. 1300–1377), the 1502 *Misse Josquin* defines a new era of authorship *tout court*, one that coincides almost exactly with the first prints of polyphonic music and that nicely forecasts the eventual dependence of authorship on printing.[7] The story of Josquin the author could hardly be told more neatly had it been invented whole cloth: the *Misse Josquin* of 1502 launched a series of three books of Masses by Josquin, all printed by Petrucci (book 2 came out in 1505 and book 3 in 1514). There followed re-editions by Petrucci and copies by other printers. By the 1540s, printing had secured an extraordinary fame for the composer; through the vehicle of the press, "Josquin" became the first early modern author of music.

The publication history of Josquin's music plots such a coherent narrative of his triumph as an author that it shines out as one of those rare and wonderful instances in which we might just let the facts of bibliography speak for themselves. But who was Josquin the author? That figure certainly cannot be equated one for one with the historical personage who sang in the papal chapel choir, worked for a time for Duke Ercole d'Este, and ultimately headed home from Italy to become provost at Condé. Obviously, the name slapped onto motets in the 1540s by unscrupulous printers cannot be taken as a sign or "signature" of Josquin, but even Josquin's authorship of the 1502 *Misse Josquin* is highly qualified—the works printed there are securely attributed, but the project of making a book of them appears to have been Petrucci's own. That is, Josquin may have composed the Masses, but Petrucci made the *Misse Josquin*. Making music and making music books misalign here, so much so that whereas Josquin clearly did write music, we need to understand his authorship as having been fabricated by others, beginning with those who printed his music.

WHAT IS AN AUTHOR?

The gap I am signaling has been worried over in numerous ways, though primarily as an editorial conundrum, not a philosophical one. Misattributions, error-ridden readings, questions about accidentals and the emendations of early editors, each of these are problems presented by the misalignment between autograph manuscripts (now lost) and the sources that survive, problems that need to be solved before consideration of a composer's works can begin. As they strive to establish a composer's corpus, scholars scrutinize the provenance, chronology, and reliability of each source. They often turn to biography to help verify attributions and establish possible dates of composition, arranging pieces on a rough timeline that can be used for stylistic comparisons. These labors stand behind the extensive critical commentaries that accompany modern editions of *opera omnia*, which regularly collate the information editors have employed in arriving at the choice of a source to use as a base text. Then the capable editor cleans up the texts, relegating works of dubious authenticity to second status, rejecting unreliable sources, correcting scribal errors or typos, realizing *musica ficta* and canons, and scoring everything up in legible modern editions with halved note values, barlines, and precise underlay of words. This secure corpus in place, musicologists are able to study a composer's output and stylistic development, and compare the works of one composer to another.

One question left unasked, though, is how well an author-bound, life-and-works approach to history suits early music. The sources themselves are very uneven in this respect: some—like Petrucci's *Misse Josquin*—contain the works of a single composer, but may have been published without the composer's knowledge. Others, most notably anthologies, only confuse our attempts to salvage a composer's corpus from the wash of pieces in collections like those printed by Hans Ott, who attributed motets of doubtful authenticity to Josquin. We fish out what we can (throwing back the rejects), dry out the keepers, and put them together in the orderly volumes that fill the shelves of the "M3" section in music libraries (at least in America). I am not disputing the value of these huge collective efforts, which each year make more music available to scholars and performers. This is music that we desperately need. What I question is the classification scheme itself—what do we miss when we adopt authorship as a fundament of music history? What cultural complexities are erased when we seek to assign written music to an author? We might salvage the makings of an *opera omnia*, but lose sight of the conditions under which the music was first disseminated. Why continue to accept those old author-privileging bibliographic necessities of name, title, date? Digitization projects and powerful search engines give us increasing access to the ocean of music still out there, but the ideologies that produced early books of mongrel, weak, and uncertain authorship nonetheless remain insufficiently debated.

Over a decade ago, in a perceptive article on "Authors and Anonyms" in the sixteenth-century madrigal repertoire, Martha Feldman exposed a series of dilemmas imposed by author-centric histories.[8] Concentrating on the printed books of madrigals coming out of Venice at mid-century, she observed that "even if printers preferred non-anonymous production, all things being equal, they seem nevertheless to have regarded certain *pieces*, certain *kinds* of pieces, and most likely pieces by certain kinds of *authors* as being categorically 'anonymous' in character."[9] She went on to conclude that anonymity in print indicated a specific status in Cinquecento Venice, not merely the printer's inability to attribute a work. Pieces closest to the unwritten tradition of melodic formulas and bass patterns often lacked attribution, as did those composed by house editors or aristocrats who may have wished to hide their identities. My own work began as a response to the challenge of Feldman's insights. The research I present here shows how ill-suited music can be to author-based frameworks, and it does so by scrutinizing the first century of music printing, during which book production began to press some (but by no means all) music into "authored" books, and bibliographies began to take authorship as their first term of order.

The history of authorship has long been of interest outside of musicology and especially among historians of the book, whose research guides my theoretical approach to the subject.[10] But even before scholars such as D. F. McKenzie and Roger Chartier published their landmark studies in the 1980s, the French philosopher Michel Foucault called critical attention to the highly contingent nature of authorship in his now-famous essay "What Is an Author?" (first delivered as a lecture in 1969).[11] With characteristic incisiveness, Foucault laid bare the distinctive conditions that pertain to authors and especially to the function of the author's name. The names of authors, he argued, have a unique discursive property that operates independently from the ordinary names used to designate individuals. He says:

Unlike a proper name, which moves from the interior of a discourse to the real person outside who produced it, the name of the author remains at the contours of texts—separating one from the other, defining their form, and characterizing their mode of existence. It points to the existence of certain groups of discourse and refers to the status of this discourse within a society and culture. The author's name is not a function of a man's civil status, nor is it fictional; it is situated in the breach, among the discontinuities, which gives rise to new groups of discourse and their singular mode of existence.[12]

Foucault posited that authorship (and the authority regularly accorded it) was not a mere fact of having written or even having been published, but a culturally constructed status. In the first place, authors' names rightly belonged only to "works"—the anonymous broadside might have a writer, but not an author; Giaches de Wert may have written and signed thirty-eight letters now archived at Novellara, but he was not the "author" of them; so, too, a shopping list in E.E. Cummings's hand would not rightly be included in his *oeuvres complètes*. Authorship rests on a sociocultural selection process that separates some texts from others, appropriating them and categorizing them under the names of authors, and circulating them in discourses divorced from the historical personages who wrote them. To reexamine the example I gave above, Foucault's concept of the "author-function" helps illuminate the series of steps that intervene between Josquin's writing down of music and the authority accorded to him by subsequent musicians, printers, and theorists. By the time of Heinrich Glarean's writing, Josquin's "works" could stand as theoretical models in the *Dodekachordon* (Basel, 1547), and Adrian Petit Coclico would dub Josquin first among the "Principes Musicorum" in his *Compendium musices* (Nuremberg, 1552).[13] The fact that Forster felt obliged to explain Josquin's absence from his otherwise "most select" collection of motets relates to the cultural significance of Josquin's name in the discursive environment of 1540s Germany and Switzerland. So too, when I list prints of Josquin's music, as I did above, the list is not simply a compilation of bald "bibliographic facts" that state a self-evident truth, but evidence of a selection process based, in the first instance, on the value scholars accord to his name. Early moderns chose what to print according to their own cultural priorities, just as ours determine what music we edit, study, perform, and record.

To maintain that authorship is a function of discourse rather than a status originating in the act of writing in no way denies the genuine fame that Josquin and other widely admired Renaissance composers commanded in real life. On the contrary, to study authorship as a discursive construct is to better understand how compositional excellence could bring fame. When, for instance, Baldassare Castiglione reported in *Il cortegiano* that a motet performed before the duchess of Urbino was found worthless until it was known to be by Josquin, his remark not only underscored the cultural capital of Josquin's name, it contributed to the formation of Josquin's authorship.[14] By defamiliarizing accounts like Castiglione's (rather taking them to be self-evident), we can better understand the creation of compositional authority in the early modern period.

PARTBOOKS, CHOIRBOOKS, AND BEYOND

Music, Authorship, and the Book is a cultural history that attends to the nodes, unevenesses, and limits of musical authorship. By the term *authorship*, I mean the fact of a composer having produced written "works" that circulated in "books" of music, so in essence, my project studies the invention of musical authorship through the medium of the book. This definition of *authorship* is the modern one, and I must note here at the outset that for early moderns, "author," "autore," "autheur," and so forth encompassed senses well beyond "writer of a book." In the sixteenth century, even as printing began to professionalize writing and book production, an "author" might still be the maker, creator, or originator of any variety of things (not necessarily written)—God as Author of the cosmos, for instance. Even the seventeenth-century *Dictionnaire universel* of Antoine Furetière (1690) gives several such definitions of "auteur" before arriving at our modern meaning of the term: "in the case of Literature, one says this of all those who have brought to light some book. Now one says it only of those who have had something published."[15] By honing in on this emerging definition, which for music means excluding oral forms of tune-smithing and music "making," I draw a line at the written that ultimately matters much more to historiography than it did to workaday musicians in the sixteenth century. After all, even Castiglione's story about Josquin's authorship recalls the performance of a motet—the "work" was judged in its sounding, ephemeral form as an anonymous sonic event. The duchess of Urbino was listening, not hovering over a score. Nonetheless, I have chosen to define authorship for music narrowly in order to cast in the brightest possible relief the limits of writing's authority in a musical world that turned on performance.

I use the term *work* deliberately here to indicate an objectified piece of music or opus, a piece of music captured in notation and able to travel on its own and survive the death of its composer. This definition of *work* is textual, but it does not presume that early moderns necessarily accorded the privileged status to written music that took hold in Europe around 1800 with the new ideologies of compositional authority that helped define the Romantic age. In that later time, scores not only allowed readers to comprehend a piece without hearing it performed, notation was believed to permit access to a composer's innermost thoughts and a "self" encoded in the written work. Gary Tomlinson, in describing this shift and the historiographical methods attending it, has remarked that by the nineteenth century, "notated music came to be viewed less as a preliminary script for performance than as the locus of the truest revelation of the composer's intent, the unique and full inscription of the composer's expressive spirit which was elsewhere—in any one performance—only partially revealed."[16] This strong prioritization of the text as the locus of meaning was foreign to the sixteenth century, though as we shall see, the bibliographic forms that enabled enduring fame for composers did first develop during the Renaissance.[17]

The written compositions studied here are primarily pieces of vocal polyphony for four or five voices (in the ranges soprano, alto, tenor, bass) in genres including Mass Ordinary settings, Latin motets, French chansons, and Italian madrigals. While I take some stock of manuscript culture, I focus on the post-Petrucci world of the sixteenth century, which saw increased production of music books and the emergence of the cultures of print that arguably allowed some composers to achieve an entirely new cultural status independent of their careers as performers. This materialistic approach to the history of authorship presumes that objects shaped the reception of a composer's works, framed their uses, and constituted their meanings. Here we should remember that written polyphony generally circulated in one of two forms: choirbooks in which all the parts were laid out to be read simultaneously by multiple singers from a single opening, or sets of partbooks that each contained a single part. As illustrated in figure 1, choirbooks were typically large books in folio containing sacred music such as Masses, motets, and Magnificats. Partbooks, by contrast, were the standard of commercial music printing in the sixteenth century, a workaday layout for anything from Masses to chansons. Cost-saving in format and far less imposing, they tended to be printed in quarto or even in octavo. It is worth noting that neither partbooks nor

Figure 1. A choirbook (above and in Chapter 2) and a single partbook (right and in Chapter 4) compared. In the choirbook, the four voices of this polyphonic piece are laid out with the superius and tenor on the left side of the opening, and the altus and bassus on the right. The partbook, by contrast, contains only the bassus part of a four-voice piece—the other parts were printed separately in similar booklets.

choirbooks presented the parts laid out in vertically aligned scores. This suggests that the synoptic reading facilitated by scores was not a priority at the time—rather, musical texts functioned first and foremost as performance parts. Choristers gathered around large choirbooks set on lecterns, standing near their respective parts on each opening, and—outside of church—musicians sang or played from partbooks in the ways that the members of string quartets or symphony orchestras each read from individual parts today. When scores did gradually come on the scene late in the sixteenth century, they appear to have been used primarily in the study of learned counterpoint.[18] One of the very first collections issued in open score, *Tutti i madrigali di Cipriano di Rore a quattro voci* (Venice: Gardano, 1577), made a point in its title of noting its usefulness to "qualunque studioso di contrapunti" (any student of counterpoint), and when Carlo Gesualdo visited Ferrara in 1594, he reportedly "show[ed] his music in score to everyone to induce them to admire his art."[19] In score, the musical work acquired a physical layout that facilitated silent study of its composition and admiration of the composer's art. Ultimately, scores became the composer's own medium of design, perfection, and preservation, but they were an anomaly before 1600, when "reading" happened in the noisy, shared, disputed renditions of a choir or consort.[20]

Partbooks and choirbooks make perfect sense from the performer's standpoint, but they complicate the history of authorship for music. Partbooks easily went missing from sets, leaving the composer's text incomplete, and even music printed in folio often seems to have been used unbound like sheet music, meeting the same quick demises as the sonatas sitting on our music stands or stored in the piano bench.[21] Some collectors gathered their little sixteen-folio partbooks together and had them bound according to voice type—soprano, alto, tenor, bass—and many of the partbooks that survive today are preserved in such "binder's volumes" or volumes in which more than one title is bound together. (Other terms for this sort of book are *tract volume* and *collector's volume,* and I use them interchangeably; foreign terms include *recueils factices* and *Sammelbände.*) But even for binder's volumes, often only one part survives. Music resisted the bookishness that defined authorship for verbal texts, resisted the codex and codification, and even as some composers such as Josquin des Prez, Clément Janequin, Cipriano de Rore, and Orlande de Lassus, did clearly gain reputations in print that extended well beyond their immediate physical orbits, much music met its textual demise as quickly as the anonymous poetry printed up in chapbooks and sold by street vendors.

My account of musical authorship seeks not only to problematize the relationship between music books and their authors, but to put bookmaking into confrontation with music making of the time. Composers often became authors without their knowledge or cooperation, their music and names pressed into service by bookmen who operated according to their own precepts. Editors, scribes, printers, and booksellers followed practices dictated by their own trades, capturing music and presenting it in forms that suited their enterprises, designing and standardizing the size, shape, and content of music books, marketing music in material forms that would be comprehensible to buyers, not all of them working musicians. The transformations made in the scriptorium and print shop likewise took place within cultural economies sometimes quite separate from the court, chapel, and cathedral settings in which composers pursued their musical careers. Yet one of the bluntest truths of music historiography is that as scholars, we rely almost entirely on prints and manuscripts of music as source material. Choirbooks and partbooks comprise most of our witnesses to music making in Western Europe in the sixteenth century (with paintings, letters, printed descriptions, and archival materials making up the rest), yet the very nature of these sources is rarely studied in and of itself. Scholarly energy has been poured into cataloging source materials, studying the provenance of individual manuscripts and the history of printing, yes, but there is still much work to be done if we take a larger view and try hold the written music that survives in printed books and manuscripts in balance with what laid beyond it. Among the most central questions are: What kinds of music were resistant to print? Did composers ever intentionally write for printed publication? What musical practices does writing exclude? How much authority did early moderns vest in written music?

Posing these questions inevitably encourages an attitude in which the study of written music is not an end in itself, but a beginning, one that raises ancillary questions of how the sources before us came to be made. It is to attend to Foucault's "author-function"—how the names of authors organized musical discourse—but it is also to embark on a project that Foucault might have dismissed: contextualizing authored "works" and examining them against the much larger background of the musical texts that surrounded them before they became discursively significant. It is also to measure the cultural significance of "works" against the musical practices of the day. Let us imagine the black and brown notes on those sixteenth-century pages as tears in the paper and vellum, tiny portals onto a world in which composers of polyphony—those habitual writers of music—were busy working with chapel choirs, violin bands, and poet-improvisers, giving lessons to amateur singers, and passing their days doing much more than composing. Josquin des Prez, Claudin de Sermisy, Jacques Arcadelt, Giovanni Pierluigi da Palestrina, Orlande de Lassus, and Guillaume Boni (to cite just a few) are simply the musicians of their age who are most visible to us, partly because they operated in a "writing culture" that renders their activities more or less traceable. As boys they attended cathedral schools where they learned to sing, read, and write polyphonic music in a style for which Franco-Flemish schools were particularly renowned. They worked in the highly literate environment of the Catholic Church, knew Latin and often multiple vernaculars, and spent at least some of their time composing the pieces for which we now know them. But they also would have been adept at improvising polyphony by employing practices that did not rely on writing, practices that, fortunately, we can imagine thanks to written accounts of descant, fauxbourdon, and other improvisations even more elaborate.[22] This is to say, even writers of polyphony worked in environments cohabited by musical aesthetics entirely indifferent to the written forms upon which authorship depended.[23] As organists and chapelmasters, their day-to-day duties likewise centered on performance, often requiring their daily presence at Mass and management of a choir. Most were singers, though the parts they sang are often unknown and rarely discussed.

What do we actually know about the lives these men led? Sometimes virtually nil. Much of what we know about Josquin des Prez, for instance, has been painstakingly gleaned from the records of ecclesiastical benefices, a type of church appointment that provided property and income to its holder.[24] Josquin was apparently ambitious about seeking them, and in some instances, his application for or receipt of a benefice has provided the principal source of information concerning his whereabouts in the 1480s and 1490s. Here it is worth noting that benefices are an arcana rarely cited by any but ecclesiastical historians, yet biographers of Josquin rely on them heavily. The fact that dedicated music historians have been forced to trawl through records of benefices for shards of biographical information shows up the scarcity of sources from which we can reconstruct the lives of early musicians, to be sure, and it drives home a larger point about the ephemerality of music itself, its immateriality as an art form, and the difficulties we have writing histories of performers when their day-to-day concerns centered on music making. Composers could write, to be sure, but many of them were nonetheless doers as their first calling, producers of events. Who knows what sort of records Josquin kept, whether he carried with him a portfolio of his compositions or simply left them behind with patrons and employers when he moved from place to place? And what, moreover, do we know of the musicians who sang with Josquin? What chorister was he berating in Cambrai for adding ornaments to his compositions?[25] Whom did he laugh at for misinterpreting the tenor of his *Missa l'homme armé?*[26] David Fallows, Josquin's most recent biographer, concludes his monumental study of the composer's life and works with the astute remark that "in some ways it would be easier to write the story of

Josquin by starting at his death in 1521. After that the information is more abundant, the main trends easier to see and put in focus."[27] The paucity of archival and musical source material dating from the composer's lifetime is striking.

I freely admit that like most histories of Renaissance music, this one is predominately populated by the tiny group of musicians who wrote polyphony. This is a history of "composers" and quite deliberately so, but it is not written at the expense of all other musicians. On the contrary, I wish to understand the factors that conjoined to separate "composers" from other musicians and turn them into the "authors" that are so central to our histories.[28] Moreover, by interrogating the nature of authorship itself—its limits and the history of its very particular construction—we can more easily move beyond its confines to construct histories that do not take authorship as their starting point. These alternative histories not only concern non-composing musicians (many of them the superstar performers of their day), but a deep appreciation of the bread-and-butter activities of "composers" whose writing was often highly occasional and only one part of their musical lives.

THE CULTURES OF PRINT

The chronological boundaries of my study are those of the sixteenth century, with the first printed book of polyphony at its beginning, Petrucci's *Harmonice Musices Odhecaton A* (1501), and just after its end, one of the first attempts to launch something resembling a complete works edition—the *Magnum Opus Musicum* (Munich, 1604), a gigantic set of 516 motets by Lassus brought to light by his sons Ferdinand and Rudolf. Though far from complete, the *Magnum Opus Musicum* neatly introduces the word *opus* in its title and, along with the seven magnificent Lassus volumes in the *Patrocinium musices* series (Munich, 1573–98), monumentalizes Lassus's works in a spirit consistent with modern notions of authorship and the *opera omnia*.

Authorship for music did not depend on print, but there is no question that printing accelerated the separation of texts from their makers and allowed for the formation of a new public sphere in which authors and their "works" took on lives independent of their creators. In printing can also be found the origins of literary property, a concept that first pertained to the ownership by bookseller-publishers of the material they printed. These legal protections were guaranteed by the privilege systems of the sixteenth century and were eventually transferred from bookmen to authors, but not until well after the period of this study.[29] For music, the great exception to this rule is Orlande de Lassus, who obtained an extraordinary series of personal printing privileges, first from the king of France and later from Emperor Rudolf II.[30] Lassus is one of the first composers to have established and maintained a career in print throughout his lifetime (ca. 1532–94), and his publications represent an early model of musical authorship. Finally, with printing came the professionalization of literary activity, the business of writing for print, one example of which is the literary career of Anton Francesco Doni, an arriviste in the great printing capital of Venice who revealed the secrets of its private musical gatherings in his *Dialogo della musica* and compiled the first bibliography of music in his *Libraria* as an aid to collectors and bibliophiles.[31]

The legal, literary, and cultural practices that coalesced around the new technology of printing touched writers of music in various ways. Josquin's posthumous reputation is a fine example of this phenomenon, but perhaps the most beautiful example—now frequently reproduced in textbooks—is the title page of Palestrina's first book of Masses from 1554, in which the composer is shown kneeling with his book in hand, presenting his Masses to the pope (figure 9). There, the relationship between composer and book seems direct, unproblematic, and complete, but a careful reading of the image and a deeper understanding of the cultures of print into which Palestrina's book issued reveal considerable gaps between the act of composition, the production of the book containing those compositions, and the cultural capital ascribed to the book as an object.

It is certainly true that the invention of the printing press was hailed in its own time as a veritable godsend. Martin Luther proclaimed that printing was "God's highest and extremest act of grace" and the French satirist François Rabelais attributed the invention of printed books to "divine inspiration," but it is always a danger to take such hyperbole at face value.[32] Some modern scholars—most notably Elizabeth Eisenstein and her followers—were quick to echo this early modern rhetoric of praise, and in her influential book *The Printing Press as an Agent of Change* (1979), Eisenstein even went so far as to declare that without the press to stabilize knowledge, the scientific revolution would not have been possible. Subsequently, however, scholars such as Adrian Johns have questioned the extent to which any inherent authority can be claimed for printing, showing instead how bookmen conspired to fabricate the truths modern readers regularly take as given: that the person named as the author of a book did indeed write the text it contains, that the book was printed where it says it was, and that one copy is the same as the next.[33] Sixteenth-century readers, by contrast, could hardly make such assumptions. Falsification and piracy were commonplace, and to take but one notorious example cited by Johns, it is now known that Martin Luther's translation of German scripture was beaten into print by its first false edition—shockingly, the proportion of unauthorized to authorized editions produced during the sixteenth century was roughly ninety to one.[34] Faced with overwhelming obstacles to accreditation in print, in seventeenth-century England, authors took to signing books by hand as a guarantee of their authenticity.[35] The body, physically present in the form of the author's signature, authorized the text.

The revisionist history Johns charted in *The Nature of the Book: Print and Knowledge in the Making* (1998) built on several decades of scholarship challenging presumptions about authorship in early modern Europe. Whereas Foucault had explicitly bracketed questions of how authors attained their unique status and what kinds of texts could sustain authorial discourse, other scholars picked up on the leads suggested in his essay and worked toward a new history of authorship that considered the cultural dimensions of book production and their role in shaping authors' works. One definitive contribution to anglophone scholarship was Robert Darnton's "What Is the History of Books?" (1990), in which Darnton mapped the "communications circuit" through which works coursed as they traveled from author to readers.[36] Publishers, printers, shippers, booksellers, and even readers left their mark on texts as they became books designed within the cultures of print. Darnton's object was to disrupt scholarly fixation on the content of texts ("the text itself") and focus instead on the forms in which texts reached their readers (the book), complicating our understanding of the seemingly direct relationship between author's text and the handwritten, engraved, or printed objects made of it.

In *The Order of Books* (1994), the social historian Roger Chartier advanced a claim even more categorical than Darnton's (and one that proved foundational to Johns's study): that book production of virtually any sort, manuscript included, compromised the ideal of a "direct and authentic relation between the author and the reader," the sort of "perfect textuality" that could only be guaranteed by autograph writing.[37] Books, Chartier argued, are not specula into the creative imaginations of their authors. Yet they *are* revealing, for the material forms in which texts are presented on the page have much to tell us about their authors as social and cultural figures. "Understanding the reasons and effects of such physical devices [in the printed book] as format, page layout, the way in which the text is broken up, the conventions governing its typographical presentation, and so forth, necessarily refers back to the control that the authors but sometimes the publishers exercised over the forms charged with expressing intention, orienting reception, and constraining interpretation."[38] The book itself is a medium of cultural expression in which we can discover the first discursive formulations of authorship.

If, according to such histories, texts cannot escape the uneven world of the objects in which they are captured, exchanged, gifted, commodified, preserved, and destroyed, authors too lose their sovereignty when their works are seen as part of the commercial, artistic, and social systems within which print operated. In the musical domain, the best-studied example of such compromised authority is opera, a genre that has long prompted reflection on the fragility of composers' control over their work. The intensively collaborative environment of musical theater, with its pastiches, shifting casts of singers, suitcase arias, and the various requirements of local economies, required flexibility that left its imprint on source materials, particularly in the eighteenth and nineteenth centuries. Prompted initially by problems of textual criticism when confronted with mismatching continuity drafts, fair copies, piano-vocal scores, performing parts, and rehearsal scores, many editors of operas came to question the extent to which even revered composers such as George Frideric Handel and Giuseppe Verdi achieved true autonomy as they worked. Opera scholarship does not announce the death of the composer any more than this study will, but it does neatly confront fantasies of authorial control with the realities of theatrical collaborations, the demands of impresarios, the cuts and interpolations calculated to please audiences, and the needs or fancies of singers.[39] The resulting textual instability is part and parcel of the genre. While nineteenth-century operatic culture is far removed from the sixteenth-century cultures of print considered here, its implications for the history of authorship are similar—in both cases, contemporary systems of production and consumption left legible marks on the author's text. For the sixteenth-century, the methods of book historians provide one means of reading them.

FROM MASS TO CHANSON

Nowhere is the fractured relationship between authors and books more evident than in the musical domain, which for centuries was dominated—textually—by miscellanies and anthologies, books, in short, that were "authored" by scribes, compilers, editors, and printer-booksellers, often without the direct involvement of composers or concern for attributing music to those who wrote it. Pieces were regularly separated fascicle to fascicle or book to book by genre, a scheme arising from practical matters of liturgical use, repertory, and layout, but authorship was not a means of organizing materials. Early printed books of music, like the manuscripts that preceded them, were cast in forms reflective of the scriptorium and print house. In an initial stage-setting chapter, "The World of Books" (chapter 1), I chart the obstacles to authorship posed by the book trade, in which privileges accorded ownership to printers, printers controlled book production, and music books often constituted authority for composers only weakly if at all.

Authorship first became significant in sacred repertoires and—as exemplified by the 1502 *Misse Josquin*—in collections of Mass Ordinary settings, a mindset already apparent circa 1500 in the organization of the Chigi Codex (I-RVat Chigi C. VIII. 234), a book devoted to the Masses of Jean de Ockeghem, which are grouped together on the first 136 folios of the manuscript. My history of authorship thus begins by tracing its emergence in books of cyclic Mass settings, particularly those copied or printed in folio, like Palestrina's First Book of 1554. Chapter 2, "Music Books and Their Authors," questions whether composers "authored" books in ways analogous to poets and writers of verbal texts and examines the very particular circumstances in which they could be said to have done so. Detailed analysis shows that books like Palestrina's were rare, the financing of them often fraught, and their production limited to a few distinct cultural spheres, primarily Habsburgian and Roman. Moreover, the phenomenon of these large, single-composer codices appears to date to the sixteenth century, evolving concurrently in manuscript and printed production.

While the high-art and ritually essential genre of Mass Ordinary settings eventually became the stuff of single-composer codices, polyphonic genres at the lowest end of the sacred-to-secular hierarchy proved more resistant to authorship. Songs in the vernacular, dances, and instrumental arrangements were regularly thrown together in manuscripts and prints with no attributions at all, at least early in the century. Thus, the "rise of the author" seen so magnificently in Roman Mass prints by 1550 occurs later and more weakly in vernacular genres. But it is against the background of vernacular genres that authorship and the Mass must be considered, for prints of chansons, frottole, and madrigals were the mainstay of music printing as a commercial venture. In Venice, the swiftest path into print was with a madrigal; in Paris, Lyon, and Antwerp, it was with a chanson. Each of these capitals sustained unique cultures of print, each with its own attitudes toward writers of vernacular music. In Venice, for instance, madrigalists could ride the waves of Petrarchism that canonized the fourteenth-century Tuscan poet as the model for vernacular lyric and—by extension—conferred authority on musical settings of Petrarchan sonnets. From the outset of high-volume music printing in the *Serenissima* in the late 1530s, printers such as Girolamo Scotto and Antonio Gardane regularly issued madrigals and chansons in single-composer prints and marketed anthologies under titles featuring the names of authors, as in *Di Constantio Festa il primo libro de madrigali a tre voci, con la gionta de quaranta madrigali di Ihan Gero . . . aggiuntovi similmente trenta canzoni francese di Janequin* (Venice: Gardane, 1541).

By contrast, the chansonniers produced in Paris long proved virtually immune to the authority of composers. The so-called Parisian chansons printed by Pierre Attaingnant beginning in 1528 were a publisher's repertoire par excellence, and Attaingnant made good business of packing chansons into partbooks with the number of songs listed in the titles (*Trente et une chansons musicales a troys parties, Vingt et huit chansons nouvelles en musique,* and so forth), but not the names of composers. In chapter 3, "Authors of Lyric," I argue that Attaingnant and his contemporaries did not consider these chansons "works," nor their composers "authors," an assessment borne out by close analysis of their musical style and the conflicting attributions they received. Even chansons as popular as "Aupres de vous" and "Tant que vivray" (both usually presumed to be by Claudin de Sermisy) appear to have had musical identities that functioned entirely on their own without an authorial presence to validate them. This imperviousness to authors, I go on to suggest, relates to the nature of French lyric poetry at the time: designed for song and published through performance, the essence of lyric resided somewhere between the voice and the page.

Authors do become strongly visible in lyric cultures in France at midcentury, in the extremely self-conscious publishing projects of the Pléiade poets: Pierre de Ronsard, Joachim Du Bellay, Pontus de Tyard, Jean-Antoine de Baïf, Rémy Belleau, and Estienne Jodelle. Their novel publishing ventures contrasted dramatically with the habits of prior poets such as Clément Marot and the court poet Mellin de Saint-Gelais, a poet-lutenist who sang his verse but did not undertake projects to have it printed. The transition from Saint-Gelais to Ronsard, who succeeded Saint-Gelais at the French court after the latter's death in 1558, marks a shift from oral publication to print and signals the rise of a new lyric economy in which poetic authority could be relocated from performance to the page.

Ronsard's publications invest authority fully in books. But I open chapter 4, "The Book of Poetry Becomes a Book of Music," by questioning whether this triumph of the book was as swift or complete as Ronsard's record in print might suggest. Musicians, for instance, were slow to set his verse; chansonniers from the 1550s and 1560s include little of his poetry. Ronsard's books of poetry did eventually become important sources of song texts for chanson composers, initially in a scattered, organic fashion involving his strophic texts (odes and *chansons*), and then suddenly in 1575 in a series of chansonniers entirely dedicated to settings of his sonnets, particularly those from *Les Amours* (1552). This glut of sonnet settings is striking because the sonnet had never appealed to lyricists in France, certainly not in the bookish Petrarchan form preferred by Ronsard. The chansonniers setting Ronsard's sonnets thus stand out as particularly literary, and they form the core repertory studied in this chapter. In presentation, they were almost unprecedented in their large formats, spacious typography, extensive paratexts (dedications, prefaces, liminary poems), and emphasis on authorship, both Ronsard's and the composer's. Those by Guillaume Boni and Anthoine de Bertrand in particular witness the arrival of the book as an organizing concept for chanson composers and their pursuit of a new almost literary authority through the medium of the book.

With this tracing of authorship from Mass to chanson, my history might have been complete, but in chapter 5, "Resisting the Press: Performance," I close by briefly considering musical authority from outside the printed repertoires in which it arguably was constructed. The chansonniers of Boni and Bertrand beautifully package their Ronsardian sonnets in strikingly authoritative forms, and they have long dominated research into the late sixteenth-century chanson. But I end by disputing their cultural currency, particularly in Paris and at the court of the last Valois, where the *air de cour* and the improvised performances of star singers and instrumentalists dominated strains of musical production only dimly emergent in print. They provide no access to the wealth of music making at the French court, which has to be researched through perspectives that let go of books, exchanging authorship for collaboration, performance, and improvisation. Thus the bibliographic seductiveness of the Ronsard chansonniers underscores the point that *Music, Authorship, and the Book* reaches at numerous turns: written material often obscures just as much as it reveals. Ultimately, it encourages us to question assumptions about the value accorded to printed music, the compositional authority projected by music books, and the importance of the "composer" at a time when musicians were prized for their ability as performers and music was written down in forms designed for performance, not study.

1.   The World of Books

By comparison with the printing of verbal texts, music printing got off to a slow start. Whereas Gutenberg's forty-two-line Bible came off the press in 1455, almost fifty years elapsed before Ottaviano Petrucci printed the first book of polyphony in Venice in 1501, the *Harmonice Musices Odhe-caton A*, a collection of almost one hundred chansons for three and four voices. Other prints followed, fairly establishing Petrucci's claim to have been the first to print polyphony on any significant scale, but even so, his double-impression method proved time-consuming, and production was slow. Each sheet had to be printed twice on each side, first with the staves, and then with the notes and text. Petrucci averaged only three titles a year across his twenty-year career in printing.[1] Genuine scale arrived with the invention of single-impression printing and Pierre Attaingnant's commercialization of the technology in Paris beginning around 1528.[2] In this method, each note or rest carried with it a small set of staff lines, allowing all elements of the music to be set typographically and each page to be printed in a single run through the press.

By 1550, music printing had expanded the European market for polyphony, and printer-booksellers in a number of major cities were producing quantities of music. The firms with the largest output include the following (with the date of the firm's first single-impression print in parentheses): Jacques Moderne in Lyon (1532), Antonio Gardane (1538) and Girolamo Scotto (1539) in Venice, Valerio Dorico in Rome (1544), and Tielman Susato in Antwerp (1543). Germans were especially quick to adopt the new technology, among them Christian Egenolff in Frankfurt (1532) and three printers in Nuremberg: Hieronymus Formschneider (1534),

Johann Petreius (1536), and the partnership of Johann vom Berg ["Montanus"] and Ulrich Neuber (1542). Taken together, production in Paris, Lyon, and Venice topped 480 editions of polyphonic music before 1550, and this figure does not even include instrumental music and intabulations.[3]

The exponential increase in the production of musical texts across the 1530s and 1540s helped establish the cultural significance of printed music, and with it a new medium of patronage and fame opened up for composers. But the world of books and bookmen turned under its own forces. The systems editors, publishers, and printers used to compile pieces and fill their partbooks often took little stock of authorship as a defining factor. Anthologies dominated the world of commercial printing, and this collective form of book greatly diminished the material projections through which composers could attain renown.

In Northern Europe, the high-volume industry of commercial music printing was dominated by chanson anthologies. Brief, tuneful, and apparently available in great quantity, "Parisian" chansons were a perfect fit for the little oblong partbooks that eventually became the standard format for all sorts of music in the sixteenth century. Beginning with Pierre Attaingnant in the late 1520s, chansonniers churned from European presses, steadily developing the market for printed polyphony even as they filled it. Almost half of Attaingnant's publications were chanson prints, and in the second half of the century under Le Roy & Ballard that proportion increased to sixty percent.[4] The statistics are similar for Nicolas Du Chemin (who began printing in Paris in 1549), Tielman Susato, and the first half of Jacques Moderne's irregular forays into printing polyphony.[5] Even the large Venetian presses of Scotto and Gardane did not neglect the chanson. One of Gardane's first publications was an Attaingnant-style chansonnier, and Scotto hit upon a best seller with Jan Gero's *Primo libro dei madrigali & canzoni francese a doi voci* [1540], a set of newly composed madrigals and chanson paraphrases for two voices that ultimately ran to twenty-five editions. Profitable enough to attract imitators, we know that Attaingnant's *Vingt et neuf chansons* of 1530 was on its way to Venice to be copied by Francesco d'Asola when the shipment of books was stolen in the Alps.[6] Printer-booksellers throughout Europe took such a strong interest in the chanson that when they wrote music themselves (as did Gardane, Susato, and Adrian Le Roy), they composed chansons, often—as we have seen—in the popular two-voice arrangements they needed to fill out their catalogs.[7] Right around 1530, we can imagine the world of printed music as a world dominated by chansons, brief works that bookmen jumbled together in collective prints aimed to please with music that was easy to sing and play.

Successful chansonniers benefited printers and printer-booksellers, but they brought composers relatively little renown, for single-composer chansonniers were rare. The beginnings defined by Petrucci's chanson anthologies, the *Harmonice Musices Odhecaton A* (1501), *Canti B numero cinquanta* (1502), and *Canti C numero cento cinquanta* (1504), actually extended the practices that governed the assembling of manuscript chansonniers such as Florence, BNC 229; the Cappella Giulia Chansonnier; Uppsala, Universitetsbiblioteket MS 76a; Brussels, Bibliothèque royale MS 11239; and Copenhagen, Royal Library MS 1848, to name but a few of the most substantial and well-studied chansonniers from the period 1490 to 1520.[8] And in the same way that manuscript anthologies regularly failed to name the composers of the chansons they contained, so too printed anthologies often dispensed with attributions. Petrucci's ABC series of chansonniers provides a case in point: in those prints, about half of the chansons are anonymous, even though elsewhere Petrucci maintained that he did his best to ascribe pieces and took offense at assertions to the contrary.[9] Attaingnant, for his part, apparently conceived of the chanson anthology as a type of print that did not require names at all, at least initially, since the first seven of his surviving collections are entirely without attributions.[10] Instead, Attaingnant's prints highlighted the material quality of the chansons they contained, transforming them into objects traded for money, commodities. Title pages advertised novelty and sheer quantity, hawking their wares with titles such as "Twenty-Seven New Songs" or "First Book of New Songs"—standard formulas in a sector of the music market that presumably consumed the latest, and lots of it. Indeed, print had actually become productive of lyric by the 1540s and printers scrambled for new material to fill anthologies, yet the titles advertise not who wrote the songs but how many of them there were (see figure 2.)[11]

Motets, too, were regularly printed in anthologies such as Petrucci's *Motetti A, B,* and *C* series, the *Motteti del fiore, Motteti del frutto,* the German prints of Hans Ott, Melchior Kriesstein, and Georg Forster, and the fourteen-book series of motets Attaingnant published between 1534 and 1539. Some very early Roman and Parisian prints from the 1520s and 1530s even tossed motets together with chansons in miscellanies, though separation by genre was the norm even then. The important point for the history of authorship is that printers issued smaller works—motets included—in anthologies of their own device. The identity of composers

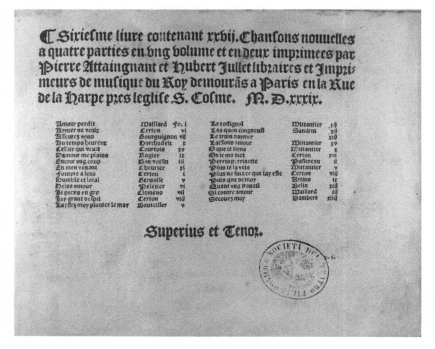

Figure 2.   Title page, *Sixiesme livre contenant xxvij. Chansons nouvelles a quatre parties en ung volume et en deux* (Paris: Attaingnant, 1539), superius and tenor. Photo courtesy of the Accademia filarmonica di Verona, shelfmark 207/1.

was of only secondary importance, and sometimes even genre did not operate as the primary means of organization.

THE NAMES OF AUTHORS

One place where attention to musical authorship proved more pronounced was Venice, a printing capital that eventually surpassed Paris as a center of music printing. In general, the book trade in Paris tended toward university textbooks, trade books for lawyers and theologians, and prayer books such as the Book of Hours *(Heures)*, of which printers churned out truly vast quantities (at least 395 editions of the *Heures* were published between 1501 and 1535, which meant that perhaps as many as 400,000 copies were produced in a city with a population of approximately 300,000).[12] In the first half of the century, vernacular production mostly comprised chivalric romances, handbooks of various sorts, and little poetry collections, books in which authorship counted for little if anything. It is hard to say why the culture of print and authorship differed so much in Venice. Perhaps the business model of the Aldine press created an environment in which authorship particularly mattered, for Manutius specialized in fine, affordable editions of classical texts that were inevitably issued as authored volumes. In the vernacular, the linguistic politics of Pietro Bembo's *Prose della volgar lingua* (1525) promoted the works of Petrarch, Boccaccio, and Dante as classics in their own right, further stabilizing the terrain that would provide such rich soil for the florescence of modern authors in Italian such as Baldassare Castiglione, whose handbook to court life, *Il cortegiano* (Venice, 1528), proved quite popular in small-format editions. So it was that when Andrea Antico, Ottaviano Scotto, and Antonio Gardane began printing madrigals in the 1530s, they issued them in single-composer volumes, of which Philippe Verdelot's *Libro primo a 4* (1533) and Jacques Arcadelt's enduringly popular *Primo* and *Secondo libro a 4* [1539] were among the first. Significantly, these early madrigal prints each included madrigals not by Verdelot or Arcadelt—they, too, were anthologies, but anthologies being sold as "authored" volumes. They seem to come directly from the desks of composers, but they, too, were created by an editor. Their authors' names do not guarantee their authenticity. Rather, the prints sport names like marketing banners on which "Arcadelt," "Verdelot," and other "famosi" pitch the contents to an increasingly name-conscious public, never mind that the collections were actually filled out with pieces by *altri eccellentissimi musici*.[13]

In the printed record, Arcadelt and Verdelot remained silent, despite the evident value accruing to their names with each reissue of their music. Printers, by contrast, set upon each other in struggles to stake claims of ownership to these books of music. One notorious case surrounds the publication of Arcadelt's second book of madrigals. Just a month after Scotto and Antico brought out their edition of Arcadelt's *Secondo libro de madrigali a quatro voci* (January 1539), Gardane issued a new edition under the title *Il vero secondo libro* ("The True Second Book"), accusing Scotto and Antico of falsely issuing madrigals by other composers under Arcadelt's name.[14] Here Gardane seems to be protecting "truth" and Arcadelt's good name, but presumably the value he defended was his exclusive right to Arcadelt's music. Both title pages include the line "Con gratia, & Privilegio," thereby asserting that the printer possessed a privilege from the Venetian Senate. So far, no such concessions have come to light, but Gardane's aggressive tone suggests that the right was his.[15] In a similar salvo, Gardane—who was especially proprietorial about his Arcadelt prints—denounced a printer in Milan for copying his edition of Arcadelt's *Primo libro*, but legally

Gardane had no recourse, since a Venetian privilege would only have pertained within the Republic.[16] Notably, one voice missing from all of these exchanges is Arcadelt's. There is no evidence that Arcadelt collaborated directly with any printers in these editions, nor did he assert rights to the music.

Printers operated according to needs and laws all their own, and nothing prevented them—legally—from printing music without the accord of its composer. Moreover, some negative evidence suggests that not all composers could afford to participate in commercial ventures, at least openly. Paradoxically, those composers with the most prominent appointments in Paris and Venice—that is, those composers working just steps from the hearts of the music publishing industry—were also the least likely to contribute signed dedications to prints of their music. Such reticence to add their authorial voices to these publications leaves historians hard-pressed to recover any sense of a composer's wishes directly from printed books. Most composers' dedications from before 1550 appear in Venetian prints, but they inevitably come from provincial musicians, who may have sought exposure in the new "virtual" environment of print. We have dedications from lesser and peripheral composers such as Gabriele Martinengo, Gian Domenico La Martoretta, Pietro Paolo Ragazzoni, and Claudio Veggio.[17] But from the most printed and reprinted composers of the age, such as Jacques Arcadelt, Clément Janequin, Claudin de Sermisy, Adrian Willaert, and Cipriano de Rore, we have not a single printed dedication, though sometimes prints of their music include dedications written by others. Like the centuries of authors whose prefaces explain that they brought their works to light only at the insistence of friends, the "Grande Arcadelte," "Famosissimi Adriani Willaert," and "Eccellentissimo Verdelot" remained in the shadows; if they collaborated with printers at all, they avoided public exchanges with patrons, which might have been inappropriate in environments like that of Venice, where the volume and proximity of print made publication all too revealing.[18] By contrast, Anton Francesco Doni, a newcomer to Venice who made his business trading in revelations, packed his *Dialogo della musica* of 1544 with no less than four dedications, one in each partbook, no doubt in an attempt to maximize returns on his labor. But then, Doni operated primarily as an editor and author, deliberately exploiting the opportunities of print. A braggart who claimed to have conquered Venice after his move from provincial Piacenza, he openly displayed his spoils by bringing to light unpublished pieces by Arcadelt, Willaert, and Rore in the *Dialogo*, much to his advantage.[19]

The scenario sketched above, in which the activities of music suppliers, editors, publishers, printers, and the legal values of the privilege system itself severed music from its composers, is not unlike the one that prevailed in the printing of play texts in Elizabethan England. As theater historians have shown, scripts belonged to the acting companies that played them and—there too—privileges went directly to the publisher. Playwrights had no legal say in the matter, and many of them evidently cared little to secure privileges themselves and assert their rights over the little six-penny pamphlets that contained cut-down versions of their scripts, scripts that in any case only lived when played out on the stage. Half of William Shakespeare's plays were printed during his lifetime, but none in an edition Shakespeare declared to be his own.[20] The evidence is negative, but it suggests that Shakespeare located his work elsewhere, in the collaborative environment of the playhouse, where actors improvised, vamped, and added phrasing, timbre, gesture, and facial expressions to the words they embodied. The very different conventions that ruled in the playhouse and printing house also suggest that scholars accept the vast gulf separating printed versions of plays from what was played on the stage. Institutional structures, guild memberships, financing, and the day-to-day activities and skills of the participants in each environment all separated theater from printshop. In his study of the disjunctions isolating the stage and the page, Roger Chartier sees their distinctiveness emerging from "an aesthetic incompatibility between the natural destination of plays which were written to be acted, seen, and heard, and the printed form which deprived them of their 'life.' "[21] The theater historian Stephen Orgel has put it even more emphatically: "If the play is a book, it's not a play."[22]

The discontinuities between plays and books did not prevent some playwrights from bringing their own works to light. Indeed, given that plays were occasionally sold to printers in mangled transcriptions made by listeners in the theater, some playwrights felt forced to involve themselves in the process.[23] One author speaking out in a preface of 1604 expresses glum resignation to the fact that if the scenes he had invented to be spoken "should be inforcively published to be read, . . . the least hurt I can receive, is to do my selfe the wrong."[24] Shakespeare's great contemporary, Ben Jonson, actively engaged in printing his own works, which evince considerable authorial self-consciousness. Keenly aware of the enduring fame to be had in print, he transformed his scripts into literary texts made for reading and printed in authoritative editions that removed interpolations made by collaborators and restored cuts made in the theater.[25]

Authorship, which for Shakespeare came at the hands of pamphleteers, was not unavailable to early modern playwrights, but it did require a set of ambitions and even financial investments that not all playwrights entertained.

The contrasting attitudes of Shakespeare and Jonson exemplify the legal and material gulfs that separated the performative world of the theater from the business of turning profits in print, and they can help clarify why composers, too, often remained uninvolved in the printing of their works. Those who neglected print may simply have been most engaged in the embodied performances through which they served their cathedrals, chapels, and patrons and for which their music was written in the first place. This is not just a matter of the separation of the activity of writing and performing, but derives from the nature of music itself as, in essence, an act that does not necessarily require texts at all. Even imitative polyphony could be improvised, as could ensemble performances of songs and dances, leaving historians of music at very much the same philosophical spot articulated by Orgel—if music is a book, it's not music. The singer-musicologist Richard Wistreich, speaking to this duality, reminds us that music is "notoriously ill-suited to entextualization—embodied; mobile; spatially, temporally and timbrally contingent; massively over-determined; and doggedly resistant to capture and authorial control."[26] Music itself, as an act, resists the press, and this very reality strongly inflects its uneven entextualizations during the first century of music printing.

Some composers did seek opportunities in print, registering claims to their compositions and attempting to rescue them from the commercial environment exemplified by the multiple editions of Arcadelt's madrigals, in which printers traded music as a commodity, often with missing, conflicting, and incorrect attributions. The lengthy dedication Francesco Corteccia contributed to Scotto's edition of his *Libro primo de madrigali a quattro voci* (1544) reveals that he was driven to print an authorized edition of his madrigals in order to correct the wrongs of earlier printers who misattributed his madrigals to others and those of others to him, and this is to say nothing of sloppy printing that left his pieces full of "scorrezzioni bruttissime & d'importantissimi errori" (the ugliest defects and most grave errors).[27] Corteccia likely obtained financial backing for the publication from his patron, Cosimo I, the duke of Florence and the book's dedicatee, who must have seen some advantage in aiding his chapelmaster to consolidate his identity in print.[28] The circulation of madrigals in Venetian prints had intensified so greatly that in 1546, Jacquet Berchem complained in the dedication of his *Madrigali a cinque voci* of thieves who steal the madrigals of others like "Corvi che si vestono bene spesso la piuma del Cygno" (crows that often deck themselves out like swans).[29] Venetian printers occasionally reassured readers that they worked from the composer's own copy of the music ("da li suoi proprii exemplari fatta"), but only prints with explanatory dedications from the composer might truly be called "authorized."

The one composer to have attained significant authorial control during the sixteenth century is Lassus. Born around 1532, his music first appeared in 1555 with an Italian edition of his *Primo libro di madrigali a cinque voci*, and, in Antwerp, Susato's edition of the *Quatoirsiesme livre a quatre parties contenant dixhuyct chansons italiennes, six chansons francoises, et six motetz faictz (a la nouvelle composition d'aucuns d'italie) par Rolando di Lassus*, a collection of chansons, madrigals, and motets that musicologists have dubbed his "Opus 1," doubtless to rescue it from the obscurity of the numbered chanson series in which it first appeared.[30] Lassus, who was in Antwerp at the time of publication, may himself have sought to promote his status as author, for Susato released, in the same year, a second version of the print with the authoritative Italian title *D'orlando di Lassus Il primo libro* . . . and a personal dedication from Lassus to Stefano Gentile, a Genoese banker resident in the city.[31] After this auspicious start, prints of Lassus's music issued from presses in Venice, Louvain, Nuremberg, Paris, Munich, and even London.[32] Across his long career, he consistently wrote in every major genre and vernacular language (except English), and, unlike most eminent composers of the preceding generation, he publicly dedicated prints of his music to notables ranging from the Veronese music lover Mario Bevilacqua and the duke of Ferrara to the king of France and Pope Clement VIII. Certainly the practices of gift giving implied by printed dedications changed as the century wore on, but Lassus also placed a unique premium on the value of his printed works. Nothing testifies to this more dramatically than the personal printing privileges he acquired from King Charles IX of France in 1571 and from Emperor Rudolf II in 1582.[33] These concessions accorded printing rights directly to him, effectively recognizing his legal ownership of his compositions, both those already written and those that he might write in the future. Thus, the protection granted to Lassus pertained to printed books, but the rights he secured also covered his output as an author, and in this respect the privileges differed categorically from those that musicians sometimes obtained when they partnered up with printers in various publishing ventures.[34] Lassus could choose his own printer, and in

France, he worked with the Royal Printer of Music, Le Roy & Ballard. As of that juncture, Le Roy & Ballard began to issue Lassus's music in single-composer volumes in a new, large quarto format with enhanced typography, splendid initial letters, and slews of panegyric verse. In Germany, Lassus took the opportunity of his new imperial privilege to have motets previously issued by Adam Berg in Munich reprinted by Katharina Gerlach in Nuremberg. A lawsuit ensued between the two printers, but Lassus was fully within his rights to bring out new editions of his music, and Gerlach won the case.[35]

Lassus's authorial privileges were extraordinary for the age, by any measure. In France, only the court poet Pierre de Ronsard possessed as comprehensive a right to control the printed dissemination of his works. Granted by letters patent in 1553, the long privilege advances a series of arguments clearly informed by Ronsard's own ideologies of language, literature, and authorship—presumably Ronsard drafted it himself. It expresses the king's dismay at the state of publishing in France and admonishes printers who bring works to light "au desceu des autheurs, & sur telz exemplaires au'ilz en peuvent recouvrer, sans regarder s'ilz sont veritables ou faulx & corrompuz" (without the knowledge of authors, and working from such copies as they may find, without regard as to whether they are accurate or false and corrupted).[36] Such textual errors, the privilege continues, endanger the quality of French literature (*bonnes lettres*), and, moreover, by their multiplication in print, they risk corrupting the truth and purity of the French language itself. To forestall such dire consequences, the patent accords Ronsard the right to choose his own printer for all his works, past and future, since the best guarantee of correctness and fidelity was for the author to supervise the printing process. The very fate of the French language hung in the balance.

As we shall see in the chapters that follow, Ronsard's self-promotion in print proved a watershed in the history of French lyric. His command of print likewise established a significant model of authorship for French chanson composers. In 1576 the composer Guillaume Boni would be accorded a royal privilege like the one awarded to Lassus, and—notably—in order to correct a corrupt edition of his *Sonetz de P. de Ronsard, mis en musique a quatre parties.*[37] But Boni's privilege is the only other author's privilege known to have been given to a musician in sixteenth-century France, and even among literary authors, Ronsard's privilege was unique. Looking ahead, in the eighteenth century the great encyclopedist and Enlightenment philosopher Denis Diderot would still be arguing for legal definitions that honored the rights of authors.[38] In his "Letter on the Book

Trade" of 1763, he asks: "Indeed, what can a man possess, if a product of the mind, the unique fruit of his education, his study, his efforts, his time, his research, his observation . . . if his own thoughts, the feelings of his heart, the most precious part of himself, that part which does not perish, that which immortalizes him, cannot be said to belong to him? . . . Who has more right than the author to use his goods by giving or selling them?"[39] Diderot's rhetorical question was novel even in 1763, a philosopher's deliberate provocation to a book trade secure in its centuries-old licensing system. Then, as in the sixteenth century, the short answer to Diderot's question would have been: books belong to those who make them. Thoughts counted for little, absent the tangible objects that gave them substance. From the perspective of the printers and publishers who financed book production and the typecutters, engravers, type founders, compilers, press operators, proofreaders, and shop hands whose labor created the music books we study, the initial imagining of a piece of music and any struggles a composer may have undergone to perfect it may well have seemed incidental compared to the messy work of compiling the type, locking it into a frame with wooden spacers and any woodblocks being used for initial letters, and impressing hundreds of moistened sheets of paper with this inked forme. The labor of printers fixed music to the page, and just as the history of musical ownership must take account of its legal framing by the book trade, so too, the very history of authorship depends extensively on the practices of the printshop and the men and women whose livelihoods centered on the presses.

2. Music Books and Their Authors

EDITORS AND CRAFTSMEN

Though the notion clashes with modern definitions of authorship, one could say that it was not composers who authored printed books, but printers, printer-booksellers, and editors. These individuals acquired the music, compiled the books, titled them, and issued them, often in series of their own device. In short, they made the books upon which authorship depended. Perhaps the most vivid illustration of the authorial status claimed by bookmen is the *Liber quindecim missarum*, an anthology issued by Andrea Antico, a woodblock cutter in Rome. The *Liber quindecim missarum* is dated May 9, 1516, and was dedicated to Pope Leo X. On the title page, a diminutive Antico kneels before the pontiff and offers him a book of music, presumably the *Liber quindecim missarum* itself, which contained Masses by Josquin des Prez, Antoine Brumel, Antoine de Févin, Pierre de La Rue, Jean Mouton, and others (see figure 3). In the image, the book is open to a canon on the text "Vivat Leo Decimus, Pontifex Maximus," and inside the actual volume there are further "Leonine" elements, such as the lion that forms the stem of the initial "K" for the Kyrie of the first Mass. The bid for patronage from Leo X organizes most of the paratextual portions of the book, and the title page replicates the scenes of princely dedication commonly found in presentation manuscripts, in which an author kneels before the throne of his prince or king.[1] The pope extends his blessing in the same manner that Christ or the Virgin blessed mortal donors in the iconography of contemporary altarpieces, reaffirming the relationship between sovereign and author as one of Christian fealty. The hierarchy imagined here attributes to the pope ultimate authority over the volume before him, one for which his subvention is being sought through the luxuriousness of the object itself.

The unprecedented splendor of the music book's title page, the coordination of the historiated initials with the subject of each Mass, the size, number, and craftsmanship of the woodcuts, and the expansiveness of the "royal" sized paper *(carta reale)* on which the hefty tome was printed were surely paired with a fine leather binding and possibly hand-coloring of the sort evident in the copy of the *Liber quindecim missarum* held by the Biblioteka Uniwersytecka in Toruń, Poland. The presentation copy may well have been printed on parchment, as gifts often were. In sum, the material form of the book aimed to capture the uniqueness and allure of the most beautiful illuminated manuscripts from the age of scribal production. It surely pleased Leo, who sang and played the lute and harpsichord and whose patronage of music was legendary.[2]

Antico's prominence on the title page is, however, a modern touch consonant with the shifts in authorship that coincided with the invention of printing. His solitary audience with the pope accentuates his importance, heightening his individual relationship with the pontiff by excising the crowds into which poets and other writers so often disappeared in manuscript miniatures of throne-room gift giving.[3] At the same time, Antico's anthology suppressed the literary authority being formulated by writers in the years around 1500 as their works moved from manuscript to print. The names of Josquin, Brumel, and others feature prominently in the table of contents fronting the *Liber quindecim missarum,* but it is Antico who seizes authorship of the book itself. Such depictions of the relationships between "author" and dedicatee remind us of how print revised the gift economy regulating patronage by introducing a new host of intermediaries that included publishers, xylographers, type designers, printers, booksellers, and their publics. Composers eventually involved themselves in printing ventures in various ways, finding financial backers for their publications, convincing patrons to bankroll printing costs, collaborating with bookseller-publishers to broker deals with printers, sometimes financing publications themselves (though rarely), working as house editors for compensation that may have come in the form of prints, and even moving into the printing trade themselves, as Gardane did after having already been published by Jacques Moderne. But in the early decades of the century, the authority available to composers in print was not comparable to that achieved by writers.

This chapter proposes several hypotheses as to why music was so resistant to the forms of authorship available earlier in literary and scientific

Figure 3. Title page, *Liber quindecim missarum* (Rome: Andrea Antico, 1516). In this image, the Roman woodcutter Andrea Antico kneels before Pope Leo X, offering him the book of music it took him nearly three years to manufacture. The book held by Antico falls open to a canon on the text "Vivat Leo Decimus, Pontifex Maximus." Biblioteca Nazionale Centrale, Florence. By permission of the Ministero per i Beni e le Attività Culturali.

publications. Certainly one part of the answer has to do with the fact that, as an industry, music printing lagged behind printed production of other sorts of books owing to the particular processes it required and the limited market for polyphonic prints. But alongside these impediments, it needs to be understood that it was not "the music itself" for which authorship was being claimed in these books. Nor did composition adequately account for the balance of labor that went into producing the object being sold. When Antico entered the music trade as a contender to Petrucci, the dynamics of these material claims to the printed book of music came to be cast in sharp relief through the language of privileges and dedications as each sought to stake out proprietary rights, and so it is worth lingering over the *Liber quindecim missarum* and its well-documented publication history for a moment because it has so much to reveal about the financing of early music editions, the role of patronage and privileges, and the involvement of composers in these initial stages of the new business, which operated independently from the business of music making.

The *Liber quindecim missarum* was one of a series of exchanges between Antico and the pope in which the engraver's gift of music was neither the first nor the last. According to the privilege printed at the back of the *Liber quindecim missarum*, on January 27, 1516, Leo X had awarded Antico a ten-year grant to print polyphonic music in "magno volumine ac regalis Chartis."[4] Significantly, the privilege was not for a specific repertoire, but for Antico's new process for printing folio choirbooks on "royal" sheets of paper. (Paper came in four standard sizes called, from largest to smallest, "imperialle," "realle," "mezane," and "rezute," so Antico planned for his book to be relatively large.)[5] Leo X likely took a genuine interest in the project, for not only did he prove an excellent patron to Antico, he awarded more book privileges than other popes, most often to assist scholars.[6] The papal indult also prohibited Petrucci from printing such books, making clear the threat that Antico posed to Petrucci's virtual monopoly.[7] By 1516, Antico had already issued three collections of frottole reprinting repertoire from Petrucci's frottola books, which were protected only with a Venetian privilege.[8] But these were modest ventures—small prints of just forty or fifty folios in quarto or octavo format. The Mass anthology was by contrast infinitely more ambitious. It was, in fact, a polyphonic print of a magnificence that had never been realized and, as such, made the perfect offering to flatter the humanistic pope.

In the preface to the volume, Antico deploys phrases common to the language in which printers, publishers, and authors petitioned for privileges, clarifying that his investment included not just capital, but ingenuity, craftsmanship, and labor.[9] He emphasized the novelty of the printing technique ("I have cut the notes in wooden tablets [which no one before me has done], and I have executed them with a new method of printing"), the unprecedented size and beauty of the music books ("I have published them in royal volumes by great care and long labor"), and the years he expended bringing the anthology to light ("I have devoted nearly three years to this forthcoming business from its inception").[10] The book is truly a remarkable achievement. Printed by Antonio Giunta (with the costs shared by Ottaviano Scotto), it employed a single-impression method in which the music and staff lines were cut into the same block, the text underlaid in type supplied by Giunta, and the whole forme printed in one go (this by contrast with Petrucci's multiple-impression method, in which the musical notes were typeset and imposed on preprinted staves). At 162 folios, it was an impressive tome indeed, and it is worth observing here that it was the first book of Masses printed in choirbook layout. Unlike the quarto partbooks of Masses issued by Petrucci, the *Liber quindecim missarum* really was a "book"—a single volume that could be bound as a textual unit. Its regal format invited the glamorous title page it received, in which the book itself takes center stage.

Antico's dedication of the *Liber quindecim missarum* quickly brought the returns for which he had hoped. Before the year was out, the pope had cancelled Petrucci's unused privilege for printing organ tablatures and transferred it to Antico instead.[11] Less than a month later, Antico issued the *Frottole intabulate da sonare organi,* a publication that must already have been under way in anticipation of the pope's favoritism. This was the first print of Italian keyboard music—another printing first—and here too, the privilege sought by Antico has as much or more to do with the technology involved (printing keyboard tablature from woodcuts) than it does with repertoire, which is not specifically mentioned in the grant. In this respect the privilege is like the one awarded to the *Liber quindecim missarum,* which protects not the contents (it is for "books of polyphony") but the novel format (folio volumes printed on *carta reale*). The two enterprises share further similarities: the title page of the *Frottole intabulate* features a portrait of Antico, here playing a harpsichord. Once again, Antico visually claims authorship of the volume, even though it is devoted almost entirely to the frottole of Bartolomeo Tromboncino (see figure 4).[12]

Although Leo X is absent, the woodcut reaffirms Antico's loyalty by including the Medici coat of arms on the music desk, precisely where the

Figure 4.   Title page, *Frottole intabulate da sonare organi* (Rome: Andrea Antico, 1517). Antico plays the harpsichord, and the Medici coat of arms embellishes the music desk, a reference to Pope Leo X and his protection of Antico's printing venture. With permission from the National Library, Prague.

book of music would rest. Next to the harpsichord sits an apple or squash that might represent the "fructus laborum suarum" protected by his privilege. The image may also level an amusing jab at Petrucci by depicting him as a monkey playing the lute. Next to the music desk, a lady holds open a book of music in upright quarto, a common format for frottola manuscripts. She looks away from the music and points at the monkey—if it is Petrucci who is being ribbed, the scene may make fun of him because he only managed to publish instrumental music for the lute, not the keyboard tablatures for which he had just lost the privilege.

Antico's gratitude for the pope's favors continued to be acknowledged, though his final "dedication" is really for insiders only: the title page of the *Canzoni, sonetti, strambotti et frottole libro quarto* printed the same year features the music for the "Vivat Leo Decimus" canon engraved in a circle around a head crowned with laurel wreaths (see figure 5). Whether the Apollonian figure in the center refers to the Mount Parnassus flourishing under Leo's rule or is intended as a portrait of Cardinal Giulio de' Medici (later Pope Clement VII) is less important than the recognizable canon, which even without its text added a final repartee to the exchanges between Antico and his patron.[13]

Figure 5.   Title page, *Canzoni, sonetti, strambotti et frottole libro quarto* (Rome: Andrea Antico, 1517). Here the canon on "Vivat Leo Decimus" reappears without its text. Biblioteca Nazionale Centrale, Florence. By permission of the Ministero per i Beni e le Attività Culturali.

Antico's title pages, prefaces, dedications, and privileges reveal a business operating somewhere closer to the gift economy of patronage than full-fledged commerce. In the first instance, papal privileges required social angling and possibly an audience. Successful petitions resulted in a papal breve formulated as a letter from the pontiff to the supplicant and Holy See full of praise for the recipient and his work.[14] They forbade anyone to print or sell the work without permission on pain of excommunication, a fine, and confiscation of the offending copies. Papal privileges were powerful indeed. Not only did they carry the threat of excommunication, in principle they were valid throughout Christendom. In reality, too, printers outside the Papal States were occasionally prosecuted for infringements with positive results; the pope's authority was felt as far away as Paris.[15] Papal privileges were, moreover, awarded in far fewer numbers than those in effect in the Venetian Republic, which were granted so liberally and in such great numbers by so many authorities (the Ducal Councillors, the Senate, and the Council of Ten) that by 1517 they had paralyzed the book trade completely enough to force the Senate to revoke all privileges not issued on its own authority. Henceforth, privileges for whole categories of prints and for long periods would no longer be awarded: they were limited to new titles and awarded only with a two-thirds vote of the Senate.[16] Privileges such as the twenty-year grant Petrucci received in 1498 to print "canto figurado et canto fermo" were typical only of this first stage of commercial printing and only for Venice. In Paris, the norm in the first part of the sixteenth century was two to three years at most.[17] Royal privileges for music prints were generally granted for ten years in the latter half of the century.

Antico's deference to the pope and the flattering language of the privileges he received evince the most courtly dimension of the social commerce between sovereigns and their subjects. But it should not obscure the fact that very real money changed hands in such transactions, for at that time papal privileges came at a price as high as thirty ducats or florins.[18] Would-be publishers often invested considerable sums just in trying to present their supplications. In 1533, the composer Elzéar Genet—known as Carpentras—paid an intermediary twenty crowns to seek a French *privilegium regium* from François Ier for the publication he had under way of his complete works (his agent was unsuccessful).[19] Presumably he had already asked Pope Clement VII for a privilege, since he had dedicated two volumes to the pope in 1532. The *Liber primus missarum Carpentras* (Avignon, 1532) and the *Liber lamentationum Hieremiae prophetae Carpentras* (Avignon, 1532) bear only the words "Cum Gratia et Privilegio" on the title pages, though the short formula is in itself not evidence that Carpentras was unsuccessful in petitioning the pope for his favor.[20] Indeed, Carpentras had already given Clement VII his Lamentations in manuscript, which apparently pleased the pope.[21] Perhaps the sumptuous manuscript, now cataloged as Cappella Sistina 163, was designed to broker the deal for the printing privilege. Dedications and the privileges they secured could alleviate a portion of the risks involved in high-investment undertakings, making them of vital interest to bookmen. Privileges brought no subventions, but the imprimatur of the pope did protect books against piracy, and technologies against theft.[22]

However privileges were obtained, they added to the considerable costs of publication, most of which went to the purchase of paper.[23] Antico, we must remember, had to organize a sizable coalition of backers to bring out the *Liber quindecim missarum*. In addition to hoping for the pope's grace, he negotiated contracts with members of two of the most successful publishing dynasties in Italy—the houses of Giunta and Scotto. Ottaviano

Scotto advanced Antico the money to print 1,008 copies and agreed to take care of selling the books, splitting the profits with Antico after he recovered his initial investment of over six hundred ducats.[24] Scotto brought to the deal his family's extensive distribution network, which included bookshops in Naples, Milan, Mantua, and Rome, and the agency of yet more family members who traveled across Italy working for the press.[25] The House of Scotto—a large firm with the financial muscle to invest in innovative publishing ventures such as Antico's choirbook—also established syndicates with other merchant-printers to aid in the distribution of books. Antico's other partner, Antonio Giunta, came from an established family of printers and booksellers, one with whom the Scottos had regular dealings during the sixteenth century. The Giunta family originated in Florence, but by 1520 they had branches in Venice, Rome, Lyon, and Spain (these latter would eventually reach from Burgos and Salamanca to Madrid).[26] The firm specialized in liturgical books, and many of their editions marked "firsts" in printing. The most imposing example is surely Luc'Antonio Giunta's editions of the *Graduale romanum* (1499/1500) and *Antiphonarium romanum* (1503/4); they were issued in humongous broadside volumes in which each sheet of paper was bound unfolded, making them the largest printed books of any sort of the age.[27] Although Antico only engaged Antonio Giunta to print the *Liber quindecim missarum* for a flat fee, the family's eminence in the production of supersized books for Catholic rites and the international scope of their enterprise no doubt proved useful in the sale of the Mass prints. Antico's subsequent dealings with the Giunti continued apace—Antonio's father, Jacomo di Biagio Giunta, financed editions of the second and third books of *Canzoni, sonetti, strambotti et frottole,* both printed by Giacomo Mazzocchi in 1518 with woodcuts by Antico.[28]

Such cooperative relationships among editors, merchant-printers, and printer-booksellers sustained an industry rife with financial peril. They also reveal the professional origins of those who pioneered the business of music publishing—though many had or acquired some musical literacy, none were composers. Rather, they were inventors, printers, engravers, woodcutters, type founders, and booksellers, developers of a new technology. Petrucci claimed to have invented a method for printing music; Antico specialized in cutting woodblocks and later went to work for the Scotto press in Venice; Giunta and Scotto came from established publishing dynasties that dealt in music only as a sideline; Pierre Attaingnant was a "libraire" who married the daughter of a Parisian printer and engraver, Pierre Pigouchet, and seems to have established his firm through his wife's inheritance; and Jacques Moderne was a bookseller-printer who added music to his production in 1532 but continued to print ordinary texts at twice the rate of his musical output. Moderne probably engaged as music editor Francesco de Layolle, a brilliant Florentine organist resident in Lyon, and possibly "P. de Villiers" as well.[29] Like Moderne, Antonio Blado, Valerio Dorico, Johann vom Berg, Ulrich Neuber, and Jean de Laet were all printers or printer-booksellers with no evident expertise in music. Attaingnant may have engaged Pierre Blondeau, a singer and scribe at the Chapelle royale, to edit music for him, and in the last years of the firm we know that Claude Gervaise worked as editor, arranger, and corrector in the Rue de la Harpe.[30] Nicolas Du Chemin, who began to add music books to his production after marrying into Attaingnant's extended family, engaged a series of musicians in his printshop beginning in 1548. The first of his house editors, Nicole Regnes, lodged with Du Chemin and received a monthly salary in return for which he was expected to proofread the music books and to teach Du Chemin "the art of music and . . . to sing and hold his part."[31] After 1551, Claude Goudimel worked for Du Chemin; between 1561 and 1568 Du Chemin issued four anthologies "veüs et corrigées par Loys Bisson"; and Henry Chandor, a choirmaster from Grenoble, is similarly credited in a print from 1576.[32]

Of all these early music printers, Antonio Gardane was unique for having worked as a professional musician before he became a booksellerprinter in Venice in 1538 (though it should be noted that Antico included two of his own frottole in his *Canzoni . . . libro tertio* of 1513). Only with the second generation of music publishers who set up shop in the 1540s and 1550s do we find a significant number of bookmen entering the trade from the music profession. Individuals such as Tielman Susato (a sackbut player), Hubert Waelrant (a singer), Adrian Le Roy (a lutenist), and Antonio Barrè (a singer in the Cappella Giulia) could compose, edit, and make their own arrangements or intabulations. Nonetheless, they did not dominate the trade. Composers still sought positions in cathedrals or as chapelmasters for their livelihood, and those musicians who did go into publishing still often felt it necessary to pair up with printing entrepreneurs and vice versa, which is how the firms of Waelrunt & Laet and Le Roy & Ballard were formed.

The prints of craftsmen such as Robert Granjon, the great designer and cutter of type, further demonstrate the extent to which the musicpublishing business relied on technical ingenuity in dealing with unusual graphic forms, not musical expertise. Granjon's publications in *caractères de civilité* set a new standard of beauty in chansonniers at mid-century, even though much of the music he printed with the new type came from Attaingnant. The same could be said of Granjon's solution to some graphic problems that made it difficult to print tablature: his typographic innovations unleashed a veritable flood of lute and guitar intabulations into the Parisian booktrade.[33] Many printing trends depended on technology, not just desire, market, or the availability of repertoire. Indeed, the entire system of book privileges emerged from the means by which other inventors patented new machines and techniques for processing silk, manufacturing glassware, and the like. Even into the eighteenth century, technology defined the shrinking limits of the printing privilege held by the Ballard family, which kept them churning out music set with clunky movable type and broken staff lines long after competitors took over the market with beautifully engraved scores made using copper plates. In the eighteenth century, they printed the works of André Campra and Jean-Philippe Rameau and exercised their prerogative as Royal Printers of Music to issue grand folio scores of Jean-Baptiste Lully's *tragédies en musique*. But in the end, even the glory of royal music, the king's imprimatur, and the names of famous authors could not sustain the prestige of the press when its book design was so badly dated, and the Ballard firm barely limped through the demise of the ancien régime.

At the beginning of this chapter, I suggested that in the anthology-dominated world of music publishing, merchant-printers "authored" books of music. Despite their collective lack of musical training, they took charge of the creation of music books not by writing the music but by authoring the processes and technologies by which music came to be printed. The men who worked during the first decades of music printing parlayed mechanical skills, entrepreneurship, adventurousness, a bit of wealth, and no doubt a measure of flair into objects that came to be valued and traded in their own rights. That they claimed authorship of those books fits a material culture in which the physical object and the ingenuity required to produce it competed for precedence with the text or texts it contained. My argument is not that authority was located exclusively in books; rather, it aims to establish the separation between books and compositional authority at the time. The music itself—the sounding object—and those who produced it inhabited a realm of performance only loosely intersected by these textual witnesses. Moreover, those sources close to performance and close to the day-to-day working environment of composers show little sign of being centered in a scriptural culture where authority was vested in the production of a written corpus.

Some evidence for this can even be drawn from books themselves. The late fifteenth- and early sixteenth-century choirbooks of the Sistine Chapel, for instance, were constructed from single sheets of *carta reale* made into bifolia by being attached to strips of parchment and then gathered together. In this form, they probably served as performance materials for the choir even before being bound.[34] Vatican manuscripts such as C.S. 44 (containing motets arranged according to the church year) and C.S. 45 (containing Magnificat settings and motets arranged according to psalm tone) may show large-scale planning, but despite their textual coherence, as bibliographic objects they are essentially collections of sheet music to which new pieces were added as they were composed or acquired. Not unlike the ringbinders used by musicians today, the design of the choirbooks allowed the chapel to maintain a repertoire in flux, to rearrange compilations of sheets and remove or replace folia with some ease. Such textual instability evinces the dynamics of a high-caliber performance institution. Significantly, there is no evidence that the music penned by the more illustrious composers in the choir was handled any differently than the rest of the repertoire. Their works were anthologized, copyists left works unattributed, and at least one composer even complained that copyists mangled his works.[35]

Folio prints such as Antico's seem to be of a completely different nature than the manuscript "loose-leaf" choirbooks they were made to resemble, as though Antico's editorship conceptually united the volume in the same way that leather-covered boards were used to bind gatherings into the hefty codices we have today. And yet there is no telling how folio Mass prints were actually used in the sixteenth century, or whether they were always bound. Nicolas Du Chemin printed a whole series of individual Masses in folio in choirbook layout, and although they survive exclusively in tract volumes, each print was only ten to sixteen folios long, and almost all of them were designed to be sold (and presumably used) independently of one another, each with its own title page.[36] Having issued sixteen of them in this form in the late 1550s, though, by 1568 Du Chemin clearly had healthy numbers still in stock and was keen to move them along, so he printed up a couple of title pages announcing the publication of a *Liber primus* and *Liber secundus* of Masses that suggested the entire series to collectors in two volumes.[37] As an extra incentive, buyers of the Masses listed in the *Liber primus* were rewarded with a "free" motet that occupied the central opening of the single bifolio title page, an "Asperges me" *a 4* by Cristóbal de Morales. Thus we see how closely even large printed anthologies sometimes approached the flying folios of the papal chapel and the textual mobility that could render print too ephemeral to support grandiose claims of authorship for composers.

Composers did eventually formulate identities in print, dramatically appropriating models such as those Antico carved out in the *Liber quindecim missarum*. As we shall see, in 1554 Palestrina advanced a year's salary to have his *Missarum liber primus* printed on the model of Antico's luxury Mass anthology. But such systems of authorial projection had not always been in place. For this new textual authority to emerge, certain material forms proved more useful than others, namely, the single-composer print (instead of the anthology) and, to a lesser extent, the folio choirbook (rather than quarto partbooks).[38] Taken together, they formed a bibliographical object to which a composer's name might be attached with the same prominence Antico had advertised his achievements in the *Liber quindecim missarum* and the *Frottole intabulate*. Finally, for composers to engage in the printed publication of their works, social conditions affecting their profession also had to change in ways that made printing remunerative, either in cash, patronage, or by contributing to reputations formerly founded almost exclusively on performance. In the following sections, then, I trace the textual appearances of the composer as author, a path that will take us first to liturgical music and—in the following chapters—to the secular anthologies that fed the presses of high-volume commercial printing.

CHOIRBOOKS, MASSES, AND FAME

The first prints devoted to the works of a single composer were Petrucci's series of Masses, which began with the *Misse Josquin* of 1502. This choice on Petrucci's part has long affirmed modern notions of Josquin's greatness, the esteem he commanded, and the idea that Petrucci hoped to feed a nascent market for polyphony with a blockbuster trading on Josquin's name.[39] But as we have already observed, nothing suggests Josquin's involvement in any of the printing ventures essayed during his lifetime.[40] Nor is there evidence that Petrucci collaborated with any of the other composers whose Masses were to follow: Jacob Obrecht, Antoine Brumel, Johannes Ghiselin, Pierre de La Rue (all 1503), Alexander Agricola (1504), Marbriano de Orto (1505), Heinrich Isaac (1506). Moreover, Petrucci's prints hardly seem formulated as vehicles of fame for their authors. In the first place, Petrucci printed the Masses in modest sets of quarto partbooks, possibly because he wished to avoid having the individual Mass sections run across too many openings, as they would have had he retained the

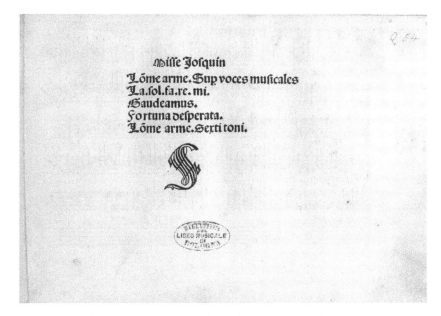

Figure 6.   Title page of superius partbook, *Misse Josquin* (Venice: Petrucci, 1502). Josquin's name appears nowhere else in the edition, not even on the title pages of the other partbooks. Photo courtesy of the Museo internazionale e Biblioteca della musica, Bologna.

same choirbook layout he had used for the *Odhecaton*.[41] Unlike Antico's luxury choirbook, the prints were not single volumes in royal folio. Second, attributions were barely visible on the actual volumes, where the composer's name appeared on the title page and often in the running headers of the superius partbook, but not in the other parts (see figure 6). This omission clearly frustrated at least one early owner of a binder's volume now in Munich (Bavarian State Library, Mus. Ant. Pract. D224), who added "Misse Josquin" by hand to the title pages of the lower voice parts.[42] Binder's volumes further obscured Josquin's authorship—if the surviving copies of Petrucci's editions of Josquin's Masses are any indication, owners were just as likely to bind them together with the works of other composers as they were to bind them together in a set.[43]

It is hard to presume on the basis of these prints that contemporaries associated musicians such as Josquin and Obrecht with books of music, or that print was a natural locus of authorial identity. Indeed, the circumstances surrounding the production of Petrucci's first four Mass volumes suggest that those who sought social gains in early printed books were not composers but publishers and courtiers. As Stanley Boorman has argued, the sequence and dates of Petrucci's first Mass volumes mirror several evolutions in the attempts of the Ferrarese court to permanently engage a chapelmaster. The *Misse Josquin*, for instance, were printed seven months before the composer arrived in Ferrara in late April 1503, appearing just at the time a dispute was raging over whether to hire Josquin or Heinrich Isaac to lead the chapel.[44]

Misse Josquin: September 27, 1502	Josquin arrives in Ferrara late April 1503
Misse Obrecht: March 24, 1503	Obrecht succeeds Josquin in 1504
[Misse] *Brumel:* June 17, 1503	Brumel appointed by Alfonso in 1505
[Misse] *Joannes Ghiselin:* July 15, 1503	Produced in anticipation of Ghiselin's arrival in Ferrara in 1503

Boorman posits that the publications received financial backing from Ferrara and were intended, in the first instance, to garner support for the appointment of Josquin over that of Heinrich Isaac. In this scenario, the *Misse Josquin* would have been used by the chapel in Ferrara and distributed to other courts, "whence," according to Boorman, "people might write to Ferrara and praise the music," thus amplifying support for Josquin's candidacy over that of Isaac.[45] Obrecht and Brumel, to whom the next two volumes were devoted, were also favorites with the court at the time of publication and subsequently engaged as chapelmasters. In the case of Ghiselin, Boorman has demonstrated that the book was produced while Ghiselin was en route to Ferrara, presumably "to flatter him" upon his arrival and "to encourage him to think he would be highly esteemed in Italy."[46] It is impossible to know how avidly the music was received and whether the books were performed from or simply admired as a bibliographic curio, but whatever the reception, Boorman's scenario nicely corrects presumptions that Josquin enjoyed worldwide renown and reigns in presumptions about Petrucci's choices by explaining them in local terms.

The careful framing of Boorman's argument draws attention to the novelty of print and its limited cultural reach and it deserves to be taken one step further here. For while Boorman suggests that print would circulate Ghiselin's Masses widely "and glory would be reflected back on the

Figure 7.   One of several versions of the printer's mark
"Fama" used by Ottaviano Scotto. From Giulio Bonagionta
et al, *Canzone napolitane a tre voci, secondo libro* (Venice:
Scotto, 1566), title page. By permission of the Jean Gray
Hargrove Music Library, University of California, Berkeley.

court," such glory would have been restricted indeed.[47] Fame in print arrived only later in the century and primarily in printing capitals like Venice, where poets and literary authors came to espouse print by the 1530s,
even though skeptics continued to prefer manuscript circulation of their
works and many authors hid their own involvement in printing their works
behind claims that friends had brought them to light.[48] The Scotto press
employed a series of printer's marks featuring *fama* with her trumpet
astride a globe (one of which is given as figure 7), but the glory Petrucci's
prints might have brought to Ghiselin or the d'Este court in 1503 is nonetheless an uncertain commodity.[49]

Unlike literature, theology, and scientific writing circa 1500, music appears to have had no tradition of books by a single composer. Whereas
works such as Petrarch's *Canzoniere,* Dante's *Divina Commedia,* and Mar-
silio Ficino's *De vita libri tres* were conceived of as books upon writing,
music was in one sense always "occasional"—destined for performance as
part of the liturgy, devotional practices, court ceremony, entertainment,

dance, and other social events. The large surviving sets of choirbooks from Milan Cathedral, the Vatican, and the d'Este court chapel all take the church calendar and other liturgical forms as their mode of organization, which is unsurprising given the ceremonial origins of much polyphony. Even the most abstract and self-standing genres were not necessarily bookish in the sense of being transmitted in manuscripts of a single composer's oeuvre. Many composers devoted considerable energy to writing cyclic Masses, in which the otherwise independent sections of the Mass Ordinary were linked through the use of a common cantus firmus or other musical device into a single whole. Polyphonic Masses were sizable, enjoyed significant prestige by comparison with motets and vernacular songs, and composers usually wrote at least the three that would be required to fill out a thin bound book. They are precisely the genre most often invoked in discussions of musical genius in the Renaissance.[50] Yet manuscripts containing Mass Ordinary settings, which did not need to be grouped according to tone or feast days, show little sign of having then taken authorship as a basis for forming a book. Prominent composers with large oeuvres worked for church and chapel, yet their traces are not to be found in the manuscripts including their music.[51] The Vatican library does include the Lamentations that Carpentras presented to Pope Clement VII sometime between 1524 and 1530 (C.S. 163), as well as the manuscript C.S. 18 (ca. 1538), a collection of polyphonic hymns and Magnificats by Costanzo Festa, who sang in the papal choir from 1517 until his death in 1545. Yet these sources, which date from the third or fourth decade of the century, are the earliest examples in the Sistine *fondo* of manuscripts containing works of a single composer from the chapel. One of the most beautiful music manuscripts at the Vatican, the so-called Chigi Codex (Chigi C. VIII. 234), dates from right around the turn of the century and opens with thirteen cyclic Masses and a requiem by Jean de Ockeghem, making it the principal source of his sacred music. It is as close as one comes to an *opera omnia* from the time, yet Ockeghem's works occupy only the first half of the manuscript.[52]

Anthologies were the rule for secular manuscripts as well. The early frottola sources dating from the decades around 1500 invariably include the works of many composers, and many transmit the music without attributions. The same is true for chansonniers, no matter what their provenance. Those from the Loire Valley are all anthologies, and only Laborde and Dijon 517 provide attributions.[53] So too, Florentine manuscripts such as the elaborately illuminated Florence BNC 229 (ca. 1492–93) or the pretty Berlin Chansonnier (ca. 1473), which was a wedding gift to a Florentine couple, anthologize their chansons with little regard for authorship or attribution.[54] There is, in fact, no correlation between the artistry of the music's rendering on the page and a concern for compositional authority. If anything, the most beautifully produced books devote their inscriptions, occasional pieces, acrostics, portraits, and coats of arms to marking the identities of their original owners. Thus we not only lack "personal" verbal texts from the hands of early composers—things analogous to the letters of Petrarch, Dante, or Ficino, the biographical allusions threaded through literary works, and the facts included in prologues and dedications—we also lack the traces of their lives that might have traveled along with their music had there been a tradition of preserving polyphony in authored books.

Two great exceptions to this generalization prove the rule: The works of both Adam de la Halle (b. 1245–50) and Guillaume de Machaut (ca. 1300–77) survive in complete manuscript editions that witness their authors' concern for written codification (in the most literal sense of the word).[55] They merit a few pages of consideration here because the regular reference to them in histories of music has virtually naturalized their forms, whereas in the context of the long history I am constructing here, they stand out as quite unique. The most dramatic case is that of Machaut, who compiled his works in what he called "le livre où je met toutes mes choses" (the book where I put all my things).[56] In a famous passage from his long narrative poem titled *Le Voir Dit* (1363–65), he describes the material state of his "book" in a letter to his beloved "Toute Belle," who was always begging him for songs:[57] "My very sovereign lady, I would have brought you my book in order to amuse you, in which are all the things I have ever written; but it is in more than twenty parts [gatherings?]; for I have had it made [copied] for one of my lords, and I am having it notated [the musical notation entered] and therefore it is convenient for it to be in parts. And when it is notated, I will take it or send it to you, God willing."[58] Machaut apparently prepared the first archetype or master copy of his works around 1349 and updated the collection several times; at least three large manuscripts containing only his works have been dated to the period of his lifetime, a fourth to near the time of his death, and two more date from the end of the fourteenth century.[59] They include his output in all genres: narrative poems, lyrics without music, monophonic songs, polyphonic songs, motets, and his famous Mass Ordinary setting.[60]

The large number of Machaut manuscripts that survive, the dates they were copied, and anecdotal evidence such as the passages in the *Voir Dit* verify that Machaut actively "published" his works by preparing an authoritative exemplar and having it copied by professional scribes.[61] In this respect, he adopted procedures similar to those of his Italian contemporaries Petrarch and Boccaccio.[62] Petrarch, for instance, had sets of exemplars made by scribes, which he proofed by having someone read the final version of the text to him aloud while he read and corrected the copies. He then published his work—the language of the time is to "send it out to the public" *(emittas in publicum)*—by sending it to patrons or friends who were then at liberty to have further copies made. Boccaccio actually counted on recipients to disseminate his works; the presentation copy of the *De Casibus Virorum Illustrium* that he gave to Maghinardo dei Cavalcanti was accompanied by a letter in which he invited Maghinardo to "correct whatsoever is not fitting" and then to "share it with your friends and finally send it forth to the public under your name."[63]

Clearly, presentation copies functioned dually as gifts to patrons and as exemplars that could be used for publication, something born out by the bibliographic evidence of the Machaut manuscripts *Vg, B,* and *E,* which has been carefully studied by Margaret Bent. The earliest of the set, *Vg,* is a deluxe presentation manuscript decorated in the early 1370s that may have been owned by Gaston Fébus, the Count of Foix.[64] Most of *B* was copied from *Vg* by several of the same scribes; unlike the master copy, it is on paper (instead of parchment), in cursive (instead of textual hands), and lacks illuminations, aspects that have led scholars to conclude that it was made in haste. From this apparently unbound exemplar, scribes copied *E* and added a work to *Vg.*

The differing quality of the manuscripts and their relationships to one another recall the practices of scribes involved in the publishing of university texts in thirteenth- and fourteenth-century Paris.[65] Official stationers held copies of texts that had been checked for accuracy, which they rented out to students and scribes for copying. These exemplars were left unbound so that several portions of the same text might be copied simultaneously, for which they were called *pecia* (quires). The *pecia* system ingeniously solved the problem of errors compounding as manuscripts were copied from copies of copies, by making available in a central location a single authoritative exemplar. Although the Machaut manuscript *B* has been said to be of "poor quality,"[66] it is sooner unattractive than inaccurate. We might also question whether *B* and its successors represent a pirate edition made by "unscrupulous individuals," as Lawrence Earp has supposed.[67] Machaut probably did not oversee the production of *B* and *E,* but once a "first edition" was finished, its dissemination was probably understood. The complaints of fourteenth-century authors about unauthorized copies of their works usually concern partial or unfinished works such as Petrarch's epic poem *Africa,* of which an excerpt of thirty-four verses circulated in his lifetime without his permission, or Boccaccio's *De Genealogia Deorum,* which escaped his hands before he had a chance to revise it.[68] Much later, in the sixteenth century, Carpentras made a similar complaint at the opening of his Lamentations, saying that copies of his pieces had been made without his consent and before the final touches had been made, to say nothing of some badly corrupted passages.[69] Machaut, by contrast, had already presented one of his lords with a copy of his *livre,* as we learn from the passage of the *Voir Dit* quoted above. He had already "published" a first edition of his complete works: the earliest surviving manuscript, BnF f. fr. 1586 (Ms. C), is believed initially to have been prepared around 1349 for Bonne of Luxembourg, wife of the future King Jean le Bon.[70] The relationships between *Vg, B,* and *E* describe a mode of dissemination in keeping with what we can discern of scribal publication in the fourteenth century.

Less remarkable than the Machaut manuscripts but still worthy of mention is BnF f. fr. 25566 (La Vallière manuscript), an edition of the works of Adam de la Halle that contains virtually all of his works, arranged by genre. Probably copied between 1291 and 1297, the manuscript appears to date from the lifetime of the composer and present his works in an authorized form.[71] Like the Machaut manuscripts, it contains works in a variety of genres: epic, lyric without music, monophonic songs, plays with musical interpolations, and polyphonic rondeaux and motets. Unlike the Machaut manuscripts, only the first quarter of the book (as it now stands) is devoted to de la Halle—the rest contains prose and narrative poems by other thirteenth-century writers. In both cases, though, the nonmusical texts explain a lot. Adam de la Halle and Machaut were poet-composers, and the preservation of their musical works in books owes (most certainly in the case of Machaut) to a writer's sense of authorship and a literary investment in bookish materiality. Machaut worked as *notaire* and then *secretaire* to Jean de Luxembourg early in his career, appointments for which he would have been expected to draft, witness, and safeguard legal documents as well as compose other sorts of texts, including literary ones. His training as a notary doubtless honed the textual practices of working out drafts on paper and producing annotated copies on parchment that led to his extraordinary degree of concern for constructing an "author's book" of his works.[72]

Beginning in the mid-fifteenth century, we can trace the work of a number of career musicians such as Dufay and Josquin, who made their livings more directly through music than did Machaut.[73] Nino Pirrotta called them "mercenary professionals" and identified them as a new breed of musician.[74] Yet, despite the value contemporaries placed on their music, there is no evidence that they engaged in the scribal publication of their works.[75] There is certainly no shortage of beautiful music manuscripts from the time—to the aforementioned examples of the Florence 229 and the Chigi Codex, we can add the heart-shaped Chansonnier Cordiforme compiled for Jean de Montchenu ca. 1477, the delicately illuminated Newberry-Oscott Partbooks prepared as a gift for Henry VIII ca. 1527–29, and the lavish manuscripts produced by the Alamire scriptorium active in Mechelen and Brussels between 1495 and 1535, including the Occo Codex commissioned by Pompejus Occo of Amsterdam (d. 1537), the chanson albums of Marguerite of Austria, the Vatican manuscripts C.S. 34, 36, and 160 (presents given to Pope Leo X), and British Library MS Royal 8 G. vii, another gift for Henry VIII.[76] Henry VIII, like Leo X, was an amateur musician of some ability, who could sing, play the organ, lute, and virginal, and even composed a number of songs and instrumental pieces.[77] And like Leo, Henry amassed an impressive library during his reign (1509–47), which is documented in an inventory of 1542.[78] Music literacy and a passion for books made presentation copies of music manuscripts and prints appropriate gifts to these and other patrons, to be sure, yet there is no evidence that any of these manuscripts were commissioned or presented by composers, despite the role such a book might have played in cultivating a potential benefactor.[79]

Books might be among the most enduring artifacts of patronage, but they were not the only means of engaging patrons, particularly for musicians. Leo X patronized performances with the same enthusiasm he directed at books, even to the point of eliciting surprise: in 1517 Marino Zorzi wrote to the signory of Venice that the pope "is excellent above all other musicians, and that, if he sings with any artist, he pays him a hundred ducats and more," a sum equivalent to half a year's salary for a chapelmaster.[80] In his eighteenth-century vita of the pope, Angelo Fabroni records with some shock that Leo rewarded musicians as generously as he did men of letters.[81] Josquin may not have cared to publish his works in print or manuscript, but he was not shy about using performances of his compositions to advantage. Heinrich Glarean tells in his *Dodekachordon* that Josquin composed "Guillaume se va chauffer," with its imbecilic tenor, at the request of Louis XII, who wanted to sing along with his musicians.[82]

Glarean's story about "Guillaume se va chauffer," true or not, reminds us of the centrality of performance in musical exchanges between patrons and their beneficiaries, and the degree to which music-making created social bonds between nobles and the performers who enlivened gatherings at the Roman Curia, the households of cardinals, and the courts of dukes and kings. We know that Orlande de Lassus played Pantalone at the request of the young Wilhelm V in an impromptu commedia dell'arte show for the duke's wedding in 1568, a sort of performance he must have given fairly often, since Massimo Troiano tells us that he was a "vero virtuosissimo" in the role of Zanni as well.[83] Lassus played alongside four courtiers and musicians from the ducal chapel, and they probably sang pieces like those published in his *Libro di villanelle, moresche ed altri canzoni* (Paris, 1581). This was an age when nobles sweated it out alongside professional musicians, thespians, and dancers, rehearsing together for carnival ballets and other more ephemeral productions and establishing a camaraderie of the same sort that noble parents angled for when they sent their sons and daughters to the French court at great personal expense to be raised as *enfans d'honneur* or ladies-in-waiting. Personal fidelities emerged through day-to-day exchanges, and the surviving letters between Lassus and Wilhelm show that the composer was a genuine friend to the young duke, who was about fifteen years his junior. Their relationship is not unlike that between Louis XIV and Jean-Baptiste Lully, who came to the king's attention during performances of the *Ballet royal de la nuit* in 1653, in which Louis famously appeared in the role of Apollo or "Le Soleil." Lully was just twenty, and Louis but fourteen; Lully subsequently parlayed his abilities as a dancer and mime into a stunning career that evolved through their shared experiences dancing side by side in the entrées of ballets. Only later did composition and direction become a primary activity for him at court. The point is that while historians have to work from written records, the production of notated music was only one aspect of a musician's career in the early modern period. Printing did not liberate career composers from the constant need to perform and organize performances, whether for a church, noble household, or—eventually—the operatic stage. Nor did it supplant performance as a primary means of publication.

The history I have sketched here is one in which composers seem paradoxically at odds with books. It is a history defined by absence—the absence of single-composer codices, of presentation copies, of books that might support compositional authority. It may be that we have lost telling sources from the fifteenth century; it may also be that because various genres required different layouts on the page, anthologies organized by genre came to be the most practical approach to book production. In fact, if

Figure 8.   Carpentras, "Lamentations," in the manuscript version prepared by the composer for presentation to Pope Clement VII, Rome, Vatican, Manuscript Cappella Sistina 163, fols. 3v-4r. By permission of Biblioteca Apostolica Vaticana, with all rights reserved.

the surviving copies are any indication, Machaut's own author's book was organized in this way, with each genre confined to separate fascicles.[84] For longer genres such as the cyclic Mass, five Masses by a single composer might have nicely filled a sixty-folio manuscript choirbook, yet only with Petrucci do we find Masses being grouped in single-composer editions. And ironically, it was precisely at this juncture—when Masses came into print—that their material form seems to have inspired Petrucci to shift to the partbooks that would further distance the textual presentation of music from the grander, unified books containing theological, classical, literary, and scientific texts. In physical dimensions, Petrucci's partbooks were the virtual equivalent of sheet music. Consider, too, that as music printing accelerated and Petrucci, Antico, and Giunta began to issue music in octavo, many prints got even smaller. The little sixteen-folio octavo prints in sets of four volumes that sold under the titles "Premier livre des chansons," "Missarum liber primus . . . ," or "Motetti libro primo . . ." may have announced themselves with the word *book* in their titles, but they were really pamphlets, no bigger than the almanacs, canards of fabulous news, and little ABCs that shared the baskets of traveling vendors with mirrors, bits of ribbon, and other odds and ends.[85]

This is not to say that composers were antitextual. The very elaboration of musical notation witnesses the culture of writing in which chant and then polyphony developed. (Dance, for instance, still lacks a satisfactory notation.) But reading and writing music does not necessarily presume an interest in books, printing, codification, and preservation. One last example that can help us reflect on composers' textual habits is the sad case of Carpentras, whose beautiful presentation manuscript was mentioned above. Cappella Sistina 163, containing his Lamentations of Jeremiah, was copied sometime between 1524 and 1530 and presented to Pope Clement VII (see figure 8). As the composer explains in the printed dedication of 1532, he had originally set the Lamentations at the request of Leo X, whom he served as chapelmaster until the latter's death in 1521.[86] Concerned to correct some badly copied versions made without his knowledge, he took the opportunity to improve his work and made a gift of the revised versions to the new pope—the gorgeous manuscript still housed in the Vatican today.

The gift of polyphony in a fine copy, the choice of the pope as a recipient, the self-effacing rhetoric that identifies the pope as a true connoisseur to whose judgment the author humbly submits ("he fears the judgment of a wise Pontifex"), these were to become the standard traits of exchanges between composers and their patrons as the century wore on, and they are already in evidence in Antico's *Liber quindecim missarum*. Nonetheless, Cappella Sistina 163 marks a turning point in the history of music, for it is the first book of polyphony that we know to have been prepared as a gift from composer to patron. In fact, it is one of very few manuscripts of music to contain the works of a single composer dating from before 1530, and the only one commissioned by the composer himself.[87] We will never know exactly what prompted Carpentras to make such an unprecedented gift given the evident disinterest of other composers in books of their music—perhaps he was impressed by Leo X's appreciation of books and thought such a gift would please another Medici pope.

Unfortunately, the most likely explanation was his affliction with tinnitus in 1526, which made performance impossible and forced him into retirement in Avignon. This must have been a terrible blow for a man who was the first musician elected to serve as master of the papal chapel. Tormented with a "continuous hissing" in his head that "agitate[d] the brain like winds fighting among themselves," he spent years consulting doctors, but without relief, finally turning his attention to the composition of music "that continuous sadness might not consume my heart."[88] These quotes come from the dedication (also to Clement VII) of Carpentras's folio print of Masses (Avignon, 1532), one of three volumes of liturgical music completed after his withdrawal from musical life in Rome. In the end, the din of tinnitus and his isolation motivated this initial turn to the book. Like Beethoven penning his works in silence, Carpentras wrote most of his music only after the hissing in his ears forced his departure from Rome. His Masses, hymns, and Magnificats, three books of music, found their inspiration in disability and were born into the silence of a life without performance. As intoxicating as any bibliophile could find the beauty of Cappella Sistina 163 or Jean de Channey's folio prints with their graceful teardrop-shaped note heads, their mute pleasures also present a temptation worth resisting, for they document a scriptural turn that might satisfy the textual intensity of historical research in the humanities, but is in many ways at odds with the music we might hope to understand.

THE REAL STORIES BEHIND SINGLE-COMPOSER CHOIRBOOKS

Despite the tragic personal circumstances behind their production, Carpentras's presentation manuscript and the four large folio prints of his works represent a dramatic shift in the attitude of composers toward the book of music. Had he not been the first composer—apparently—to undertake such publishing projects, the honor of precedence might well have fallen to another of his colleagues in the papal chapel, which was one locus for the new interest in books.[89] In 1536, for instance, Costanzo Festa asked Filippo Strozzi to suggest a Venetian printer who could bring out his music, and two years later he secured a privilege for "Works of music, that is to say, Masses, motets, madrigals, basses, counterpoints, Lamentations, and some of his own composition."[90] In the same years, two large manuscripts of his sacred music were prepared, Cappella Sistina 18 and 20, perhaps in conjunction with the publishing project.[91] Festa's was one of the first Venetian privileges to have been applied for by a composer rather than a printer, engraver, or publisher, earlier ones having gone to Bartolomeo Tromboncino in 1521 for "Canti de canzone, madrigali, sonetti, capitoli et stramboti, versi latini et ode latine et vulgar, barzelete, frotole, et dialogi" and Marco Antonio Cavazzoni in 1522 or 1523 for organ tablature.[92] Festa's sacred music was never printed, and certainly not in large folio choirbooks as Carpentras's was, but the privilege still witnesses the intensification of publishing interests that, for books of music in folio, ultimately came to be centered in Rome. Whether the books were in manuscript or print was perhaps not an issue at the outset, for the cache of single-composer books in this form appears in both manuscript and print at about the same time.[93] Table 1 lists all of the books in folio that contain the works of only one composer dated 1400–1554, whether printed or manuscript.[94]

What emerges so dramatically from this table is the extent to which folio choirbooks were a local phenomenon, something particularly prized in papal circles and at the Habsburg-Burgundian Court in Flanders. The La Rue manuscripts were gifts produced by the Alamire scriptorium. They seem not to have been commissioned by La Rue (who had retired at sixty-three in 1516), but rather by his employers, who wished to share or show off the music of the Habsburg-Burgundian chapel. Two of them were gifts to Leo X, one a gift to the archduke of Austria, and the last possibly a gift as well.[95] The Appenzeller and Manchicourt manuscripts also came from Flanders. The rest of the books have Roman connections. Festa (C.S. 1517–45?), Morales (C.S. 1535–45), Palestrina (Cappella Giulia 1551–55; 1571–94), and, later, Animuccia (C.G. 1555–71), all served in the Cappella Sistina (the papal chapel) or the Cappella Giulia (the choir of St. Peter's) at the time their books were produced. Carpentras dedicated his *Liber primus missarum* and the Lamentations (both the manuscript and the printed editions) to Clement VII, and Festa's gorgeous manuscript C. S. 18 may have been a gift to Paul III, for it features his coat of arms. Some of

TABLE 1. Chronology of Books in Folio by a Single Composer,
1400–1554

Manuscript or Print	Shelfmark or Printer, Date
Pierre de La Rue, Masses	Rome C.S. Ms. 34 (1515–16)
Pierre de La Rue, Masses and Mass sections	Rome C.S. Ms. 36 (1516–18)
Pierre de La Rue, Masses	Vienna N.B. 15496 (1515–16)
Pierre de La Rue, Masses	Montserrat Ms. 773 (1516–34)
Heinrich Isaac, Masses	Munich Ms. 3 (1523–25)
Carpentras, Lamentations	Rome C.S. Ms 163 (1524–30)
Carpentras, *Liber primus missarum*	Avignon: Channey, [1532]
Carpentras, *Liber lamentationum Hieremiae prophetae*	Avignon: Channey, [1532]
Carpentras, *Liber hymnorum*	Avignon: Channey, [1533–34]
Carpentras, *Liber cantici Magnificat*	Avignon: Channey [1536]
Costanzo Festa, Hymns and Magnificats	Rome C.S. Ms. 18 (ca. 1538)
Costanzo Festa, Motets	Rome C.S. Ms. 20 (ca. 1539)
Appenzeller (Benedictus), Masses, motets	Montserrat Ms. 765 (ca. 1540)
Pierre Colin, *Liber octo missarum*	Lyon: Moderne, 1541
Cristóbal de Morales, *Missarum liber primus*	Rome: Dorico, 1544
Cristóbal de Morales, *Missarum liber secundus*	Rome: Dorico, 1544
Pierre de Manchicourt, Masses	Montserrat Ms. 768 (1545–55)
Cristóbal de Morales, *Missarum liber primus*	Lyon: Moderne, 1546
Cristóbal de Morales, *Mariae Cantica Vulgo Magnificat dictâ*	Lyon: Moderne, 1550
Cristóbal de Morales, *Missarum liber secundus*	Lyon: Moderne, 1551
Giovanni Pierluigi da Palestrina, *Missarum liber primus*	Rome: Dorico, 1554

these books, then, were made for other parties, but as time went along, more were demonstrably produced for composers such as Carpentras, Morales, and Palestrina, who contracted directly with scribes or printers and put up much of the money themselves.

Printed examples of this Roman style of book have received much attention from scholars, making them seem far more common than they really were. Usually a set of Masses in choirbook layout and in large folio reminiscent of Antico's *Liber quindecim missarum,* these were impressive books and almost always dedicated to potential patrons. Probably the most frequently reproduced title page of any Renaissance music book belongs to

Palestrina's first book of Masses, published by Dorico in Rome in 1554 (see figure 9). It has become a popular textbook example of the deals brokered by musical offerings in the sixteenth century. The woodcut—modeled on the Antico—conveniently symbolizes the place of Palestrina's book in a series of exchanges that began with Julius III's appointment of Palestrina as *maestro di cappella* in 1551.[96] Palestrina reciprocated with the gift of Masses in 1554 and was in turn rewarded a month later with membership in the Cappella Sistina.[97]

On the title page, Palestrina holds his book open to view, affirming the identification of the composer with the material object bearing his name. It is probably not by chance that scholars have preferred to study single-composer prints rather than anthologies, for books like Palestrina's appeal to modern notions of authorship. Its large size (393 × 262 mm), the portrait of the composer, the borders filled with classical imagery, and the large font reserved for Palestrina's name all support the perception that Palestrina was a composer of great importance. His name is emblazoned on the book in a style that satisfies latter-day notions of the cultural authority books could support. The cyclic Masses within, moreover, conveniently recall the abstract large-scale forms of the Beethovenian symphony and they play—should we so desire—toward the myths of musical genius contemporary with the formation of musicology as a discipline in the nineteenth century.[98]

The arrival of the authored book into the world of professional musicians would seem to be complete. Palestrina's *Missarum liber primus* has co-opted the patronage relationship once cultivated by Antico, and in very much the same terms. In fact, this turn had occurred even earlier, with the edition of Morales's *Missarum liber secundus* printed by Valerio Dorico in 1544. Dorico produced two choirbooks of Masses for Morales in that year, the second of which copies Antico's page ornaments, historiated initials, and title page, on which Morales kneels before Pope Paul III.[99] Dorico's books were, in turn, so remarkable that they were slavishly copied by Jacques Moderne in 1546 and 1551, from the decorative initials heading each Mass right down to the style of note head, the signatures, and the dedication (though not the title pages).[100] More than ordinary pirate prints that used the layout of the music in the original as a means to skip the business of counting off lines of type, these were real facsimile editions, not just of the music, but of the book itself. Dorico too ended up copying his own work, for the woodcut image from title page of Morales's *Missarum liber secundus* formed the basis for that of Palestrina's *Missarum*

Figure 9. Title page of Giovanni Pierluigi da Palestrina, *Missarum liber primus* (Rome: Dorico, 1554). Printed choirbooks containing the works of a single composer were luxury items that had a certain currency in Rome but were nonetheless extraordinary, even in the Eternal City. Photo courtesy of the Museo internazionale e Biblioteca della musica, Bologna.

liber primus—the faces and the papal arms are reworked, but, ironically, Palestrina is left holding Morales's music in figure 9.[101]

In the high-powered circles of the Roman Curia and among the ultra-Catholic elites of Europe, these books were fashionable enough for composers and their backers to initiate printing projects and take the significant financial risks to bring them out, which in the case of Palestrina's first book would have cost a year's salary for an edition of 500 copies.[102] Table 2 lists all the known single-composer books of polyphony printed in folio in the sixteenth century. The preponderance of Mass prints and liturgical works would seem to confirm the artistic importance contemporaries accorded to cyclic Masses and sacred music, tying a nice bow on the story by which printing participated in the propagation of Renaissance polyphony and brought renown to the "biggest" composers, whose printed corpuses could represent their grandeur with supersized books.

As bibliographic standouts of the century, the books listed in table 2 attract considerable scholarly attention. They transistion easily to volumes in modern *opera omnia* and make for nice chapters in studies of a composer's life and works. As a group, however, they cannot be taken as a cross section of the world of music books in the sixteenth century, for that would entirely misrepresent the extent of musical authorship at the time. In the first place, printers themselves overwhelmingly preferred lighter genres such as motets, madrigals, and chansons, and even for their Mass prints, Venetian printers insisted on quarto partbooks. Folio prints of music were rare—particularly those devoted to the works of a single composer—and in almost every case some special set of circumstances conjoined to bring these choirbooks to light.

We can begin our analysis with Cristóbal de Morales, whose *Missarum liber secundus* has just been discussed, and for whose *Missarum liber primus* the original printing contract of 1544 survives.[103] Morales organized a coalition including two publishers, Antonio de Salamanca and Giovanni della Gatta, with Dorico engaged to handle the printing. Morales underwrote around half of the costs, in exchange for which he received the lion's share of the pressrun of 525 copies; the contract further stipulated that he could distribute up to 275 copies in Spain, but no more than 50 in Italy, and—doubtless to preserve the sales of his partners—he could not sell his own copies to book dealers. The principal financial risk fell to Morales, then, but it would be too much to call the print a "vanity publication," not just because he could expect to receive some cash remuneration for copies he offered to cathedrals and churches, but because such books represented a form of professional currency in Roman Catholic circles. He dedicated

Carpentras, *Liber primus missarum*	Avignon: Channey, [1532]
Carpentras, *Liber lamentationum Hieremiae prophetae*	Avignon: Channey, [1532]
Carpentras, *Liber hymnorum*	Avignon: Channey, [1533–4]
Carpentras, *Liber cantici Magnificat*	Avignon: Channey [1536]
Pierre Colin, *Liber octo missarum*	Lyon: Moderne, 1542
Cristóbal de Morales, *Missarum liber primus*	Rome: Dorico, 1544
Cristóbal de Morales, *Missarum liber secundus*	Rome: Dorico, 1544
Cristóbal de Morales, *Missarum liber primus*	Lyon: Moderne, 1546
Cristóbal de Morales, *Mariae Cantica vulgo magnificat dictâ*	Lyon: Moderne, 1550
Cristóbal de Morales, *Missarum liber secundus*	Lyon: Moderne, 1551
Giovanni Pierluigi da Palestrina, *Missarum liber primus*	Rome: Dorico, 1554
Pierre Colin, *Liturgicon musicarum duodecim missarum*	Lyon: Moderne, 1556
Jacques Arcadelt, *Missae tres*	Paris: Le Roy & Ballard, 1557
Claudin de Sermisy, *Missae tres*	Paris: Le Roy & Ballard, 1558
Pierre Certon, *Missae tres*	Paris: Le Roy & Ballard, 1558
[Rocco Rodio, *Missarum decem liber primus*	Rome: Dorico, 1562]
Cristóbal de Morales, *Canticum Beate Mariae*	Venice: Gardane, 1562
Jacob de Kerle, *Sex misse*	Venice: Gardane, 1562
Francisco Guerrero, *Canticum Beatae Mariae*	Louvain: Phalèse, 1563
Diego Ortiz, *Liber primo hymnos*	Venice: Gardane, 1565
Francisco Guerrero, *Liber primus missarum*	Paris: Du Chemin, 1566
Giovanni Animuccia, *Missarum liber primus*	Rome: Dorico, 1567
Giovanni Pierluigi da Palestrina, *Missarum liber secundus*	Rome: Dorico, 1567
Giovanni Animuccia, *Canticum Beatum Virginis*	Rome: Dorico, 1568
Giovanni Pierluigi da Palestrina, *Missarum liber tertius*	Rome: Dorico, 1570
Francesco Corteccia, *Responsoria*	Venice: Gardano, 1570
Francesco Corteccia, *Responsoria . . . residuum*	Venice: Gardano, 1570
Orlande de Lassus, *Patrocinium musices . . . prima pars*	Munich: Berg, 1573

(continued)

TABLE 2. *(continued)*

Orlande de Lassus, *Patrocinium musices . . .* secunda pars	Munich: Berg, 1574
Orlande de Lassus, *Patrocinium musices . . .* tertia pars	Munich: Berg, 1574
Orlande de Lassus, *Patrocinium musices . . .* quarta pars	Munich: Berg, 1575
Placido Falconio d'Asolo, *Introitus et alleluia*	Venice: Gardano, 1575
Tomás Luis de Victoria, *Liber primus qui missas, psalmos . . .*	Venice: Gardano, 1576
Orlande de Lassus, *Patrocinium musices . . .* quinta pars	Munich: Berg, 1576
Orlande de Lassus, *Missae variis concentibus ornatae*	Paris: Le Roy & Ballard, 1577
Costanzo Porta, *Missarum liber primus*	Venice: Gardano, 1578
George de La Hèle, *Octo Missae*	Antwerp: Plantin, 1578
Alard Gaucquier, *Quatuor Missae*	Antwerp: Plantin, 1581
Tomás Luis de Victoria, *Cantica B. Virginis vulgo Magnificat*	Rome: Zanetto and Basa, 1581
Tomás Luis de Victoria, *Hymni totius anni*	Rome: Zanetto and Basa, 1581
Jacob de Kerle, *Quatuor Missae*	Antwerp: Plantin, 1582
Francisco Guerrero, *Missarum liber secundus*	Rome: Zanetto, 1582
Tomás Luis de Victoria, *Missarum libri duo*	Rome: Gardano and Basa, 1583
Francisco Guerrero, *Liber vesperarum*	Rome: Gardano, 1584
Tomás Luis de Victoria, *Motecta festorum totius anni*	Rome: Gardano and Basa, 1585
Tomás Luis de Victoria, *Officium Hebdomadae sanctae*	Rome: Gardano and Basa, 1585
Orlande de Lassus, *Patrocinium musices . . . Magnificat* [vol. 7]	Munich: Berg, 1587
Philippe de Monte, *Liber I Missarum*	Antwerp: Plantin, 1587
Orlande de Lassus, *Octo cantica*	Paris: Le Roy & Ballard, 1587
Orlande de Lassus, *Patrocinium musices . . . Missae* [vol. 8]	Munich: Berg, 1589
François Sales, *Patrocinium musices . . . Officia* [vol. 9]	Munich: Berg, 1589
Giovanni Pierluigi da Palestrina, *Hymni totius anni*	Rome: Tornieri & Donangeli, 1589

TABLE 2. *(continued)*

Giovanni Pierluigi da Palestrina, *Missarum* *liber quintus*	Rome: F. Coattino, 1590
Pietro Paolo Paciotto, *Missarum liber primus*	Rome: Gardano, 1591
Blasius Ammon, *Patrocinium musices . . .* *Missae* [vol. 10]	Munich: Berg, 1591
Caesar de Zacchariis, *Patrocinium musices . . .* *Intonationes* [vol. 11]	Munich: Berg, 1594
Giovanni Pierluigi da Palestrina, *Missae* *quinque . . . liber sextus*	Rome: F. Coattino, 1594
Giovanni Pierluigi da Palestrina, *Missae* *quinque . . . liber septimus*	Rome: F. Coattino, 1594

NOTE: This table lists polyphonic prints of thirty folios or more, thereby excluding the series of sixteen individually printed Masses issued by Nicolas Du Chemin. It does not include posthumous prints, which would add Cipriano de Rore, *Tutti i madrigali di Cipriano di Rore a quattro voci* (in score) (Venice: Angelo Gardano, 1577); Juan Navarro, *Psalmi, Hymni, ac Magnificat totius anni* (Rome: F. Coattino, 1590); and Giovanni Pierluigi da Palestrina, *Hymni totius anni* (Rome: F. Coattino, 1598). Also noteworthy is the series of ten individually printed Masses issued at or near the time of Clemens non Papa's death: *Missa cum quatuor vocibus . . . Tomus I–X* (Louvain: Phalèse, 1556–60). My deepest thanks go to Jane A. Bernstein, who shared with me her forthcoming research on Roman prints of the late sixteenth century and who kindly reviewed and emended this table.

the *Missarum liber primus* to Cosimo I de' Medici and the *Missarum liber secundus*, with its splendid title page, to Pope Paul III. As far as we know, no career moves resulted from the dedications, but Morales may have hoped for an outcome analogous to the promotion Palestrina would obtain in 1554 following the printing of his own *Missarum liber primus*.

Palestrina consistently sought to have his sacred music printed in folio, and his seven books in folio account for a large number of the editions listed in table 2. Jane Bernstein has shown how Palestrina would have been able to finance these publications in part through his advantageous second marriage in 1581 to Virginia Dormoli, the wealthy widow of a Roman furrier.[104] Whereas before that time he counted on rewards from well-chosen dedicatees (Julius III and Philip II of Spain), during the years that followed, he parlayed profits from the fur trade into a self-financed career in print. He clearly prized his Masses in the self-financed volumes, but that may be because he was having trouble publishing them elsewhere: Bernstein calculates that within Palestrina's lifetime, only 43 out of 104 of his Masses were published, most of them languishing in manuscript.[105] Indeed, for many composers, the evidence of surviving prints misrepresents their actual output, shifting the balance unevenly toward secular genres. None of Giaches de Wert's Masses were printed in his lifetime, notwithstanding the remarkable popularity of his madrigals in print; the same scenario holds true for Costanzo Festa, none of whose liturgical music (four Masses, a Magnificat cycle, and a set of Lamentations) came to light before their modern editions. Only one of the ten Masses written by Nicolas Gombert came into print during his lifetime, and even Lassus, whose music commanded an almost unique salability, only managed to see two-thirds of his Masses into print before he died in 1594.[106] Volumes 2 and 8 of the *Patrocinium musices* series put out by Adam Berg contain eleven of Lassus's Masses between them. It is unclear who financed the later volumes of this veritable Denkmal der Tonkunst in Bayern, but the set was initiated at the request of Duke Wilhelm V and the first five volumes apparently paid for by him, a luxury he presumably gave up when he went bankrupt in 1575.[107] Largely aggrandizement for the young Wilhelm, these prints named him prominently on the title page, included his portrait on the verso, and typographically established his ownership of the musical establishment at the Bavarian court, where Lassus was employed.[108] Horst Leuchtmann even believes that the *Patrocinium musices* began as Wilhelm's bibliographic rejoinder to a costly series paid for by his father, Duke Albrecht V, and likewise printed by Adam Berg in large folio, the *Historien der lieben Heiligen Gottes* by Laurentius Surius.[109]

Of the other luminaries of the century, Francisco Guerrero was one who found the lure of monumental books irresistible no matter what the costs.[110] Not only did he present manuscripts of his liturgical works to Seville Cathedral, Toledo Cathedral, and Charles V, and engage Nicolas Du Chemin to print his *Liber primus missarum* on *carta imperiale* (the largest size paper available), he traveled to Rome to proofread copies of the *Missarum liber secundus* (1582), personally placed a presentation copy in the hands of Gregory XIII, and probably took the opportunity at that time to begin arranging the publication of his *Liber vesperarum* (1584). That book was dedicated to the canons of Seville Cathedral, who supported his lavish publishing ventures—though sometimes quite belatedly, for in August 1591 Guerrero was thrown into prison over the debt he owed on the 1584 publication, to be rescued only the following month when the chapter voted to pay off his creditors. Clearly the monetary rewards and professional prestige reaped from folio publications were uncertain—in fact, gifts of them were sometimes openly refused, a fate that befell Tomás Luis de Victoria on more than one occasion.[111]

Many of the composers whose sacred works found their way into spectacular folio choirbooks managed to avoid debtor's prison by finding subventions for their publishing projects. In 1567 Giovanni Animuccia received fifty ducats from the Cappella Giulia for the printing of his *Missarum liber primus* (works commissioned by the chapel that he had written in a style sympathetic to Tridentine aesthetics).[112] Cardinal Giulio Feltro della Rovere likely underwrote the publication costs of the folio prints dedicated to him by Placido Falconio (1575) and Costanzo Porta (1578), since we know that he not only paid for the printing of Porta's *Missarum liber primus*, he paid the composer's expenses to travel to Venice to oversee the printing.[113] Philippe de Monte, we know, advanced Christopher Plantin sums of money for the publication of his Masses of 1587, presumably in anticipation of the rewards that regularly came from Maximilian II and Rudolf II for the music dedicated to them.[114] Jacob de Kerle was likewise compensated for publishing costs directly by the Imperial Court, though surviving copies of the *Quatuor Missae* bear different dedications, the first to the archbishop of Cologne (1582), a second one newly printed by Plantin to the emperor (1583), and a third printed elsewhere to Pope Gregory XIII (1583).[115] Taken together, they witness how unsettled de Kerle was in those years: war forced him to leave Cambrai Cathedral, from which he moved first to Cologne and then into imperial service. Finally, Arcadelt's *Missae tres* exposes with particular clarity the host of interests that might operate behind this corner of the book industry: in the preface to the print, Adrian Le Roy explains that the publication was part of a deal brokered with Charles de Guise, Cardinal of Lorraine— Charles agreed to intervene on Le Roy's behalf to obtain the king's permission to print Masses by musicians in the royal chapel, in exchange for which Le Roy consented to print the Masses of the cardinal's own musician, Arcadelt. Arcadelt's role in the arrangement is vague at best, and here is another case in which we would have lost every trace of a composer's Masses had a patron not wished to publicize his or her possession of them in print. Authors, dedicatees, and printers all might have stakes in these publications, but market-driven they were not. In almost every case, very particular interests coincided when polyphony appeared in these monumental formats.

The scenarios we can recover from these books of Masses in folio show composers operating with various degrees of initiative behind the scenes. Among the most adventuresome were Morales, Palestrina, Guerrero, and Monte, who fronted the money for prints themselves, sometimes partnering up with financiers, publishers, or booksellers. Their investments might pay off in rewards from dedicatees or grateful recipients or losses might land them in the poorhouse. Other composers managed to shield themselves from risk by convincing their employers to finance a publication, a long-standing type of arrangement that can be inferred from a number of obsequious dedications from composers to their patrons, but one that we know to have been the case for Animuccia, Placido Falconio, and Costanzo Porta. Lassus, we know, enjoyed tight relationships with numerous printers and well-placed patrons, which he parlayed into author's privileges giving him extraordinary control over the choice of printers for his works, but the nature of the financing of them is less clear. At the most opaque end of the spectrum, yet again, sits Jacques Arcadelt, about whom we still know so little, despite his having been one of the most printed and reprinted composers of the century. The stuff of a direct negotiation between the Italophilic cardinal of Lorraine and the printer Adrian Le Roy, his *Missae tres* were the pawn in someone else's game. Shot through with social relationships and cultural hierarchies, the capital outlay necessary to produce a choirbook in large folio brought together whole hosts of personages with independent interests that often aligned in the author's favor. Barter economies, clientage systems, gift exchanges, and the commodification of music overlap in striking configurations in the cultures growing up around print, sometimes crystallizing brightly around a figure like Arcadelt, Lassus, Morales, or Palestrina.

No constellation of events is more unique than that behind the publication of George de La Hèle's magnificent *Octo Missae*, in which the Masses of a young, unpublished composer went down in history as the first music to come off the presses of the master printer Christopher Plantin, whose *Officina Plantiniana* in Antwerp initiated the publication.[116] The story is this: After the technological success of Plantin's *Biblia regia* (1568–72) and the *Biblia polyglotta* (1569–73), which had been supported by Philip II of Spain, Plantin received a royal privilege to print all Roman Catholic liturgical books required throughout Philip's extensive empire, which included Spain, Portugal, and the Netherlands. As part of these dealings, Plantin agreed to print an elegant antiphoner for the king in royal folio, despite the difficulties Philip seemed to be having settling his accounts. Plantin ordered 1,800 reams of unusually high quality *carta reale* in preparation for the printing and had several alphabets and a huge number of decorative capitals made by the foremost artists and engravers of his day (Gérard van Kampen, Pierre van der Borcht, and Antoine van Leest). But by 1578, it became clear that Philip's financial difficulties were far graver than

Plantin had previously suspected, and the royal court turned a deaf ear to all appeals for money. Having already purchased paper for the book of chant—not to mention the phenomenal alphabets—Plantin ended up plunging more money into music type and decided to bring out the Masses of La Hèle, a young musician of interest to Philip through whose music Plantin hoped to remind the king of his forgotten debts. La Hèle contracted with Plantin to purchase forty copies at a reduced price, but put up no money for the project, leaving Plantin to bear the risk alone. In 1581, by which time La Hèle had been appointed royal chapelmaster, Plantin had given La Hèle four copies of the Masses, received no money for them, and still had reams of the antiphoner paper to hand, "all to my great loss in this unfortunate time, in which I am oppressed and burdened by the rest of this paper" (le tout à mon grand dommage en ces temps malheureux etc. ausquels je me trouve fort oppressé et chargé du rest desdicts papiers).[117] The debt owed him by Philip II amounted to the phenomenal sum of 46,960 florins. He went on to use the same paper, type, and decorative elements for the Masses of Kerle, Monte, and Gaucquier, the last being dedicated to Archduke Mathias, governor of the Low Countries, whom Gaucquier served as chapelmaster. These arrangements show Plantin negotiating with his patron (Philip II) and casting about for others (Archduke Mathias), and using the music of La Hèle and Gaucquier as substitutes for the antiphons he was to have printed in royal folio. Clearly the composers were intermediaries, but the books were very much Plantin's to give as well. The deal arranged for Monte's Masses concluded with Plantin's sending thirteen copies to the composer, but not before making a personal gift of three copies to the Bishop of Antwerp.[118] A money-losing venture of the highest order for Plantin, the Masses in folio that began as a project to flatter the ultra-Catholic king of Spain ended as a series of attempts to mitigate the financial disaster of the abandoned antiphoner by printing another sort of choirbook. This is how Plantin got into the music business, entirely to his regret.

The overlapping interests bringing together printers, composers, local dignitaries, and dedicatees of international stature, the exchanges transacted using compositions and printed books as commodities, the wealth sought in the form of subventions, and the gifts of dedications repaid with jobs, money, benefices, and goodwill (so crucial in a time of war), taken together, these scenarios deny the characterization of the luxury prints of the sixteenth century as simple vanity prints financed by composers or as the product of a vital culture through which composers pursued careers as "writers." Rather, these unusual books illustrate the choppy histories behind the typo- and xylographic marvels we admire today and the fits and starts through which music printers, composers, and patrons discovered a role for the book of music in the economies of Renaissance patronage. The bibliophilia of the Medicis, the dukes of Bavaria, and the Catholic princes of Europe, the expansion of the printing trade and its distribution networks, the needs of Catholic reformers for new sorts of music, the waning of the benefice system and composers' turns to other means of income, the expansion of cathedral and chapel choirs and the size of the books they read from, and the sheer beauty of high-end printing, all conspired to create a set of conditions that allowed certain books of music to acquire social meaning and even political currency. But it did not happen overnight, it did not happen everywhere, and that it should have happened at all was far from self-evident at the time.

3. Authors of Lyric

"The king has a greater desire to have you than ever," wrote Adrian Le Roy to Orlande de Lassus in 1574.[1] Beginning in 1570, Le Roy had made something of an industry publishing Lassus's chansons in France, and he surely would have been delighted had Lassus accepted the royal invitation; indeed, he may even have solicited it—he was the one who presented Lassus's "musique cromatique" to King Charles IX, music that ravished the young monarch beyond words and prompted the offer of employment. Charles even ordered Le Roy to print the music, "so that it would not be lost," and accorded to Lassus the extraordinary "author's privilege" he received in 1571.[2]

The "chromatic music" that intensified the king's desire to have Lassus for his own was probably from the *Prophetiae Sibyllarum*, and in the end, not only did Lassus refuse Charles's invitation to make a permanent move to France, the music remained withheld from publication as well, despite the king's commandment to print it. For the *Prophetiae Sibyllarum* belonged to Duke Albrecht V of Bavaria, to whom Lassus had made a gift of them sometime around 1560. The set of four partbooks now in Vienna (Österreichisches Nationalbibliothek Ms. Mus. 18744) were prepared under Lassus's supervision, and each includes a portrait of the composer and miniatures of the twelve sibyls painted by Hans Mielich.[3] This private repertory was never printed in Lassus's lifetime, appearing only posthumously in 1600.[4] It is a favorite example of "musica reservata" or "reserved music," a term used inconsistently in the sixteenth century but one strongly associated with text expression and chromaticism and specifically with Lassus's own works. Samuel Quickelberg, Lassus's first biographer and a familiar at the court in Munich, famously described the composer's Seven Penitential Psalms in swooning language, so affecting was the music, and he ended by remarking that they called such music *musica reservata*.[5] Discussions of *musica reservata* thus rightly try to pin down what particular devices defined the genre, but we might also take the term literally, for like the *Prophetiae Sibyllarum*, Lassus's Penitential Psalms were, as objects, private books for the duke's personal pleasure. Composed around 1560, the Penitential Psalms had been copied into a presentation manuscript for Duke Albrecht, one very much like that containing the *Prophetiae Sibyllarum*. They were not printed until 1584, well after Albrecht's death in 1579. Thus, they resided at the innermost reserve of the court. That their unavailability added to their cachet is perhaps attested to by their theft in 1563 by Jean Pollet, the duke's copyist, a "leak" of enough significance that the great bibliophile and music lover, Johann Jakob Fugger, told of the theft in a letter to Cardinal Antoine Perrenot de Granvelle that same year.[6]

These examples of songs that were kept back from print remind us that printed publication was sometimes inappropriate. It could tarnish a work. Indeed, many pieces apparently intended for exclusive company came to light only posthumously or at the very end of their composers' careers, including works such as the exploratory motets and madrigals in Adrian Willaert's *Musica nova* (published in 1559 when the composer was in his sixties), the *musica secreta* for Alfonso II d'Este's *concerto delle donne* in Luzzasco Luzzaschi's *Madrigali* for high voices (published in 1601, after the death of the duke and the disbanding of the ensemble), and the *chansonnettes mesurées à l'antique* from the Valois court in Claude Le Jeune's *Le printans* and *Airs* (published in 1603 and 1608, respectively, three decades after the death of Charles IX and years after Le Jeune's death).[7] In many cases, these are the very works for which those composers are best known today, yet in their own time, the fame they garnered for their makers came not through printed dissemination, but in concerts held behind closed doors, such as the performance of "musique chromatique" Le Roy organized for Charles IX. Like opera, which throughout its history depended on manuscript scores and parts, for some genres print was not only impractical, it subverted the manuscript system that allowed composers and theaters to retain physical control of the music. Many of the famous examples of printed opera scores—that of Claudio Monteverdi's *Orfeo* and the *oeuvres complètes* of Lully printed in large folio by Ballard—monumentalized court productions after the fact, serving the patrons who sponsored them.

A second problem engendered by print was textual corruption, an exacerbation of the ruinous results of copying decried by Carpentras in the dedication of his Lamentations. As the sixteenth century wore on and some composers began to invest time and resources in publishing projects, success in print often meant that their works were reprinted willy-nilly without authorial oversight. Print expanded the circulation of music exponentially beyond the system of manuscript production. But out on the choppy waters of commercial printing, where privileges guaranteed only the rights of printers, unauthorized editions were not only legal, but the norm, particularly for lighter genres. Even at the highest level of book production, none of the modern guarantees of authorship were in place—that Palestrina holds Morales's music on the title page of his *Missarum liber primus* should raise suspicions concerning the involvement of authors in the production of books bearing their names, even those they had paid for. For some books we know that composers checked proofs.[8] Stop-press corrections and corrections between the first two issues of the first edition of Lassus's "Opus 1" suggest, for instance, that he oversaw its printing at Susato's shop in Antwerp.[9] But many books were knockoffs, even some expensive folio editions. Moderne copied Dorico's prints of Morales's Masses, which were only protected by a ten-year privilege within the Kingdom of Naples, the Republic of Venice, and the Papal States; Francesco Corteccia seems to have been driven to publish his first book of madrigals after a number of them came out attributed to other composers and riddled with printing errors; in 1561 Philibert Jambe de Fer launched legal proceedings against Jean d'Ogerelles for publishing a volume of his psalm settings without naming him on the title page—the list goes on and on.[10] No wonder composers implored dedicatees to protect their works with the "shield" of their good names.[11]

Lassus complained to the emperor about prints of his music so garbled that he could barely recognize his own work, begging for an imperial privilege to match the one he had secured during his visit to France.[12] This way he could oversee the reprinting of his works, which otherwise were literally out of his hands and became, with each edition, more and more corrupt. But just as printers regularly operated within their legal rights when printing music without the composer's consent, nothing prevented them from using a good name to sell some music. After mid-century, publishers were adding composers' names to the titles of anthologies in a nascent example of brand-name marketing—"Arcadelt & autre autheurs" and later "Lassus & autre autheurs" were favorite choices for chansonniers in France—yet no author guaranteed the accuracy of these works in an environment of opportunism, copies, and bald lies. Centuries later, to take just one notorious example, Franz Joseph Haydn suffered considerably at the hands of printers who sold spurious works under his good name, capitalizing on his renown to pitch chamber works to a public hungry for new music in Haydn's light, playable (and falsifiable) style.[13] It is symptomatic of the problems with print that already in 1556 Hermann Finck maligned the false glory of publishing as something available to any hack composer: "In the span of half a year, [they] manage with great toil to produce a little song of whatever quality with scarcely three consonances in it, and immediately take care to have it printed, so that their great and glorious name can be known to the whole world."[14] Finck chose an apt example, for "little songs" were the bread and butter of the music printing business, and many of them were knocked out for profit. Perceptions of the stylistic registers that distinguished genres from one another played strongly into the degree of authority each might command in print, with books of Masses at the top (as demonstrated so vividly by the preponderance of Masses in table 2) and secular songs at the low end of the scale.

This chapter concerns a unique moment in the history of the chanson, a turning point at which French vernacular song was caught up in the literary campaign of the Pléiade poets to remake the French language. It represents a particularly self-conscious and writerly slice of chanson culture in France, not the whole by any means, but it is significant for the way it expanded and stratified the stylistic registers of song production, creating a new zone for compositional expression in the vernacular. Interestingly, the impetus behind the creation of this ambitious type of lyric came not from musicians, but from the group of young poets who came of age around 1550—most notably Pierre de Ronsard, Joachim Du Bellay, Rémy Belleau, Pontus de Tyard, Jean-Antoine de Baïf, and Estienne Jodelle. They saw in lyric poetry a vehicle for the advancement of their careers, and musicality was a central component of their aesthetic. From the very start, their poetics invoked musical metaphors in which the lyre symbolized the poetic act of creation inspired by the Muses. The image of ancient poets singing their verse to the lyre that is so frequently called up by Horace, Anacreon, and others led Ronsard in particular to fashion an entire language equating writing with singing and his "lyre."[15] Ronsard turns again and again to the lyric metaphor, particularly in poems like "À sa lyre," which closes the first book of *Odes* from 1550.[16] Holding a lute, he is seized with a Platonic furor that promises to inspire poetry worthy of expressing France's glory. Full of future tenses and prophetic metaphors (he was only twenty-five after all), Ronsard's "singing" generates a new French and a new France.[17] In this way, Ronsard's appropriation of the lyre refits the ancient myths of Orphic magic and Apollonian supremacy to his own corpus and to an emerging ideology of Gallic superiority.[18]

The Pléiade pursued their reformation on two fronts: at court and in print. We know, for instance, that Ronsard frequented the court and presented his verse there, but a slew of contemporaneous publications worked a second angle. This self-promotion in print supplemented (or sidestepped) the performances though which poets usually first presented their work in public and especially at court, skipping directly to the bookmaking that more naturally came at the end of a poet's career, if at all. For instance, the great predecessor of the Pléiade, Clément Marot, issued his lyric poetry in print only after it had enjoyed some success in musical performances, and it was Clément who brought a good share of his father's poetry to light after the latter's death. By contrast, the Pléiade poets clearly saw an advantage in printed publication, and even conceived of their poetry in "books," rather than the scattered rhymes that typified the production of poets who wrote all sorts of verse for gifts, special occasions, to please a patron, and for day-to-day delectation.

Chanson composers were slow to set Pléiade poetry to music, and it is probably fair to conclude that for all Ronsard's talk of music in odes such as "À sa lyre," his poetry was not a staple of singers, certainly not initially. Ultimately, however, Pléiade poetics opened up a new arena for chanson composers: not only did these poets promote lyric production as a cultural priority, their use of print to capture authority for their movement ultimately enhanced the potential of polyphonic chansons to support claims of authorship for composers. By 1575, amid the continuing production of nondescript anthologies of chansons, some French composers were making their debuts in print with single-composer chansonniers in large quarto formats with pages and pages of liminary verse, dedications, woodcuts of the composer, and luxurious typesetting. These substantial books of polyphony are the subject of the following chapter—in the present chapter, I dig into their prehistory with the aim of showing how poorly chansons supported claims of authorship, even when some of the most prominent poets had penned their verse and well-known composers their music. The so-called Parisian chansons, *voix de villes*, and *airs de cour* that dominated lyric production in France for much of the century were the stuff of performers, and I will argue that their "authority" (inasmuch as it could be claimed for these genres at all) resided in performance, not in the textual vestiges or supports to performance that were printed by Attaingnant, Du Chemin, and others. It is not self-evident that prints of chansons were things composers particularly cared to put their names to, or that those prints were received with admiration by publics who thought of chansons as "works." This chapter, then, attempts to show how little musicians and printers seemed to care about the authorship of printed chansons and—by looking at the publication patterns of lyric poetry more generally—how these attitudes aligned with those toward lyric as a whole. That the Pléiade poets managed to build lyric personas for themselves in print is thus all the more remarkable an achievement, as we shall see, and it set the stage for chanson composers to do the same in the last part of the century.

The polarities I explore between print and performance and between writing and speaking or singing apply equally to musical and literary production, and by approaching the written records of lyric (poetry collections, treatises, and books of music) from the perspective of performers, I hope to offer a new history of lyric as active, embodied, and performed, one that I believe could complement more deliberately textual scholarship on French lyric by literary historians. For printed books of poetry shine in a different light when they are put into dialogue with the lute songs and polyphonic chansons their creators would have enjoyed as living, breathing examples of Orphic beauty. First we shall consider the chanson and its composers, and then the poet as lyricist.

THE PARISIAN CHANSON AND COMPOSERS AS "AUTHEURS"

More than Mass, motet, or madrigal, the chanson resisted becoming a vehicle of public renown in print. Part of this had to do with the tenacity of the anthology as the standard form for chansonniers. From its outset in 1539, the Venetian press of Girolamo Scotto had been printing motets and madrigals in (ostensibly) single-composer editions, with madrigals by Arcadelt and Rore leading the way and motets by Nicolas Gombert, Jacquet of Mantua, and Adrian Willaert in abundance. Initially the other major music printer in Venice, Antonio Gardane, kept with the French style of book he was used to from his years in Lyon, issuing a series of *Fior de mottetti* anthologies more than a little indebted to Moderne's *Motteti del fiore* and some Attaingnant-style anthologies in addition to more Venetian prints. But names evidently sold books of music more readily in Venice, where even anthologies came to be titled with formulas such as *Il terzo libro de i madrigali novissimi di Archadelth a quattro voci, insieme con alchuni di Constantino Festa, & altri dieci bellissimi a voci mudate*

(Venice: Scotto, 1539). Here the series is dedicated to Arcadelt, and a print of mixed authorship is shoehorned into it, rather than the other way around. Indeed, the status of madrigalists as authors is fairly clear, at least at the level of book production, since the genre came into print primarily in single-composer editions—editions, moreover, that became quite popular. Arcadelt's *Primo libro di madrigali a quatro voci* was unquestionably the most marketed book of the century: appearing first in 1538 from Gardane's press, it was issued over a period of 116 years in at least fifty-six editions by twenty-five different printers.[19] It opened with the beloved "Il bianco e dolce cigno," a piece that was well-enough known by 1544 for Doni to include an arrangement of it in the *Dialogo della musica*.[20] While certain chansons also became "hits" that were used to hook readers into buying prints by placing them on the opening pages, their composers seem not to have been much of a selling point.

In the North, where most chansons were printed, anthologies continued to hold sway. Attaingnant broke with this formula for only three composers: Clément Janequin, Josquin des Prez, and Claude Gervaise. Janequin's fame came to rest on a noisy set of songs that depicted birdcalls, hunting, and the sounds of battle in music. They were all extraordinarily long—at least three times the length of a standard chanson—and employed lots of fast, repeated notes and onomatopoetic texts. Perhaps because of their unusual length and typographic requirements, Attaingnant segregated these songs in a separate print when he first issued them under the title *Chansons de maistre Clement Janequin* [1528], which included only five chansons, all by Janequin. Thus the single-composer chansonnier was born for France. After that beginning, Janequin was often printed apart, though sometimes his shorter lyric works appeared as volumes in Attaingnant's numbered *Livre* series (*Huitiesme livre contenant xix. chansons nouvelles a quatre parties de la facture et composition de maistre Clemet Jennequin* [1540], and *Trente & ungyesme livre contenant xxx. chansons nouvelles a quatre, en deux volumes de la facture et composition de maistre Clement Jennequin* [1549]).[21] Considerations of page layout likewise factored into Attaingnant's publication of Josquin's chansons, a knockoff of Tielman Susato's *Septiesme livre contenant vingt & quatre chansons a cincq et a six parties composees par feu de bonne memoire & tresexcellent en musicque Josquin des pres* (Antwerp, 1545). The five- and six-part chansons simply would not fit into two partbooks of the two-in-one *Livre de chansons* series in which the Josquin print came out (as the *Trente sixiesme livre contenant xxx. chansons tres musicales, a quatre cinq & six parties, en cinq livres, dont le cinquiesme livre contient les cinquiesme*

& sixiesme parties, le tout de la composition de feu Josquin des Prez, 1550),
so as the title states quite noticeably, Attaingnant issued the music in five
volumes, the only time he did so in the entire history of the press. Attaingnant must have thought he could make some money by copying
Susato's Josquin edition, and Janequin was such a staple of French and
Italian presses that there is no question his books could turn a profit, even
in Northern markets ruled by chanson anthologies and even though Janequin himself spent most of his life in the provinces, arriving in Paris only
in 1549 when, in his sixties, he became a *chantre du roi*.[22] Gervaise, by
contrast, was an unknown, a house editor for the press, but his three-voice
chansons of 1550 were actually arrangements, a collection of others'
works.[23]

Perhaps most striking of all is a certain absence of Claudin de Sermisy
in Attaingnant's catalog. Though his chansons predominate in Attaingnant's early chansonniers and regularly received pride of place at the
openings of volumes, Claudin is never named in the title of a chanson
print. From at least 1533 until 1555, Claudin was music director of the
Chapel Royal, easily the most important musical position at court, and he
clearly had good relations with Attaingnant, who printed over 150 of his
chansons, graced his motets with a luxury edition in large quarto in 1542
*(Claudii de Sermisy, Regii Sacelli Submagistri, Nova & Prima motetto-
rum editio)*, and devoted to him the lion's share of the extravagant *Viginti
missarum musicalium* series of 1532.[24] So esteemed was Sermisy that two
composers dedicated prints to him: Pierre Certon, *Petri Certon Institutoris
Symphoniacorum puerorum Sancti Sacelli Parisiensis recens modulorum
editio* (Paris: Attaingnant, 1542) and Maximilian Guilliaud, *Rudiments de
musique practique* (Paris: Du Chemin, 1554). He was praised by Claude
Chappuys in his *Discours de la court* as a "père aux musiciens," and featured by Rabelais in the prologue to the fourth book of *Pantagruel* singing
a dirty song in a garden with Willaert, Gombert, Janequin, Arcadelt,
Certon, Morales, Verdelot, Pierre Sandrin, and virtually the whole host of
composers of any renown; Barthélemy Aneau named him in the *Quintil
Horatian* (1551) as "renommez," but Claudin's "renown" could not have been
generated by print.[25] Rather, his reputation preceded and—if anything—
added desirability to Attaingnant's chansonniers, not the reverse.[26] He
made his living at court and collected lucrative benefices, including a ca-
nonicate at the Sainte-Chapelle that brought with it a house in Paris and
a fair stipend, and despite the huge number of his chansons in anthologies and their popularity in arrangements, tablatures, spiritual contrafacta, and pirate prints, his authorship only really crystallized in print with

the publication of his sacred works—the motets of 1542 and the Masses printed in small batches by Du Chemin and Le Roy & Ballard at the end of his career, in 1556–58. But even these publications stand as after-thoughts, monuments to a lifetime spent singing dirty songs in gardens, rehearsing Magnificats in fauxbourdon with choirboys, leading the per-formances of motets during the daily Masses that François Ier so enjoyed, and composing in an easy style that spoke to a generation of musicians.[27]

The fact that we have not one book of songs from the composer whose chansons defined a new style of lyric setting in the 1530s seems in itself definitive of the genre. Attendant to this are significant attribution problems—Isabelle Cazeaux, editor of the chanson volumes in Claudin's *Opera Omnia*, has kept the popular "Aupres de vous" off the composer's works list in *New Grove*, and one of Claudin's most beloved chansons, "Tant que vivray," may have only barely been retained as part of his oeu-vre, since it was printed under his name only once, and then only in 1536.[28] "Tant que vivray" had appeared in the first of Attaingnant's chansonniers in 1528, was reprinted three times by Attaingnant, pirated by Scotto and Phalèse (in whose *Septiesme livre* it was reprinted—anonymously—at least twenty-four times), arranged for lute, keyboard, and lute and voice, arranged for two voices by Jan Gero, printed in a version *à 3* by Waelrant, expanded to five voices by Certon, spiritualized by well-meaning reform-ers, and made into dances, but almost invariably without his name.[29] These patterns of transmission and attribution illustrate the release of Claudin's chansons into a zone of the music trade ignorant of creative property, ownership, and "works" as the products of a compositional process that might be traced back to the labors of a single notable individual.[30] Close to the business of minstrels, who sang tuneful songs during *sotties, farces,* and morality plays at the bourgeois public theaters and picked out song accompaniments on the lute when they sang at court, Claudin's style bore the naturalness and ease of collaborative forms and the improviser's art. The huge number of arrangements enjoyed by his songs suggests that their identities as works rested primarily in great melodies, ones lightly robed in polyphonic accompaniments that might be shorn away, reduced, elaborated, or recast in two or three according to the needs of a pavane or galliard. Unlike the madrigal, where the affective setting of the text de-pended on harmonic devices employing all voices uniformly and word painting that relied on changing textures across the whole polyphonic fabric of the piece ("Il bianco e dolce cigno" is a fair comparison), Claudin's chansons were melody-oriented to such a degree that in some sense the tune *was* the piece. But when we discover, as Lawrence Bernstein has, that both Claudin's melody and Marot's poem for "Tant que vivray" are modeled on the anonymous monophonic chanson "Resjouissons nous tous loyaulx amoureux" included in the manuscript BnF f. fr. 12744, Claudin's authorship of the chanson recedes further into the murky world of formulaic lyric, memorized tunes, and standard chord patterns that allowed musicians equipped with improvisational abilities beyond those of most modern performers to make music without the aid of precomposed works.[31]

"Jouyssance vous donneray" beautifully exemplifies the ways improvisational habits shaped chansons of this type. In the first instance, the poem—by Marot—was designed for music.[32] A *chanson* of two strophes, each stanza is made up of two tercets rhyming *aab, aab,* the *a*s masculine and the *b*s feminine.[33] The pairs of "a" rhymes ("donneray," "meneray," "laisseray," "seray") give the poem formal clarity, particularly since the lines are only eight syllables long, making the rhymes arrive more quickly than they would have in decasyllables; the diction likewise forgoes enjambment, following the line endings and sticking with an epigrammatic style of utterance that turned the poem into a series of lyric quips, rather like a compressed version of the epigrams so favored by composers of the previous generation. Altogether, the naiveté of the rhyme scheme and the poem's straightforward expression of amorous fidelity infuse the hackneyed conventions of *l'amour courtois* with freshness and light. Making up simple verse like this on the spot was the stock-in-trade of poets and likely of some courtiers as well, at least judging from seventeenth-century accounts of the literary games at Parisian salons, where even the lackeys contributed lines to the poems being composed.[34]

> Jouyssance vous donneray,
> Mon amy, & si meneray
> A bonne fin vostre esperance.
> Vivante ne vous laisseray.
> Encores quand morte seray
> L'esprit en aura souvenance.
>
> Si pour moy avez du soucy,
> Pour vous n'en ay pas moins aussi,
> Amour le vous doibt faire entendre.
> Mais s'il vous griefve d'estre ainsi,
> Appaisez vostre cueur transy.
> Tout vient à point qui peult attendre.[35]

[Fulfillment will I give you, my beloved, and I will lead you where your hope aspires. While I live, I will never leave you. Even in death, my spirit will always remember.

   If my care for you is no less than yours for me, love should teach you this. But since it troubles you, ease your tormented heart. All things come to those who wait.]

In the musical setting as well, we can sight the extemporaneous practices by which a four-voice setting could be devised (see example 1). The tenor is the most logical and repetitive of the voices and probably presents the original tune around which the other voices are built (or, at least, it was likely the first voice to be devised).[36] It follows the poetry closely, with rests after almost every line and cadence tones on the final, G, at the end of lines 3 and 6 where there is semantic closure; this line-by-line declamation is punctuated in the other voices by suspension cadences at the end of virtually every line, and the G cadences at the midpoint and end of the piece are underscored by 5–1 motion in the bassus for additional finality. Add to this the simplicity of musical rhymes that follow the poetic ones (cadences on B♭ and G for the *a* and *b* rhymes), melodic repetition mirroring the rhyme scheme (music: ABCB; text: *aa b aa b*), and a refrain at the end, and the package was complete. Versification, regular cadence structures, and the standard rhythms in the melody interlocked in quickly comprehensible forms that could easily be committed to memory if they had not been drawn from a stock of memorized patterns in the first place.

If we look at the inner workings of the cadences that bind the voices together, we can see how utterly formulaic they are: they generally begin in the superius with a suspension figure on the pitch above the cadence tone five beats before the cadence (as in measures 5, 14, 18). This (usually) cues one of the lower voices to move to a dissonance on the following beat (the B♭ in the bassus against the C in measure 6; the F in the tenor against the E in measure 15; the D in the tenor against the C in measure 18, beat 3). Reaching the cadence tone three beats before the cadence, on the next beat the tenor moves to the seventh below the superius (mm. 6, 11, 15, 19, 24), and on the beat before the cadence the superius drops down to the leading tone, with all resolved as the superius moves upward and the tenor downward by step. The bassus could join in with 5–1 motion to the cadence tone (mm. 11, 19, 24) or set up the formula only to drop out, as it does in measures 6 and 15, as a way of softening those medial cadences and clarifying the tonal structure of the piece. My point in taking apart these cadence formulas in such detail is to show that improvisers could have

Example 1.   Claudin de Sermisy, "Jouyssance vous donneray," from *French Chansons of the Sixteenth Century*, ed. Jane A. Bernstein (University Park, PA: Pennsylvania State University Press, 1985), 15–16.

counted on the highly conventional relationships they establish between the voices, all of which are cued by the superius in a cascade of prescribed reactions performable in real time.[37] The melody, moreover, measures out the placement of cadences predictably, with cadences at the end of each line.

Singers were conditioned to anticipate these structures by duo arrangements of the same chansons such as those made by Tielman Susato and Antonio Gardane, as well as by improvising polyphony according to the rules of descant and fauxbourdon.[38] Fauxbourdon *à 4* is particularly relevant in this regard: tenor and superius move in parallel sixths, with the bassus improvised below the tenor in alternating fifths and thirds, the altus singing alternating fourths and thirds above the tenor, and all voices cadencing as described above.[39] Many of Sermisy's Magnificats include sections of fauxbourdon written out according to these rules, and fauxbourdon was such standard practice for harmonizing psalm tones that in 1582, for instance, Benedic Macé printed a little handbook explaining the technique so that—as he says—in all those little town and country parishes where congregations knew their chant tunes, devout Christians would be able to sing in harmony together.[40] These procedures likewise inflect many chansons of the era, not just in the cadence structures of chansons such as "Jouyssance vous donneray" and the voice leading following on from those cadences, but in entire stretches of homophonic chansons (example 3, mm. 6–9—in chapter 4—is a case in point).

Line openings in pieces such as "Jouyssance vous donneray" also resort to polyphonic commonplaces that likely reflect the habits of ensembles working from a stock repertory of monophonic tunes and standard practices for harmonizing them. Just as the cadences set up regular destinations for each voice, the beginnings of lines often take off from the cadences, using the final sonorities as starting pitches (particularly in the superius and bassus). The classic dactylic rhythm at the opening and after the "5–1" cadence in measure 12 is set homophonically (a standard choice throughout the repertoire as a whole), and the inner lines that begin with a softer rhythm and off the beat, as in measures 3, 7, 16, and 20, prompt a more ruffled series of entrances that in measures 7 and 20 form a proper little point of imitation. Working out points of imitation such as the one in measure 7 would not have been too hard for a consort, particularly given the reciprocity between composition and improvisation in a world where singers were constantly working back and forth between reading polyphonic compositions, memorizing them, and singing in various styles of improvised counterpoint, be it descant, Romanesca frameworks, or fauxbourdon.[41] The jagged little head motif we find in measure 7—a pair of descending fourths that themselves descend stepwise—was exactly the sort of thing that would have been used in any first lesson on *fuga*, and it is here deployed in its simplest form: as a stretto *fuga* at the semiminim beginning in the contratenor and imitated in the bassus (an octave below), the tenor (a fifth above the bassus), and the superius (a fifth above the tenor and with the entrance anticipated).[42] Stretto fugues of this sort were ubiquitous by 1500 and would have been in the ears of anyone who sang or played polyphony—in 2005, John Milsom was so shocked to find Lassus employing this rudimentary procedure in a motet printed in 1564 that he was prompted to ask: "Is this a student work? Is it not by Lassus at all?"[43]

My intention in the foregoing analysis is not to denigrate "Jouyssance" as the work of a student or hack, nor do I wish to claim that Claudin merely jotted down what he worked up on a preexistent tenor in collaboration with other singers. It may be that extemporaneous polyphonic performances employed the same conventions evident in the printed partbooks, possibly to a far greater extent than has formerly been acknowledged. Certainly the consistency with which improvisable forms are visible in this repertory suggests reciprocal exchanges between the practices of minstrelsy and "composition"; Lawrence Bernstein's discovery of monophonic antecedents for songs such as "Tant que vivray" further blurs the distinction between the ways musicians "jammed" on preexistent popular tunes and the supposedly newly composed chansons of Claudin. Finally, the frequent parallel tenths between bassus and superius recall the voicing and harmonies of the frottola—a genre scholars have more diligently sought to connect to practices independent of writing.[44] But in the end, "Jouyssance"—the textual version attributed to Claudin's scriptural labors—is a well-written chanson, without errors of counterpoint of the sort that might occur between outer voices when improvising on the fly around a tenor.

Scholarly debate over the origins of the so-called Parisian chanson and its relationship to the *chansons rustiques* of the previous generation has tended to turn around questions of originality and novelty, with the standard narrative according to Claudin the consummate ability to craft "graceful but quite straightforward lyrical miniatures with easy charming melodies," and "polished soprano lines."[45] But the formulaically scripted aspects of the music argue against characterizing Claudin's settings as so completely managed by a compositional genius that without his writing—without his *authorship*—they would not have come into being. Rather, the predictable forms of all Parisian chansons and the arrangements habitually made of them fruitfully call into question the whole notion of their status as single-handedly authored works in the first place. Whether or not Claudin devised the melody of "Jouyssance vous donneray" is less interesting than the world that opens up to view when we bracket attention to individual creators in favor of acknowledging the complex systems within which musicians and poets interacted with each other, the presence of conventions, and the stocks of materials (both poetic and musical) over which little ownership could be claimed. In this light, the vagaries of attribution common to the Parisian chanson make more sense.

THE LYRIC ECONOMY AT MID-CENTURY

The resistance of chansons to the modes of authority established for other genres by single-composer prints and (relatively) strong attribution patterns situated it in a netherworld of anonymous lyric populated by vernacular songs and poems of the sort heard at the theater, in the street, and at dances—not far, in short, from the cries of market vendors immortalized in Janequin's "Cris de Paris." Tunes came from here and there only to be further bandied about in versions both written and unwritten; superius lines and tenors came apart from the polyphony of four-voice settings and caught on by "word of mouth." Just like the prints that scattered songs to points far away from the performances of the composer and his or her circle, the trafficking of chansons through oral-traditional practices did nothing to affirm the presence of an author behind the music being heard. Indeed, such threats to authorship struck not just composers, but poets as well. All sorts of literary works traveled in song, severed from their authors, carried along on the currents of improvisation, caught in the eddies of a stock repertory, washing ashore here and there in written musical settings. Petrarch titled his *Canzoniere* with a windy metaphor—"Rime sparse"—alluding to the breezy appropriations to which lyric was eternally subject as song scattered it far from the pages of books. His great predecessor Dante Alighieri complained about blacksmiths singing unauthorized versions of his *Divine Comedy* at the local forge, which goes to show how grasping and assimilative the oral traffic in poetry could be, even of highly literate verse by renowned authors.[46]

Michel Foucault touched on this "anonymous" aspect of early lyric at the opening of his famous essay "What Is an Author?" in which he argued that not everything that is written has an author. Rejecting modern assumptions concerning the nature of authorship and the identification of "works" with "authors," Foucault's essay was a landmark in shifting attention away from the person of the author (as a producer of a work) and toward the cultural constructions in which the names of authors are used "to characterize the existence, circulation, and operation of certain discourses within a society."[47] Most of the essay is devoted to defining the author-function, but early on, in order to establish the sorts of texts that did not have authors, Foucault suggested that whereas scientific texts were considered authoritative in the early modern period only when ascribed to a specific author, literary texts did not require authors at all. "There was a time," he says, "when those texts which we now call 'literary' (stories, folk tales, epics, and tragedies) were accepted, circulated, and valorized without any question about the identity of their author. Their anonymity was ignored because their real or supposed age was a sufficient guarantee of their authenticity."[48] Only in the seventeenth and eighteenth centuries, he argued, did the meaning and value attributed to literary texts come to depend on authorship. In that later period and into the twentieth century, " 'literary' discourse was acceptable only if it carried an author's name . . . and literary works [came to be] totally dominated by the sovereignty of the author."[49]

My interest in Foucault is not to substantiate or revise his history of the author-function.[50] Rather, I cite the essay because his description of a time when poetry did not need authors invites critical attention to the evolution of an author-function for French lyric. During the period around 1550, French poets began to publish printed lyric oeuvres with clearly "authorial" ambitions. Such a turn did not happen spontaneously and required not just the material labeling of poems with the names of poets, but the construction of conditions that marked some texts as "works" when others were not. At the most materialistic level, scholars have sighted this transformation in the attitude of the Pléiade poets toward printed books of their works, an observation that fits with a broader assertion that print was central to the formation of authorship at the time. Yet when considered against the background of the music printing in France, the triumphant narrative of the Pléiade's self-invention in print exhibits some strain.

Music historians anxious to establish the cultural importance of chansons have regularly tied the history of song to literary history, concentrating on chansons setting the poems of "famous" poets such as Ronsard and sighting in those settings the influence of a literary culture presumed to be predominant.[51] We certainly know much more about the attitudes of sixteenth-century poets toward music than the reverse, which is unsurprising given how verbose poets could be and the number of treatises they wrote on lyric poetry. But despite the difficulties recuperating the attitudes of musicians, it is possible to reimagine the lyric field as one in which musical performance held the stage and the Pléiade poets were working at the edges. That is, we can use musical settings to reflect upon literary production (rather than the other way around). The books that Ronsard and his cohort left to us are impressive in number and form, but as sources for song they were not in the lyric mainstream, not even at court, and not even after Ronsard became court poet in 1558. By setting "literature" within a more holistic and musical context, we can discover fissures in the seemingly flawless representations of print, the patchy authority that poets were actually able to achieve outside the pages of their books, and the relative importance of music within the lyric economy as a whole.

The Pléiade poets took great advantage of the printed book as a form of self-presentation, even developing its possibilities as a ground of contestation during the emergence of their new poetics. Ronsard made his debut in print very early, at age twenty-five, with four books of *Odes* (1550) that brought him favored status at court.[52] Four years later he would solicit and receive from Henry II the author's privilege that gave him control over the printing of his works.[53] Joachim Du Bellay—also in his mid-twenties—published in 1549 a volume of sonnets *(L'olive)* and odes *(Vers lyriques)* in conjunction with the inflammatory *Deffence et illustration de la langue françoyse* (1549), partly as an exemplification of the principles expounded in the treatise.[54] Virtually all of the Pléiade poets produced printed collections in those years. The group's philosopher, Pontus de Tyard, came out with the sonnet cycle *Erreurs amoureuses* in 1549 and also included a volume of *Odes* as an appendix to his neo-Platonic dialogue on poetic furor, *Solitaire premier* (1552).[55] Jean-Antoine de Baïf, who was born in Venice the illegitimate son of the humanist, diplomat, and neo-Latin poet Lazare de Baïf, published two collections of Petrarchan sonnets early on: *Les amours de Méline* (1552) and *L'amour de Francine* (1555).[56] The youngest of the *brigade* (as they were known at that time), Rémy Belleau, published a translation of the odes of Anacreon in 1556, as well as his own Anacreontic *Petites inventions*.[57]

The "bookishness" of these lyric publications was unprecedented in France, as were the self-consciously classicizing poetics that crystallized in them.[58] By choosing the *Anacreontea*, Horace's *Carmina*, and Petrarch's *Canzoniere* as models, the Pléiade imitated book-length corpuses that, in the case of Horace and Petrarch, were closed lyric cycles more or less unified with an overarching narrative structure. The Pléiade's claims to precedence as the first to write sonnets or odes in French are overstated, it is true, but they *were* the first to realize the potential of these poetic genres to structure large-scale publishing projects.[59] Even in name, Ronsard's *Quatre premiers livres des Odes* clearly alluded to the four books of odes comprising the Horatian *Carmina*, and Du Bellay's formulaic *L'olive* patently replaced Petrarch's laurel with an olive tree.[60] By 1550, these classics had proved their success in the market for print—the Horace had enjoyed at least thirty editions in the incunabula period alone, and publishing Petrarch's *Canzoniere* defined a small industry in its own right. As with other best-selling titles, purchasers of Petrarch could choose between luxury folio editions, tiny duodecimo *petrarchini*, and even the French *Laure d'Avignon . . . extraict du poete Florentin Françoys Petrarch*, translated by Vaisquin Philieul (Paris: Jacques Gazeau, 1548). When it was published in 1552, Ronsard's Petrarchan sonnet cycle *Les Amours* came in at 240 pages, making it of a nice size for binding all on its own.

Like the *Canzoniere*, which has long attracted the attention of literary scholars fascinated by the first appearances of authorial self-consciousness, *Les Amours* presents a formulation of authorship that is virtually synonymous with books, one that allows us to ignore the context of embodied performance and the presence-oriented culture of lyric production in which these works took shape, not to mention the centuries of struggles over publishing rights and literary ownership that intervene between the Renaissance and our own time.[61] Whereas other poets proved their lyric talents in the flesh, Ronsard's musicality ultimately expressed itself in writing. Indeed, the first declaration of his lyric ideals, "À son luc" (To his lute) was composed in the early 1540s during a time of some tragedy for the young poet, who was recovering from an illness that left him partially deaf.[62] Du Bellay, too, began to go deaf around 1550.

Classicizing, polemic, and grandiose, Ronsard designed the odes to elevate French diction to the rhetorical heights achieved by the ancients and to "reawaken" French poetry to the sophistication of classical verse. In the preface to *Les quatre premiers livres des Odes,* Ronsards declares himself "le premier auteur Lirique François" and guided others toward a heroic style appropriate to the eternal celebration of glory. "I do not doubt that the variety in my poetry seems awkward to the ears of our rhymers, and especially [to those] of our courtiers, who admire only a little sonnet *petrarquizé* or some sweet little love poem that always continues in its subject."[63] Sacrificing immediate success with an undiscerning public, Ronsard rejected the ephemeral poetry written by those who would die "without renown, & reputation," attempting instead to establish a new sort of lyric that would "survive the innumerable centuries to come" and a new breed of poet to "cry the glory of princes consecrated by them to immortality."[64] The sheer pompousness of his odes reads as a new language of monarchic praise, a lyric alternative to the *histoires* traditionally produced by writers attached to the court, moving lyric away from the incidental works of entertainer-poets and toward the textual grounds upon which writers could declare their authority. The contest, then, was not just one between rival poetic forms—the vernacular *chanson* versus the Greek ode or the homegrown epigram versus the Italian sonnet—but a pitch to claim for lyric poets the authorial cachet of other literary forms. The object was not to profit from the sale of printed books themselves, for that right belonged to bookmen. Rather, the elevation of lyric could establish the Pléiade poets as worthy of patronage. In this light, we should see Ronsard's desire to control the printing of his oeuvres as still centrally motivated by the gift economy in which—to quote Du Bellay—"one can trade praise as one trades money."[65]

If we look back fifty years before the Pléiade, we can sight precursors to these mid-century attitudes in the published works of the *rhétoriqueurs*, a group of poet-historians active in the years between 1460 and 1530. In particular, the genres in which the *rhétoriqueurs* chose to print helps us locate poetry in the hierarchy of genres in which writers cast their output, and it also helps to situate song in French cultural life at court. This earlier generation experienced the advent of printing and, as shown by Cynthia J. Brown, writing took on a new dynamic at that time as literature became commodified outside of the courtly circles in which it had formerly circulated in manuscript.[66] From a traditional constellation of relationships between patron, poet, and scribe, new participants engaged in book production—the printer, the publisher, and eventually an expanded reading public—affecting authors' involvement in determining the literary and physical makeup of their books.[67] Initially, the publishing enterprise was governed by *libraires* and *imprimeurs,* and only around 1500 did authors begin to assert their ownership over book production through legal means; concomitant with this shift, authors sought to strengthen their identities in print (all of this half a century before composers took similar measures). In 1504, Andre de La Vigne, former secretary of Charles VIII, brought a lawsuit against the bookseller-printer Michel Le Noir over the unauthorized publication of his *Ressource de la Chrestienté,* which had appeared at the head of the latter's *Vergier d'honneur* of 1502–3. Pierre Gringoire, favorite of Louis XII, secured his own printing privilege for the *Folles entreprises,* the first French privilege awarded for a vernacular work and one Gringoire was sure to reprint in full in the 1505 edition of the text.[68] These unprecedented initiatives likely influenced the involvement of Jean Lemaire de Belges in the publication of his *Temple d'honneur et de vertus* (1503) and *La légende des Vénitiens* (1509), both of which marshal extensive paratexts to affirm his authorship. The title page of the *Temple d'honneur* states his (slightly misspelled) name with extraordinary prominence and links it to his mentor and patron ("Le Temple d'honneur et de vertus. Composé par Jehan Le Maistre disciple de Molinet, a l'honneur de feu Mgr de Bourbon"), whereas some editions of *La légende des Vénitiens* feature his coat of arms on the title page. Letters, dedications, and—for *La légende*—a printing privilege detail the history of each work and call further attention to Lemaire's person, his alliances with the house of Burgundy and the French crown, and the labors and expenses by which his works came to light. We should note, however, that these authorial campaigns for sovereignty over the printed book were not waged in the field of lyric verse. La Vigne's *Ressource de la Chrestienté* was an allegorical polemic written in support of Charles VIII's anticipated military expedition to Italy to capture Naples in 1494; Gringoire's *Folles entreprises* was a defense of Louis XII against the pope; Lemaire's epideictic poem *Temple d'honneur* was a *poème de circonstance* glorifying his recently deceased patron, Pierre, Duke of Bourbon; and *La légende des Vénitiens* was a polemical tract favoring the foreign policy of Louis XII.[69]

The *rhétoriqueurs* did not neglect lyric, they just staked their careers in print on other genres. Lemaire wrote a couple of the texts found in the chanson albums of Marguerite of Austria, and he seems to have had more than passing familiarity with music. He may have been a choirboy at Notre Dame-la-Grande in Valenciennes, and the fluency with which he employed technical terms and described the stylistic differences between the music of Josquin, Agricola, Compère, and Ockeghem in *La concorde des deux langages* certainly argues in favor of his musicality. The polyphonic chanson "Mille regretz" is even attributed to him in Attaingnant's *Vingt et sept chansons musicales* (1533), even though it is almost certainly by Josquin.[70] Jean Molinet, a *rhétoriqueur* employed as the official chronicler of the house of Burgundy, was certainly a composer, even though only one piece has been firmly attributed to him, the four-voice rondeau "Tare ara mon cueur sa plaisance."[71] He was named along with Guillaume Du Fay, Josquin, and other renowned composers in the motet "Omnium bonorum plena." But lyric poetry and composition constituted a sideline that is badly represented in Molinet's print publications: a series of political tracts such as the *Temple de Mars* and *Faictz et dictz*, the *Art de rhétorique*, and the *Roman de la rose moralisé* in prose.[72] Jean Marot, father of Clément and court poet to Louis XII and François Ier, wrote at least seventy-five rondeaux, a major part of his output. But they were only printed posthumously in 1536 in an edition of his son's *L'adolescence clementine*.[73]

Many of the allegories, *epistres*, polemics, and histories just cited were brief works subject to the errant transmission patterns common to occasional verse and lyric. That these particular genres were favored by the *rhétoriqueurs* for their ventures into print relates less to their suitability to become self-standing printed books than the subjects proper to them—matters of moral, religious, and political concern. Aligned with the sovereign's designs and ornamented with monarchic praise, a polemic such as *La légende des Vénitiens* surely attracted its royal privilege by sanctioning the king's controversial military policies in exchange for Lemaire's right to profit from the book's publication.[74] Lemaire was never to receive official support from Louis XII, and Anne de Bretagne hired him only several years later. For authors without remunerative court appointments, financial success was highly fugitive, and those who persisted in the attempt to earn a living by the pen in France continued to publish *histoires, chroniques,* and translations, not lyric. The best-documented case is that of François de Belleforest, who held no sustaining court appointment or benefices in his career, even after becoming royal historiographer in 1568, a position that brought with it little more than the title.[75] His most popular work—the *Histoires tragiques*—kept him quite busy: it began with translations of Matteo Bandello, to which Belleforest added his own works until the series ran to seven volumes in dozens of editions, most of them in canard-size octavo or seidecimo formats. He also devoted himself to two imposing projects in folio, *L'histoire des neuf Roys Charles de France* (Paris,1568) and the monumental *La cosmographie universelle de tout le monde* (Paris, 1575) in three thick volumes. All were works of historiography.

Against this background, the Pléiade poets' quest for greatness in the field of printed lyric is all the more striking. The *chansons,* rondeaux, and epigrams favored by the "rimeurs" at court were the stuff of amorous pastimes and songs like "Jouyssance vous donneray," not forms in which to eternalize the magnificence of a monarch or even the collectable sort of book sought by lawyers, bureaucrats, students, and bibliophiles, who generally preferred works in Latin and of cultural standing, or at the very least romans, contes, and *histoires*. Undoubtedly the classical tone of the Pléiade's lyrics caught the attention of some readers, but it is important to note—as does Michel Simonin—that Ronsard, Du Bellay, and the others of the *brigade* did not necessarily strive to please their public in the same ways freelance or court-appointed authors did. This new generation of poets came from families of the old nobility, which distinguished them from writers of the previous generation.[76] Though they often had to struggle financially, they represented the first fruits of the cultural program initiated by François Ier that emphasized humanistic education, an education the Pléiade poets exhibited with considerable indiscretion. Whereas court poets dissimulated their knowledge of literature out of respect for or acquiescence to the limited tastes and understanding of their aristocratic audiences, the young poets of the *brigade* entertained no such concerns.[77] They liberated lyric from the need to please courtiers, turning it away from love and toward their own status-seeking ends. Ronsard declared in his *Odes* that the "true object of a Lyric poet is to celebrate to the extreme he whom he undertakes to praise."[78]

By infusing the elaborate form of the Pindaric ode (made up of strophe, antistrophe, and epode) with the language of heroic glory, Ronsard set up lyric to join *histoire*, allegory, and polemic as a princely genre. His insistence on printed publication further distinguished his *Odes* from the lyric current at court, and while his *Quatre premiers livres des Odes* were not dedicated to Henry II, they did open with a series of odes celebrating the king, the queen, Marguerite de Valois, the cardinal of Guise, and the victory of François de Bourbon at Cerizoles that made clear the potential of lyric to glorify the Valois in print. In his preface, Ronsard also criticized lyricists who failed to bring their verse to light, accusing them of being "shadowboxers" (Sciamaches) who hide their work rather than offering it up to public opinion.[79] As Michel Simonin observes, Ronsard's insistence that poetry be published and judged by the public threatened to dispossess the court of its role as legislator of Parnassus.[80]

Ronsard's attack on poets who shunned the hard light of printed publication was a pointed reproach of his senior rival at court, the poet Mellin de Saint-Gelais, who had become maître d'hôtel to François Ier sometime around 1518 and served the Valois until his death in 1558.[81] In 1536 Saint-Gelais was put in charge of the royal library at Blois, and when it was moved to Fontainebleau in 1544, he was made assistant to Pierre Duchastel, the head librarian of the king, but despite the bibliographic nature of his responsibilities at court, the verse he penned is more illustrative of his activities as a performer and impresario. He was renowned as a lutenist and apparently "published" his lyric poetry by singing it to his own accompaniment. Admirers touted his prowess as a poet and musician in one, maintaining, moreover, that he was a mathmatician, philosopher, orator, lawyer, doctor, astronomer, and theologian, in short, a "panepistemon" versed in universal science.[82] "Of such as he you won't find thirteen in a baker's dozen" one curiously exclaimed.[83] In addition to love lyrics he wrote a number of cartels (poems for tourneys, usually in the form of poetic challenges) as well as occasional poems for masquerades, weddings, amorous exchanges, festive combats, and small theater pieces keyed to special celebrations. The security of his court appointment affected both the content of his oeuvre and the forms in which it is preserved, for Saint-Gelais never bothered to issue a print of his complete works, allowing them to circulate among courtiers and *lettrés* in manuscripts such as the elegant Ms. BnF fr. 885, a gift from Henry II to Diane de Poitiers and a principle source of the poet's writings. From that environment, his verse escaped into the world of commercial printing, where printers of little poetry anthologies avidly included them in their collections. The first edition of his so-called complete works, *Saingelais, OEuvres de luy tant en composition que translation ou allusion aux Auteurs Grecs et Latins* (Lyon: Pierre de Tours, 1547), offers a case in point: despite the title's claims, it includes poems by other authors, and of the poems attributed to Saint-Gelais—a mere fraction of those he wrote before 1547—many are spurious works.[84] The fact that Saint-Gelais's name could sell poetry in Lyon represents a genuine, grassroots fame that Ronsard might well have envied.

Scholars such as Simonin have interpreted the battle lines drawn up by Ronsard as pitting manuscript against printed publication, but there is no evidence that Saint-Gelais was a Petrarch or Machaut when it came to overseeing the textual forms in which his works were disseminated. Only one manuscript, Chantilly, Musée Condé 523, can be connected directly to the poet, who emended this particular copy himself. Yet despite its early date—circa 1540—Donald Stone does not use it as the basis for his edition of the poet's work, remarking that few of the corrections appear in other contemporary copies and emphasizing that Saint-Gelais's poems circulated in multiple forms during the poet's lifetime.[85] Such pernicious variants and the uncodified nature of the poet's corpus prompt suspicion that Saint-Gelais did not vest much authority in texts of his works at all, whether manuscript or print. Simonin missed what I believe to be the real point of Ronsard's challenge to the *poète du roy*: Ronsard was responding to the threat posed by song. Saint-Gelais was a lutenist, poet, and singer, a true lyricist adept at composing and performing *poésie pour musique*. Son of the *rhétoriqueur* Octavien de Saint-Gelais, Mellin had traveled abroad to study law in Bologna and Padua but soon abandoned jurisprudence in favor of song, developing his talents in emulation of the Italian improvisers Serafino dall'Aquilano and Il Chariteo, who improvised both poetry and music.[86] Back in France, his ability to sing his poetry to the lute made him appear as a latter-day Orpheus. It is easy to imagine how this combination of skills could have irritated Ronsard, who was partially deaf, played no instrument, and who once even admitted that his voice was worthless for song.[87]

The minstrelsy at which Saint-Gelais excelled may have constrained his verse, it is true, but this combination of the sister arts also defined the very nature of lyric. Indeed, not only was the lyric economy at mid-century dominated by oral circulation, recitation, performance, and song, even Ronsard's retreat to classical precedents confronted him with music at yet another turn, for it was through singing that the ancient Greeks worked their mythic effect on the passions. One singer frequently referred to by poets, artists, and storytellers in Renaissance France was Apollo, whose lyre symbolized the transcendence of the lyric art and the dominion of princes. Pervasive references to Apollo's sovereignty over Mount Parnassus and the Muses in poems, frescoes, and theater works reminded rulers of the arts' supporting role in a pacific kingdom.[88] Further stories abounded of Apollo's son Orpheus, who could move rocks or trees with his music and who charmed Pluto in the underworld in order to resurrect Eurydice. These fables, along with those of Arion and Amphion and the lyric metaphors perpetuated in Horace's *Carmina*, fueled Ronsard's desire to associate his poetry with music, and undoubtedly prompted him to announce his intentions toward music in the preface to *Les quatre premiers livres des Odes:* "And I will revive again (if I can) the use of the lyre, today resuscitated in Italy, that lyre alone which should and can animate verses and give to them the just weight of their gravity."[89] That literal declaration to promote his verse in the style of *poesia per musica* amplifies the lyric metaphor elaborated in the *Odes*, particularly in the last poem of the first book, "À sa lyre."[90]

In this light we might see the polemic of the *Quatre premiers livres des Odes* as a pitch to resituate the authority of lyric poets somewhere between performance and print and to capture for the literary author some of the singer's prestige. If so, it deepened the contest of the *chanson* versus the ode initiated the previous year by Du Bellay, another *querelle* that becomes more interesting when reexamined from a musical perspective. In *La deffence et illustration de la langue françoyse* (1549), Du Bellay famously condemned three *chansons* as "mieux dignes d'estre nommez chansons vulgaires qu'odes ou vers lyriques" (more worthy of being called common songs than odes or lyric verse).[91] Two were by Saint-Gelais—"O combien est heureuse" and "Laissez la verde couleur"—the latter being Saint-Gelais's lament of Venus at the death of Adonis, a popular *chanson* that lent its title to a Lyonnaise anthology edited by Antoine Du Moulin, the *Deploration de Venus sur la mort du bel Adonis, avec plusieurs autres compositions nouvelles* (Lyon: Jean de Tournes, 1545).[92] The third song in Du Bellay's list, "Amour avecques Psyches," was another lament at the death of Adonis by Pernette du Guillet, which was published by Jean de Tournes in the same collection under the title "Conde Claros de Adonis."[93] The three texts Du Bellay cites were all renowned as songs, a fact noted by Barthélemy Aneau in his rejoinder to Du Bellay's attack: "and if they [these three *chansons*] can be sounded on the lyre (as they are), they merit the name of lyric verse more than the barkings of your *Olive* do, which could never be sung."[94] All three *chansons* seem to have been sung to pre-existent tunes, either pavanes or galliards or the chordal progression Conde Claros, a bass pattern used by improvisers of epic verse.[95] Much has been written elsewhere about Du Bellay's citations and his invectives against Thomas Sébillet, in whose *Art poétique françois* (1548) "Laissez la verde couleur" and "O combien est heureuse" were each cited not once but twice; these salvos do not need to be rehearsed here.[96] Essentially, Sébillet maintained that the ode, *chanson,* and *chant lyrique* were virtually identical, with the exception that *chants lyriques* (Saint-Gelais's designation for works like "O combien est heureuse") had slightly shorter lines best suited for music.[97] For the ode and *chant lyrique* Sébillet suggests the following models: Pindar in Greek, Horace in Latin, and in French, Saint-Gelais, "Autheur tant dous que divin" (an author as sweet as he is divine.)[98] Thus the new genre being cultivated by the *brigade* was said by Sébillet to be just another sort of *chanson* like those of France's leading lyricist, Saint-Gelais.

In the context of the present argument, it is well worth observing that when the *Deffence* was written, Du Bellay and Ronsard were virtually unknown and had published nothing at all. To attack "Laissez la verde couleur" was not just to attack a poem by the king's poet, but to attack a song that had inspired at least one imitation ("Amour avecques Psyches"), had been printed several times, and was on everyone's lips. It is not just the song's stunning popularity, but the *kind* of popularity it enjoyed that helps explain the "vulgaire" epithet slung at it by Du Bellay, and Ronsard's promotion of a more exclusive genre of strophic verse. In the *Deploration de Venus,* for instance, "Laissez la verde couleur" stood at the head of a mélange of poems by Saint-Gelais, Pernette du Guillet, Bonaventure des Periers, and others, gathered together in an octavo print of just twenty folios. Few of the poems bear attributions and several are followed by an anonymous *response,* or poetic reply, written to the rhyme scheme of the original. The collective nature of the *Deploration* anthology, along with its anonymous and self-replicating poem–response pairs, indicates that from the very outset, "Laissez la verde couleur" was part of a repertory collected, recycled, and renewed in countless *recueils de chansons* (collections of song texts). This culture of print privileged songs like Saint-Gelais's to such a degree that the *Deploration* was expanded and reprinted in 1547, 1548, 1554, 1556, and 1561. And under the title of La Borderie's *Le Discours du voyage de Constantinople* (Paris, 1546) and the *Livre de plusieurs pieces*, which comes at the end of a reedition of *Le Discours* (Paris or Lyon, 1548), still other collections assured "Laissez la verde couleur" of wide circulation during its first decades in print.[99]

The appeal of "Laissez la verde couleur" to printers lay in their penchant for contrafacta, or new song texts written to be sung to popular tunes, and a whole genre of poetry anthologies—*recueils de chansons*—sustained the production of contrafacta, which offered new songs to buyers without costly or hard-to-read musical notation. Not without reason were bookmen in Lyon the publishers of virtually all the initial editions of Saint-Gelais's famous lament, for alongside copies of the *Deploration de Venus*, they churned out reams of cheap *recueils* packed with contrafacta, as did the Bonfons family in Paris. "Laissez la verde couleur" was a favorite in the *recueils* well into the 1580s where it inspired numerous lyrics upon its timbre.[100] Well might Du Bellay or Ronsard have wished to achieve such popularity in print, but by rejecting the *chanson* in favor of the Pindaric ode, they foreclosed the broad circulation enjoyed by more singable verse. *Chansons* were creative of other verse, their tunes were sung repeatedly and hung in the air, and as such they ill suited the practices of the Pléiade poets with their highly literate elocution and focus on authoring books.

Saint-Gelais has left us no written music, but from what we can discern of his improvisatory style, he preferred syllabic melodies and light accompaniments that would not mar the audibility of his verse. Musical settings of his poetry by contemporary composers suggest that he often used music that was already about, singing his poems to the bass patterns, dances, and popular tunes that were the lutenist's stock-in-trade.[101] Traces of these musical materials survive in polyphonic settings of his poems, such as those setting "Laissez la verde couleur," which harmonize melodies that may well bear some resemblance to Saint-Gelais's own melodic blueprint for the song. Pierre Certon, Jacques Arcadelt, and Adrian Le Roy all set the text for four voices. It was also intabulated for guitar by Le Roy, included in a monophonic chansonnier compiled by Jean Chardavoine, and a melody for it was penned into a *recueil de chansons* by an unknown writer

Example 2a. Pierre Certon, "Laissez la verde couleur" (tenor), in *Premier livre de chansons en quatre parties, par M. Pierre Certon* (Paris: Le Roy & Ballard, 1552), fol. 2r.

Example 2b. Jacques Arcadelt, "Laissez la verde couleur" (tenor), in *Tiers livre de chansons nouvellement composé en musique a quatre parties par M. Jacques Arcadet* (Paris: Le Roy & Ballard, 1561), fol. 4r.

Example 2c. Jean Chardavoine, "Laissez la verde couleur" (monophonic melody) in *Le recueil des plus belles et excellentes chansons en forme de voix de ville* (Paris: Claude Micard, 1576), fol. 72v. Melody reminiscent of that in Certon, with more regular rhythms, the fourth line transposed up a tone, and the contour of the last line altered.

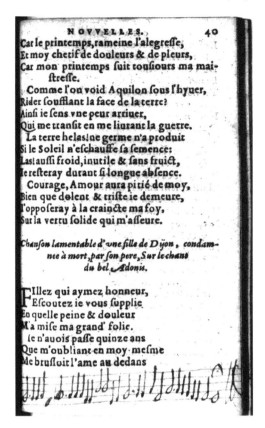

[Lais-sez la ___ ver-de cou-leur O prin - ces - se Cy-the-ré - e,

Et de nou - vel-le dou-leur Vos - tre beau-té soit pa-ré - e.]

Figure 10. *Le recueil de chansons nouvelles. Livre III* (Paris: Bonfons, 1586), fol. 40r. Bibliothèque nationale de France, Arsenal, Rés. in-8, 11345. A transcription of the music appears below the image.

sometime after 1586. The melodies from Certon, Arcadelt, and Chardavoine are given in example 2, with the manuscript tune from the *recueil de chansons* of 1586 shown in figure 10.

Most of the sources in example 2 relate to the melody written down by Certon (ex. 2a), though the late version penned by our anonymous bears some similarity to Arcadelt's melody as well (ex. 2b). Certon and Arcadelt both knew Saint-Gelais and stood an excellent chance of having heard him perform the song. As a royal musician and master of the children at the Sainte-Chapelle du Palais, Certon doubtless knew Saint-Gelais well (he set eleven of Saint-Gelais's poems to music). Likewise, Arcadelt's employer, Charles, Cardinal de Lorraine, regularly included Saint-Gelais in his musical and literary salon. Charles seems to have had a penchant for lute songs, and this taste may have inspired Arcadelt's settings of seventeen poems by Saint-Gelais, all as four-voice songs using tuneful melodies reminiscent of those Saint-Gelais might himself have employed when singing them. Indeed, Arcadelt's "Laissez la verde couleur" sets the first six stanzas of the poem in what is essentially a set of composed-out harmonic and melodic elaborations on a single tune, a precious record of the kind of improvisations Saint-Gelais might have entertained as he repeated the melody over and over for the forty stanzas of the song.[102]

It is tempting to speculate upon which melody for "Laissez la verde couleur" was closest to Saint-Gelais's own. But by far the more interesting questions, it seems to me, are raised by the version of the tune that was penned into the little *recueil de chansons* printed in 1586, almost thirty years after the poet's death (shown in figure 10). The owner of the print, *Le recueil de chansons nouvelles,* wanted to sing a new song that had been written to the tune of "Laissez la verde couleur," which by then was known as "Le chant du bel Adonis." But memory failing him or her, our singer or a friend or teacher wrote the tune in the book at the bottom of the page as a reminder of how it went. This version is not a transcription from one of the five earlier printed sources, but a conflation and reduction of them resulting, it appears, from oral transmission.

Whoever wrote down this version of the melody seems to recall features that we find in the versions of Arcadelt and Certon. The opening of Arcadelt's setting may have stuck in that person's mind: the rhythm matches, as does the choice of G with a flat as the tonality, although Arcadelt's extraordinary beginning on F♯—which is counterintuitive—has been replaced with a plebeian beginning on G. Or maybe our anonymous remembered the melody we see in Certon's setting, recalling its ascent through a minor third but not its beginning on the third scale degree of a piece in F. In any case, the manuscript tune slips away from Arcadelt's version and resorts to the melodic contours of Certon's, rising in the first phrase and dropping a third to the first cadence, a trajectory inverted in the second phrase, which descends and then ascends to the medial cadence. Similarly, the rhythm turns from Arcadelt to Certon, conflating Arcadelt's unusual rhythmic opening with Certon's more even declamation. The corresponding rhythmic formulas shared by all of these tunes or "timbres" relate them to each other and perhaps to a declamatory formula employed by Saint-Gelais in performance. Indeed, the rhythmic similarities between the anonymous timbre—surely the most representative of the oral tradition—and the versions of Arcadelt and Certon suggest that in some cases the rhythm of a timbre was less subject to distortion than its melody during its mixed transmission in both oral and written forms, which would make sense given the way the rhythm firmly hooks into the text. The narrow range of declamatory formulas is also particularly evident in the manuscript timbre, which wends its way from G to D in the first two phrases and from G to C and back in the second two, covering but a fifth in all. The wider range of the melodies written down by the polyphonists seems to shrink during a process of oral transmission or recollection that erodes extraordinary musical features and reduces the song to a little ditty in G that begins and ends in the same place.

The manuscript melody points up the longevity of timbres in the milieus where they circulated. "Laissez la verde couleur" reached an apex of popularity at court right around 1549.[103] Here it is, penned into a *recueil de chansons* sometime after 1586, albeit as an *aide mémoire*, but one presumably drawn from an aural recollection, not copied from a known printed source. Ultimately, the anonymous timbre for "Laissez la verde couleur" stands less to confirm what we know of Saint-Gelais's own musical practices than it does to point away from the sophisticated minstrelsy of a Saint-Gelais, who probably altered the tune extensively as he worked and perhaps beyond recognition.[104] Certainly the lasting popularity of the timbre in the repertory of the *recueils de chansons*—a popularity that far outstripped the longevity of Saint-Gelais's poetry in the polyphonic repertory more directly connected with the court—demonstrates that the song had a long and independent life beyond his immediate orbit.

It is hard to write a history of musical publication, for ultimately it should take stock of publication in performance as well as in manuscript or print. For musical settings of the Catholic Mass, with its strongly determined liturgical function, its institutional homes in chapel and cathedral, and its writerly musical style, the documentary evidence is fuller. But for the chanson, it is difficult to trace histories, disseminated as the genre was in sung performances. The textual witnesses to these musical acts are few and fragile, and they likely tell as little about the sound of a chanson as a fake sheet does about Dizzie Gillespie's rendition of a jazz standard.

Settings surface here and there in printed polyphonic chansonniers and *recueils de chansons* from the deep pools of memory that preserved them, and while we can be grateful for the existence of these texts, it is important to remember that they are flotsam pitching on an ocean of lost performances by Saint-Gelais and those who heard his *chansons* and sang them themselves. Currents of song and memory carried lyric along on tides we can describe only loosely based on the transmission patterns evident in written source materials, currents so forceful and long-standing that we might even wonder whether the *querelle de la chanson et de l'ode* represented the attempt of the Pléiade poets to assert the validity of written publication in the face of orality. Du Bellay decries the *chansons* of Saint-Gelais as "vulgaire," as too common, too much in circulation, not, perhaps, because Lyonnais printers featured them in *recueils,* but because everyone was singing them.

If Saint-Gelais and Ronsard represent two extremes, the one devoted to singing lyric verse and the other to writing books of it, Clément Marot stands out as a poet who worked both systems. In closing, it is instructive to consider his career, for it brings us back to Paris in the 1530s when Attaingnant first popularized chansons by Claudin, Sandrin, and Janequin in print and Claudin first set Marot's "Jouyssance vous donneray" to music. A familiar amid the *libraires* and *imprimeurs* on the Left Bank, Clément engaged in numerous literary projects, editing the *Roman de la Rose* and the works of Villon for Galliot Du Pré, translating Ovid's *Metamorphoses* into French for Estienne Roffet, and bringing the poetry of his father to light in 1536. He got his own *L'adolescence clementine, autrement, les oeuvres de Clement Marot* into print with Roffet in 1532 at the somewhat ripe age of thirty-six, and well before the authorial revolutions of the Pléiade, he promoted the word *Oeuvre* in the titles of his publications beginning with *Les oeuvres de Clement Marot . . . Le tout songneusement par luy mesme reveu, & mieulx ordonné* (Lyon: Etienne Dolet, 1538). Florian Preisig sees Marot's role in the formation of authorship for French poets as decisive, and certainly Marot's record as an editor and his own career in print supports this view.[105]

Marot stuck his *chansons* at the very end of his first publication, *L'adolescence clementine,* and this seems strange given their popularity in the settings being printed in the very same years by Pierre Attaingnant. Indeed, part of the rationale for publication of *L'adolescence clementine,* as Marot explains in the preface, was to recapture his poems from others and reprint them in an authorized edition: "I know not, my dearest Brothers, who incited me the more to bring these little youthful things to light, whether your continual supplications or the displeasure that I have had of hearing a large part of them shouted and published in the streets, all incorrect, badly printed, and more to the profit of the Bookseller than the honor of the Author."[106] Literary historians such as Preisig have read the preface as a significant historical moment, in which Marot asserts his right to profit from his own works. An insider to publishing, he was well-positioned to ply the commercial side of the book trade directly, and the book itself is evidence of his success. But what is equally striking about this preface is Marot's characterization of what has happened to his poems. They have been badly printed by others, yes, and need correction, but his first displeasure comes from hearing them "shouted and published in the streets." Not unlike Dante's complaint about blacksmiths singing stanzas from his *Divine Comedy*, Marot's remark brings us to the noise of streets, where traveling vendors sang songs to sell a few broadsides and vied for attention with market criers. Marot's poems escaped not just the typographical control though which he could ensure their correctness, they were swept up in the flurry of anonymous song verse that drifted down from oral circulation to settle onto the pages of cheaply printed *recueils de chansons*. The sonic nature of Marot's distress is palpable in his preface.

The placement of his *chansons* in *L'adolescence clementine* seems calculated to segregate his "literary" oeuvres from the song repertoire. Had Preisig taken stock of musical settings in his history of Marot's authorship, he might have read Marot's preface differently and seen printed publication as one author's attempt to contain his corpus from diffusion into the oral circulation of poetry promoted by chansonniers and *recueils de chansons*.[107] Much adored by polyphonists such as Claudin and easily put to song by minstrels, Marot's *chansons* had already been "published" in musical performances, perhaps even in the streets of Paris. All of his thirty *chansons*, rondeaux, and ballades to be printed before 1533 appear first from the presses of Pierre Attaingnant, in polyphonic settings.[108] Thus, while one can discover in Marot an author determined to turn printing to his own advantage, the print history of his *chansons* is more checkered than that of his other verse. For Marot's *chansons*, the sources look much like those for Saint-Gelais's lyric poetry, with musical prints and manuscripts of music regularly outnumbering the strictly textual sources.

It is hard to discern how Marot viewed the unattributed publication of *chansons* such as his "Jouyssance vous donneray" and "Secourez moy, ma Dame" in Attaingnant's chansonniers. The displeasure voiced in the preface to *L'adolescence clementine* may not have been directed at Attaingnant, who was, after all, Royal Printer of Music and working under privilege in the same neighborhood, though Attaingnant's prints certainly facilitated the corruption of Marot's verse as variants multiplied in settings by other composers and careless reprintings. Even Attaingnant's prints introduce variants in the poetry from year to year and setting to setting, so many that exasperated modern editors of Marot's *chansons* may well be justified in ignoring the readings of musical sources.[109]

Marot did retain the *chansons* in the authorized edition of his works, *Les oeuvres de Clement Marot . . . Le tout songneusement par luy mesme reveu, & mieulx ordonné* of 1538, at the end, in a position that evinces their marginal status as oeuvres. But while Marot may not have esteemed *chansons* as the stuff of literary greatness, as an insider to the printing trade, he did not neglect to print them. Indeed, he may ultimately have tried to capitalize on the useful advertisement presented by polyphonic prints, for in 1538 he edited his own "chansonnier," *Les chansons nouvellement assemblées oultre les anciennes impressions,* evidently at his own expense and possibly in an attempt to make good on the musical renown of his verse and its reprinting in *recueils de chansons* such as *S'ensuyvent plusieurs belles chansons nouvelles nouvellement imprimees . . . avec aulcunes de Clement Marot de nouveau adjoustées* (Lyon: Claude Nourry, [ca. 1533–34]).[110] Such a self-published *recueil de chansons* was extraordinary, so much so that it is hard to know whether to interpret it as the product of Marot's ambitions as an author or his interests in the Parisian printing trade, but whatever his intentions (and we cannot know them), one outcome is clear: *Les chansons nouvellement assemblées* established a significant precedent for authored chansonniers. The time when composers would supplement the authority of performance with printed chansonniers of their own was still decades in the future, but already in Marot's *recueil de chansons,* the trail to them had been blazed.

4. The Book of Poetry Becomes a Book of Music

Ronsard ended his first book of *Odes* with a bombastic ode "À sa lyre," a celebration of the power of lyric poetry indebted to Horace and Pindar for its language, but featuring himself quite centrally.[1] In it, he praises his lute for any renown that may come to him, and although he employs the image strictly as a metaphor, it is hard not to catch a whiff of envy if we read the glorious account of his "singing" in this poem as a confrontation with Mellin de Saint-Gelais, *aumônier* of Henry II and someone who really could sing and play and make up poetry for music on the fly. The contest between the two was no secret, after all, Ronsard the twenty-five-year-old upstart fresh from university trying to take on Saint-Gelais, the established master. Indeed, Ronsard was roundly criticized at court for neglecting to praise Saint-Gelais directly among those he flattered in *Les quatre premiers livres des Odes,* an omission that apparently struck contemporaries as just as pointed as I find his grasp for Saint-Gelais's lute in these final lines:[2]

> Par toy je plais, et par toy je suis leu:
> C'est toy qui fais que Ronsard soit esleu
> Harpeur François, et quand on le rencontre,
> Qu'avec le doigt par la rue on le monstre.
> Si je plais donc, si je sçay contenter
> Si mon renom la France veut chanter,
> Si de mon front les estoiles je passe,
> Certes mon Luth cela vient de ta grace.[3]

> [It is through you that I please, and through you I am read: It is thanks to you that Ronsard is elected the lyricist of France, and that when met in the street people point him out. So, if I please, if I know

how to satisfy, if France wants to sing my renown, if I surpass the stars by my thoughts (lit. "my brow"), surely, my Lute, it is thanks to your grace.]

Partially deaf, with no singing voice, Ronsard's verse may have pleased on the page, but I doubt it would have garnered much praise in his singing of it to the lute. Given the performance culture at court, Ronsard's pretentions to the post of "Harpeur François" might even have seemed ludicrous at the time. Saint-Gelais apparently mocked Ronsard before the king and assembled company by reading the most ambitious bits of the first book of *Odes* aloud in a dirisive voice, and it is hard to imagine that he would have skipped the fun that could be had with a pompous rendering of this all-too-fabulous ending.

Apart from the content, one thing that made Ronsard's verse so easy to mock in a performance such as Saint-Gelais's is its unmusicality. The lines quoted above, for instance, employ decasyllabic couplets more appropriate to epic poetry than lyric verse, and in many other places in his *Odes,* the elocution is tortured, the imagery confusing, and the verse forms irregular, with a result too labored to work well in song. In these initial stages, especially, Ronsard's verse was often overwrought, the very antithesis of Saint-Gelais's.

Despite the significant lip service he paid to music in his poetry, Ronsard's odes were greeted coolly by chanson composers. Lyric in name but not very singable, the few settings they did receive tended to be of isolated strophes, not entire poems.[4] It is impossible to know whether this neglect of his verse irritated the young poet, particularly given Saint-Gelais's favored status with song composers, but whatever the inspiration, Ronsard next produced a work that was explicit in its musical aspirations: *Les Amours de P. de Ronsard.*[5] It was published in 1552 by Veuve Maurice de la Porte and included a thirty-two-folio musical supplement of polyphonic settings printed by Nicolas Du Chemin. This extraordinary combination of printed polyphony and lyric poetry made a true chansonnier of Ronsard's verse in every sense of the term and it marks a genuine first in French printing.

Les Amours has been an object of study since the revival of interest in Ronsard's poetry in the late nineteenth century, with a modern edition of the text coming out in 1857 as the first volume in Prosper Blanchemain's *Oeuvres complètes,* and a musical edition of the *Supplément musical* published in 1903.[6] Even before Blanchemain's edition, Romantic composers had begun to set the poems of Ronsard, starting with Richard Wagner's

"Mignon allons voir si la rose" in 1840 and followed by Victor Massé in 1849, Georges Bizet in 1866, and Charles Gounod in 1872, a trend that expanded dramatically throughout the early twentieth century.[7] This long history of settings, initiated by the musical supplement of 1552, seems to make the musicality of Ronsard's verse self-evident, and late twentieth-century scholars of French song, writing in a context that also included Darius Milhaud's *Les Amours de Ronsard* (1934) and *Quatre chansons de Ronsard* (1940), Maurice Ravel's "Ronsard à son âme" (1923–24; orchestral version 1935), and Francis Poulenc's song cycle *Poèmes de Ronsard* (1924–25; orchestral version 1934), would have had no reason to question a history that accepted Ronsard's presentation of his oeuvre as destined for song. But as we saw already in the preceding chapter, Ronsard's bookish works stood apart from the lyric culture of his day. The pompous language of the *Les quatre premiers livres des Odes* seduces partly through its audaciousness, and *Les Amours* partly though the size of the cycle—176 poems and a book with weight in the hand—but these projections of magnificence are lost in the singing, where clear oratory and brevity are the strongest priorities. The effervescence of song cannot sustain the load of a sonnet cycle like *Les Amours*, even when composers group together three or four chansons (as in the settings of Milhaud and Poulenc). If this poetry has captured the attention of several centuries of musicians, it owes in part to print—the location of Ronsard's authority—and to the imprimatur Ronsard's authorship can confer on musical compositions.

The polyphonic songs appended to *Les Amours* launched Ronsard's musical career in a conspicuous way, staking his claim to lyric by drawing attention to the collection's potential as a source of *poésie pour musique* in the highest style, a potential already being realized in Ronsard's century for Petrarch's *Canzoniere*.[8] In Italy—and particularly in the Venetian literary circles of Pietro Bembo—madrigal culture had intensified along with Petrarchism in such a way that Petrarch's sonnets set one standard for serious madrigal verse. Bembo's elevation of Petrarch as the model for lyric poetry in his *Prose della volgar lingua* (1525) contributed early on to the growing popularity of the sonnet form among madrigal composers, who by about 1540 had adopted the Petrarchan sonnet as a vernacular form equal in stature to Latin texts.[9] The sonnet settings in Adrian Willaert's *Musica nova* (Venice, 1559) and Cipriano de Rore's *Primo libro a 5* (Venice, 1542) stand as monuments to the Petrarchan cast of the Venetian madrigal.[10] That *Les Amours* was presented as the poetic choice of French composers underscored its implicit relationship to Italian models. By extension, the musical supplement to *Les Amours* fostered the

Figure 11.   Frontispiece, *Les Amours de P. de Ronsard,
Vandomois, nouvellement augmentées par lui, & commen-
tées par Marc Antoine de Muret* (Paris: Veuve Maurice de la
Porte, 1553), fol. 1v. Bibliothèque nationale de France, Rés.
P Ye 125. In early editions of *Les Amours*, Ronsard shares
this opening of the book with an engraving of his mistress,
Cassandra, who faces him. In later editions of his works, his
portrait appears alone.

impression that an entire French musico-poetic culture parallel to that of Italian Petrarchism was already in place, with Ronsard as its Petrarch.[11] It was, after all, in the frontispiece to *Les Amours* that Ronsard crowned himself poet laureate (though with the myrtle leaves associated with Venus and a more strictly amorous immortality than the heroic wreathes worn by Caesar: see figure 11).[12]

In tandem with the frontispiece, the musical supplement works within the space of the book to portray Ronsard as a lyric poet fully realized, fabricating musicality for his verse whole cloth despite the fact that the sonnet was not widely considered poetry for music in France.

Here it is worth pausing to remark the exceptional format of the musical supplement, which was printed in a small upright octavo half the size of Du Chemin's oblong quarto partbooks, with the four voices laid out in the manner of a miniature choirbook. This layout invited singers to gather around *Les Amours*, holding the book and singing from it. Such a result required significant effort, for printing the *Supplément* entailed a complete reorientation of Du Chemin's standard forms (upright instead of oblong, octavo instead of quarto, choirbook layout instead of partbooks), one precipitated by the need to fit polyphony together in a book of poetry.[13] We should also note that the surviving copies of *Les Amours* in the 1552 and 1553 editions all include the gatherings of music, which do not have a separate title page or colophon and may not have circulated on their own. Thus, although the *Amours*-plus-*Supplément* sets appear at first glance to be mongrels pulled together by readers, the volumes actually stage themselves as compilations featuring Ronsard as one of a series of "lyricists" that included the poet-composer Muret, and the composers Pierre Certon, Claude Goudimel, and Clément Janequin, who contributed musical settings. Textured like an anthology and projecting the sociability of performance, they are not unlike the compilation titled *Hectamophile* studied by Nancy Vickers, whose research encourages us to understand heterogeneous books like these as "carriers of relationships."[14]

By the end of the century, Ronsard's musical aspirations for *Les Amours* would be fulfilled, for it is the single most important source of French chanson texts of the century. As a result, Ronsard dominates our understanding of poetry and music at the time. His book is a magnet, beautiful and attention-getting. In this chapter, I explore the musical history of Ronsard's "chansonnier" in detail, beginning with the *Supplément* and ending with the eight books of Ronsard settings issued in Paris between 1575 and 1578 and featuring sonnets from *Les Amours*. The two music books on which we will linger (and the best-studied by modern scholars)

are Anthoine de Bertrand, *Les Amours de P. de Ronsard* (1576) and Guillaume Boni, *Sonetz de P. de Ronsard* (1576). That I have chosen Ronsard as
the subject of this chapter risks—I am well aware—simply amplifying his
dominance in histories of the late sixteenth-century chanson. But my design in revisiting the subject of "les musiciens de P. de Ronsard" (as Henry
Expert titled them in his 1923 edition) is to explore how Ronsard's works
captured the attention of composers and how they in turn exploited his
authority so aptly that it still frames musicological discourse today.[15] This
chapter studies the history of *Les Amours* in polyphonic settings, particularly the fad in the 1570s for entire chansonniers based on *Les Amours*.
This extraordinary phenomenon marked a true turning point in the history of the chanson; more specifically, it marks a transformation in the
history of the chansonnier as a genre of book.

These books of Ronsard settings, then, define the culmination of the
trajectory I have been charting, one that moves from the flyaway chansons of Claudin, Certon, and others whose works were generally anthologized toward the formation of single-composer chansonniers that were
arguably conceived of as books from the start and designed for printed
publication. One strand of analysis that will gain momentum as we go
along is the significance of the book itself as constitutive of meaning. "The
book always aims to install an order," says Roger Chartier, "whether it is
the order in which it is deciphered, the order in which it is to be understood, or the order intended by the authority who commanded or permit-
ted the work."[16] We will see chanson composers carefully ordering the
contents of their books, and the Royal Printers of Music, Le Roy & Ballard, leveraging elements of book design such as layout and ornament to
assert compositional authority by visually likening music books to those
of canonized authors. Extensive paratexts comprising liminary verse
praising the composer, dedications, prefaces, and portraits of the composer
likewise reinvented chansonniers in the imposing style defined by Ronsard. At chapter's end, finally, we will test the success of these auto-
canonizing music books by tracking their reception, looking to see who
collected them and what authority they commanded in two massive bibliographies that came out in 1584 and 1585: the "Bibliothèques" of François
de La Croix du Maine and Antoine Du Verdier.[17] These "libraries" attempted to order the entire world of books in French, and by so doing they
contributed to the larger cultural project in which the musical *Amours*
played a part by elevating the vernacular to a language that could rival
Greek, Latin, and the classical literary canon. With *Les Amours*, French
chansons were swept up to Mount Parnassus in Ronsard's wake.

SETTINGS OF RONSARD'S POETRY, 1550–1570

It seems virtually certain that Ronsard or someone close to him, such as Marc-Antoine de Muret, initiated the musical project behind *Les Amours*, for the composers who contributed to the *Supplément* were all Parisian and had direct ties to Ronsard, to the court, or to the publisher Du Chemin. Pierre Certon was master of the choirboys at the Sainte-Chapelle, Janequin was at that time on his way to becoming *compositeur ordinaire du roi*, and Claude Goudimel worked for Du Chemin as house editor.[18] Muret was a greater humanist than composer—only three polyphonic songs of his survive, all written in a simple homophonic style and all published in 1552–53 by Du Chemin—but he was regent of the Collège du Cardinal Lemoine, where Ronsard had been his pupil.[19] Muret published a commentary on the mythology of *Les Amours* the following year, a paratext that, like the polyphonic settings issued with the collection in 1552, packaged the sonnets with an interpretive apparatus affirming their canonic status. The choice of composers seems calculated to establish Ronsard's credibility with court musicians, just as the *Supplément* itself shows how much music still mattered as an endorsement of a lyric poet. For composers, we should see in the *Supplément* a new publishing space, for their chansons landed in a discursive zone that constructed authorship with lyric poetry and music.

The musical supplement was not just a little polyphonic chansonnier appended to *Les Amours*, but a series of settings meant to provide music for most of the poems in the collection (for a list of the settings, see table 3).[20] Key to the inherent musicality of the cycle is Ronsard's care to restrict the rhyme schemes he employed in the sonnets and to regularize the alternation of masculine and feminine rhymes within them in such a way that the quatrains always rhyme *abba* (beginning with either a masculine or feminine rhyme word) and the tercets invariably begin with a rhyme of the opposite "gender" from that ending the quatrains, as shown in table 3. Later, in his *Abbrege de l'art poëtique françois* (Paris, 1565), Ronsard explained that careful attention to the alternation of masculine and feminine rhyme words made verse "more fitting to Music & the harmony of instruments, in favor of which it seems that Poetry was born."[21] He also admonished young poets to be sure to carry through with the "same measure" in the rest of the verses of an elegy or chanson "so that the Musicians may attune to it more easily." In this passage, Ronsard connects two practices: the alternation of masculine and feminine rhymes and strophic regularity in poems intended for music, a connection evident in his sonnets, which

TABLE 3. The Musical Supplement to Pierre de Ronsard's *Les Amours*

Composer	Form	Incipit	Masculine/Feminine Rhymes
Certon	sonnet	J'espere et crains . . .	*fmmf fmmf mmf mfm
Certon	sonnet	Bien qu'à grand tort . . .	mffm mffm ffm ffm
Goudimel	ode	Errant par les champs de la grace . . .	
Goudimel	epode	En qui respandit le ciel . . .	
Goudimel	sonnet	Quand j'apperçoy . . .	*mffm mffm ffm fmf
Goudimel	ode	Qui renforcera ma voix . . .	
Muret	sonnet	Las, je me plain . . .	fmmf fmmf mmf mmf
Janequin	sonnet	Qui vouldra voir . . .	*fmmf fmmf mmf mmf
Janequin	sonnet	Nature ornant la dame . . .	*mffm mffm ffm ffm
Janequin	*chanson*	Petite Nymphe folastre . . .	

NOTE: Asterisks (*) indicate those settings that can be used to sing other sonnets in the collection.

he wrote in two like quatrains followed by two like tercets. In this way, Ronsard made the sonnet into *poésie mesurée à la Lyre,* a feature born out by the *Supplément musical.*[22] The four sonnet settings marked with asterisks in table 3 are each followed in the *Supplément* by a list of other sonnets that can be sung to them. Most of the sonnets in the collection are assigned to one of these four musical settings by virtue of their particular pattern of masculine and feminine rhymes. The sonnet with the most unusual rhyme scheme—"Quand j'appercoy"—has only three texts assigned to its setting, while those with more common rhyme schemes— "Qui vouldra voir" and "Nature ornant"—divide the bulk of the sonnets between them (92 and 59 sonnets, respectively). In total, 168 of the 176 sonnets in the original edition are assigned music.[23]

Ronsard's decision to restrict his rhyme schemes was extraordinary for the time. Bembo, by contrast, explicitly encouraged diversity in a sonnet's rhymes in accordance with Petrarch's aesthetic, and in France, Du Bellay worked toward rich and varied rhyme schemes in his sonnet cycle, *L'olive* (which Barthélemy Aneau denounced as "barkings . . . that could never be sung").[24] Ronsard's "formes fixes" for the sonnet represent a significant departure from Petrarchan ideals, one determined by the practicalities of writing verse for music in France.

The exchangeability of texts in the *Supplément* places it amid the practices of minstrels and all those who worked with timbres or "airs" designed for the easy declamation of long strophic *chansons* or new texts written in the same form.[25] In conception, the songs reprinted in the *Supplément* are also related to the formulaic frottola designed "de cantar sonetti" (for singing sonnets) in Ottaviano Petrucci's *Strambotti, Ode, Frottole, Sonetti. Et modo de cantar versi latini e capituli. Libro quarto* [1505], and they are probably not at all unlike the performances of sonnets as *formes fixes* given by Italian improvisers such as Serafino dall'Aquilano and Ronsard's nemesis, Mellin de Saint-Gelais.[26] It would do a disservice to the conception of *Les Amours* to disregard its pretensions to Venetian models, but in fact, the outward form of these sonnets and their musical settings resemble the common stock of lyric modes employed by the lutenist-improvisers *Les Amours* purported to supplant. Moreover, the arrangement of the book—with texts and music printed separately—compels musicians to memorize the notes so that they can read the texts while they sing, very much as people must have sung from song sheets or *recueils de chansons* containing contrafacta to popular polyphonic chansons. The printed music impresses the reader as drawing *Les Amours* into an exclusive musical culture delimited by music literacy, but the way the music fits with the texts actually engages the memory instead.[27]

The settings of *Les Amours* are not Italian madrigals with French texts, but French chansons that have been fitted to the new form of the sonnet. At issue here are French versus Italian aesthetics of text expression and differing attitudes toward the authority of the poet's text over the composer's musical setting. The chansons in the *Supplément* are not through-composed; rather the music of the first quatrain is repeated for the second and that for the tercets either through-composed or repeated for each group of tercets. These repetitions nicely reduce the long texts to seven lines of music, but they foreclose any detailed word painting, since one line of music is made to serve multiple lines of text. Moreover, the repetitions create one of two musical forms, either AABB or AABC—not such a far cry, in short, from the repetitive ABCAA forms used in chansons of Sermisy's generation, or the form of "Jouyssance vous donneray" (ABCBB). Finally, the chansons for *Les Amours* are all written for four voices, like the chansons published by Attaingnant, and in a generally homophonic texture with some points of imitation and the occasional melisma at caesuras or near the ends of lines. An extreme example of this tendency toward homophony is Certon's "J'espere et crains," a virtual *voix de ville* characterized by the syllabic declamation, homorhythmic texture, and

Example 3.   Pierre Certon, "J'espere et crains," measures 1–9. From Julien
Tiersot, *Ronsard et la musique de son temps: oeuvres musicales de Certon,
Goudimel, Janequin, Muret, Mauduit, etc.* (Leipzig: Breitkopf & Härtel, and
Paris: Fischbacher 1903), 34.

triple meter definitive of the genre (see example 3); the setting also employs a good stretch of written-out fauxbourdon in measures 6 to 9, harmonies typical of the *voix de ville* and one of the features that places it
close to the practices of improvisers. It is perhaps not surprising that Certon thought of the *voix de ville* when composing his contribution to the
Supplément, for exchangeability of texts is one hallmark of that genre and
exactly what makes the tension between Ronsard's Italian pretensions and
the actual music of the supplement so striking.[28] Overall, the *Supplément*
manufactures the tuneful varieties of musical success being enjoyed at
mid-century by the poetry of Clément Marot and Saint-Gelais.

By cultivating the idioms of the chanson, the musical settings in *Les
Amours* fail to replicate the Italian attention to language evident in the

Petrarchan settings of madrigalists, who attempted to match syntax and meaning with music directly expressive of the text. The allusion to Petrarch and his authority in the madrigal repertoire is present, but a "translation" has been made, from Italian into the French musical language of the Parisian chanson and *voix de ville*. This has its parallel in Pléiade poetics. The use of Gallic models, while contrary to Du Bellay's recommendations for French verse forms in the *Deffence et illustration de la langue françoyse*, is implicit in his defense of the French language itself. For the problem, as he saw it, lay not in the nature of French, but in the negligence of those "governing" it.[29] Indeed, the cultural chauvinism of the *Deffence* was the means through which Du Bellay bolstered the Pléiade's French project against the potentially overwhelming literary merits of their idols.[30] Classicizing poets thus struggled within a paradox—the imitation of canonized models enhanced the creative process but slavish fidelity would reduce poets to mere copying. Linguistic nationalism played a key role in shoring up Pléiade poetry against complete absorption into the Horatian, Pindaric, and Petrarchan traditions; the musical style of the *Supplément* thus plants Ronsard's sonnets in the soil of French lyric and projects the Gallic pride voiced in the *Deffence*.

Although the musical supplement to *Les Amours* attempted to propagate a simplified, potentially musical, and particularly French type of sonnet, the sonnet did not take root in the repertory of polyphonic chanson prints right away. Between the publication of *Les Amours* in 1552 and 1575, only fifteen musical settings of French sonnets came into print, a statistic that is doubly curious when one considers the large number of chansons on sonnets by Ronsard to be published between 1575 and 1580, to which we will turn momentarily.[31] Certainly French composers must have found fourteen-line sonnets unpleasantly prolix compared to other chanson verse, but size alone does not explain the difference between Ronsard's sonnets and earlier *poésie pour musique*. Ronsard reinvents the language of *amour courtois* in such a way that the love inspiring his verse is sometimes almost effaced by the density of his language. While his grammatical structures tend to be parallel and linear, and to proceed by line (all of which facilitate musical setting), his poetry can be so encrusted with abstraction and classical allusion that it becomes too thick to understand upon first hearing as a chanson. The opening quatrain of sonnet 36 makes the point well:

Pour la douleur, qu'amour veult que je sente,
Ainsi que moy, Phebus, tu lamentoys,

Quand amoureux, loing du ciel tu chantoys
Pres d'Ilion sus les rives de Xanthe.[32]

[From the sadness that love wants me to feel,
As I, Phoebus, you lamented
When, in love, far from the heavens you sang,
Near Ilium on the banks of the Xanthe.]

Ronsard opens with a passing reference to the pain of love, a typical conceit of courtly love poetry. But quickly we are transported to a mythic realm as Ronsard compares his amorous laments to those of Phoebus (Apollo) accompanying himself on the lyre along the banks of the Xanthe near Ilium (Troy). The remainder of the poem draws associations between Ronsard and Apollo, both with lyre in hand, and Ronsard closes by depicting his own site of poetic inspiration along the banks of the Loire. The poet's beloved Cassandra is missing entirely, and the sonnet no longer initiates the same expectation that a song, when performed before the mistress, might function as a token of love and soften her heart.

For all of their complexities, Ronsard's sonnets did come to be set as chansons, but only with regularity in the 1570s. Before that time, chanson composers continued to prefer strophic poems or epigrams instead, and pulled only isolated tercets or quatrains from the sonnets they did set.[33] The ephemerality of lyric continued to exercise its power, disassembling sonnet cycles, tearing poems from books, and scattering rhyme on the winds of performance. Ronsard even added strophic *chansons* to his repertoire, announcing in the *Nouvelle Continuation des Amours* (1556) that he sought in them "un beau stile bas, populaire et plaisant."[34] It is noteworthy that this collection was far less stable than *Les Amours*—not only was it absorbed into the *Second Livre des Amours* and rearranged in subsequent editions of that book, but by 1571 it contained a mobile jumble of madrigals, *chansons*, sonnets, *stances*, *baisers*, and elegies. Loosely structured and amenable to errant reading practices, the collection looked more like a pirated lyric anthology than any of Ronsard's earlier books. Indeed, even *Les Amours* was modified to accord with these norms in its unauthorized versions: the 1557 edition of *Les Amours* probably issued by Christopher Plantin (with the false imprint of Augustin Godinet, Basel) added to the *Amours* series works by Rémy Belleau and Nicolas Mallot and liminary sonnets by Saint-Gelais, Baïf, and Estienne Jodelle, turning it into something close to an anthology of the latest poetry from Paris.[35]

In the end, the linguistic ambitions behind *Les Amours* may have projected cultural significance, but the musical appendix seems to have had little direct generative effect. It was dropped from the sonnet cycle in the first edition of *Les Œuvres de P. de Ronsard* (1560).[36] Intriguingly, Ronsard's failed attempts to instigate a spate of sonnet singing in France turned him back toward the *chanson*, the very genre maligned by Du Bellay in the *Deffence*. The reasons may have been practical: After the death of Saint-Gelais, the appointment as court poet came to Ronsard, and the task fell to him to write occasional verse for songs and to organize royal events such as those that took place during the fetes at Fontainebleau in 1564 and the royal tour of France in 1564 and 1565. His youthful bookish projects came undone under the pressures of performance, odes and sonnets gave way to *chansons,* and finally Ronsard enjoyed some musical success: polyphonic settings exist for thirty-six of his forty-two strophic *chansons,* and a number of them even appeared in monophonic chansonniers such as that of Jean Chardavoine, which anthologized the most popular tunes of the day.[37] His poetry had finally achieved the rich (and often nameless) currency of Marot's "Jouyssance vous donneray" and Saint-Gelais's "Laissez la verde couleur."

LES AMOURS DE P. DE RONSARD MISES EN MUSIQUE

Ronsard's sonnet cycle did finally make it into music, but in a fashion far less organic than the appropriations just described, and it had to await the time right around 1570 when composers and printers found some cultural expediency in music books. This correlates with the overall patterns of reception for Ronsard's verse: around 1570 his sonnets reached their greatest popularity and his *chansons* became a staple in cheap prints of anonymous poetry published in Paris and Lyon.[38] Four editions of Ronsard's complete works were printed in Paris between 1567 and 1578 alone. On the surface, then, two trajectories converged in the 1570s, when Ronsard's poetry finally appealed to an expanded public and composers and music printers began producing books of chansons organized around the works of individuals.

The idea that a polyphonic chansonnier might be an object of authority for composers opened up a new publishing space, one accepting of Ronsard's extremely self-conscious authorship. It also underscored the relative permanence of the printed book by comparison with the ephemerality of performance. Indeed, the durability of books and the heaviness of the printing process are thematized in the prefatory poem to *Les Amours,* in which Ronsard asks the Muses to accept his book into their temple and engrave his sentiments there "plus dur qu'en fer, qu'en cuyvre et qu'en metal" (harder than in iron, in copper, and in metal).[39] The explicit reference to iron type, copperplate engraving, and the steely tools of book production thus stand for the solidity of the words on the page even as the physical endurance of the printed word is superseded by the poetic immortality following from the canonization of Ronsard's oeuvre in Parnassus. Elaborating this duality even further is the portrait of Ronsard engraved by Jean Cousin or Nicolas Denisot reproduced in figure 11, and the French epigram that in the 1584 complete works edition replaced the Greek inscription from the original printing:[40]

> Tel fut Ronsard, autheur de cest ouvrage,
> Tel fut son oeil, sa bouche et son visage,
> Pourtraict au vif de deux crayons divers:
> Icy le Corps, et l'Esprit en ses vers.[41]
>
> [Such was Ronsard, author of this work, such was his eye, his mouth, and his face: living portrait from two different palettes: here his body, and his spirit in his verse.]

We have not quite achieved the total identification of author with his written corpus that Montaigne would seal with the line "Je suis moy-mesmes la matiere de mon livre" (I am myself the matter of my book) in his *Essais* of 1580, but the sentiment expressed in the inscription is not far off.[42] By 1560, literary authors had a keen sense of the book as self-defining. Authors' portraits became more commonplace, prefaces from authors directly "au lecteur" were replacing or supplementing dedications, and the coy acrostics and other hidden signatures often employed by writers in the fifteenth century were all but extinct.[43]

Nothing analogous can be spotted in printed polyphonic chansonniers before 1570, but after that time, self-consciously authored chanson prints become a veritable overnight phenomenon. The first large-scale publication of this sort was the *Musique de Guillaume Costeley, organiste ordinaire et vallet de chambre, du treschrestien et tresinvincible roy de France, Charles IX* (Paris: Le Roy & Ballard, 1570).[44] It was printed in oblong quarto on large sheets of paper that Le Roy & Ballard had previously only used for sacred music and was an unprecedented sixty-eight folios long, a fair-sized book on its own, even in parts, and over four times as long as prints in that printer's *livre de chansons* series.[45] In addition to its one hundred chansons for four, five, and six voices (some of which were translations of psalms) and three motets (including a "Domine salvum fac regem"—the so-called coronation motet), the *Musique* was rounded out with dedicatory sonnets to the king and the count and countess of Retz, a foreword and son-

Figure 12. Costeley at the age of thirty-nine. From the beautifully printed and grandly titled *Musique de Guillaume Costeley, organiste ordinaire et vallet de chambre, du treschrestien et tresinvincible roy de France, Charles IX* (Paris: Le Roy & Ballard, 1570), contratenor partook, fol. 1v. Bibliothèque Sainte-Geneviève, Rés. Vm 60.

net from Costeley to his friends, two panegyric sonnets from Jean-Antoine de Baïf, one from Rémy Belleau, and two different engravings of the composer (one of which is reproduced as figure 12). All in all, it was a monumental publication, the rival of the *Livre de meslanges* of 1560, the huge historical anthology of chansons in five to eight voices printed by Le Roy & Ballard and introduced by Ronsard's famous preface on music.

For Costeley's chansons to be presented with such elaborate trimmings was extraordinary for any time and place, and unparalleled for a single-composer edition of chansons. And here we might note that Costeley was the first of the composers we have considered to establish a career in print with chansons. However popular may have been the chansons of Sermisy, Janequin, and Arcadelt, all are more arrestingly represented in print by their Masses and motets, which were issued in beautiful folio editions such as the *Missae tres Jacobo Arcadet* (1557) and *Missae tres Claudio de Sermisi* (1558) or Janequin's large quarto *Sacrae cantiones seu motectae quatuor vocum* (1533—now lost). Costeley was of a younger generation of musicians who might be employed at cathedrals or chapels, but who—no matter what their day-to-day obligations—concentrated in their careers in print on vernacular song. Pierre Clereau and Nicolas de La Grotte (organist to Henry III) had similar publication records, though in material form there is no comparison between prints of their chansons and the new style of chansonnier from the 1570s.

Costeley's *Musique* figures the author in a new way for Parisian chansonniers, one indebted to the Pléiade, yet unlike Ronsard's *Les Amours*, which was initially issued in octavo, Costeley's book of music was in a substantial quarto format measuring 172 × 228 mm, with the spacious margins contemporaries took as a sign of prestige.[46] The pages of paratextual material heightened Costeley's authority even further—taken together, the larger paper, engravings, dedications, panegyrics, and the prominence of Costeley's name, his royal title as "organiste ordinaire et vallet de chambre . . . du roy," and the king's name on the title page locate the chansons at court, giving body to Costeley, and giving the book itself an importance that rivals that of the music it contains. The modern reader can almost feel the hand of the composer on each page of this edition that contains over eight hundred accidentals, a huge number, and one that could only have resulted from Costeley's direct involvement with the publication. (The 1579 edition, by contrast, omits most of them; by that time Costeley had married advantageously and moved to Evreux, and his appointment required his presence at court only from January to March.)[47] We can hear his voice with unusual clarity as well, in his dedication where he offers his music as relief to the king from the "storms" besetting the country and in the extensive neo-Platonic preface, in which he reveals his fears that the single manuscript copy of his works might be stolen by "quelque trop-follement curieux" for the thief's own profit. He details the origin of his mircotonal experiments and the ideals they represent, talks about tunings and the problems with keyboards and lutes, and explains the many accidentals in the print. Compared to the mute presentation of the music in earlier chansonniers, Costeley has invested himself dramatically in his book, revealing his thoughts in print and putting down on paper a description of his musical habits.

Costeley's book is fashioned as an object of endurance with a sense of its potential destiny as more than a set of performing parts, and in this respect, it was a sign of its times. In the following year, 1571, Lassus would secure his extraordinary privilege from Charles IX, and just a few years later, Charles would order Le Roy to print the *Prophetiae Sibyllarum* of Lassus, "so that it would not be lost."[48] Similarly, Guillaume Boni reported that in 1565, Charles IX had asked for music that he heard in Toulouse to be copied in order to preserve it; and Boni, too, received a special author's privilege from King Henry III in 1576.[49] Given the value of preservation articulated in Costeley's preface, we might see the print as part of an extensive bibliographic project that appears to have encompassed the whole series of large chansonniers produced by the Royal Printers in those years—the *Livre de meslanges, contenant six vingtz chansons, des plus rares, et plus industrieuses qui se trouvent, soit des autheurs antiques, soit des plus memorables de nostre temps* (1560), its reedition as the *Mellange de chansons tant des vieux autheurs que des modernes* (1572), Costeley's *Musique*, and the *Mellange d'Orlande de Lassus contenant plusieurs chansons, tant en vers latins qu'en ryme francoyse* (1570). That the king's printers strove to create a canon of chansons is nowhere more evident than in the retrospective 1572 *Mellange de chansons*, which drew its repertory from across the breadth of sixteenth-century chanson production. Ronsard's preface to that edition constructed a genealogy of chanson composers beginning with Josquin and his "disciples" (Mouton, Willaert, Richafort, Janequin, Maillard, Claudin, Moulu, Jaquet, Certon, and Arcadelt, in that order) and culminating in Lassus, who—according to Ronsard—transformed the music of his predecessors, making honey from all the most beautiful ancient flowers.[50] The language of progress, retrospection, and increasingly self-conscious historicizing employed by Ronsard reveals the dimension of state building evident in the Pléiade's emulation of the classics, and shows how music contributed to the definition of French court society as it came into print.

Costeley's *Musique* appears to be a fine example of a composer emulating Ronsard's style of authorship, but here it is crucial to recall that Costeley did not compose the songs as a set. Indeed, in his preface, he says that he had composed "Seigneur Dieu ta pitié" some twelve years before, and the organization of the print gives no indication that it was conceived a priori as a book destined for the press. This fact is a rather crucial point, since it tells us much about Costeley's intentions as an author and about the nature of his book, whether it presents and preserves a miscellaneous oeuvre written across a career, or whether it was imagined from the outset— like Ronsard's *Amours*—as an object destined for print. To understand the full ramifications of this distinction in musical terms requires delving briefly into modal organization.

Looking back through the chanson anthologies printed by Pierre Attaingnant, Tielman Susato, and their successors, one finds that the songs are ordinarily arranged according to musical characteristics of the eight church modes.[51] In the broadest outlines, pieces in D came at the beginnings of collections and those in G at the ends, roughly following the order of the modes given by medieval theorists, who posited four pairs of modes with finals on D, E, F, and G, respectively. Medieval sources number the modes 1 through 8; each pair included two different ranges, the authentic range an octave above the final (modes 1, 3, 5, and 7) and the plagal range in an octave encompassing the final (modes 2, 4, 6, and 8). Sixteenth-century musicians would have known the modes from the eight psalm tones still very much in use and from Magnificat settings, in which polyphony alternated with plainchant in one of the eight modes. But the modes did not necessarily apply to polyphonic music, which usually had a range much larger than an octave and often had finals of A and C, both theoretically disallowed in medieval theory. These significant inconsistencies meant that modes could not operate in the manner that keys did in the common practice period, and it was entirely possible for someone to sit down to write a piece of music with a final of D and a tenor part in the range d–d' without necessarily thinking of it being in "mode 1" or "Dorian" or any mode at all. In fact, the disjunctions between modal theory and polyphonic practice precipitated numerous attempts to recast the system of modes in the sixteenth century, such that by 1575 several systems existed at once (the traditional eight church modes, an eight-mode system with Greek names, Heinrich Glarean's twelve-mode system with Greek names, Gioseffo Zarlino's revised twelve-mode system beginning on C, and so forth).

Whereas composers could and did write music without recourse to modal theory, editors found modes highly useful, for they offered a system by which to organize the contents of music books. The conceptual categories "mode 1," "mode 2," and so forth became an editorial rule of thumb for sorting the twenty or thirty pieces to be included in a print. Mode was a rough form of alphabetization, but it was only partially abstract, for each modal group cohered through musical commonalities such as final pitch, the presence or absence of a flat in the signature, and overall range.[52]

As Harold S. Powers demonstrated in his landmark article from 1981, "Tonal Types and Modal Categories in Renaissance Polyphony," pieces with significantly different tonal configurations ("tonal types") might all be assigned to the same modal category by editors seeking to rationalize pieces in a variety of tonal types according to the rudimentary theories originally designed to make sense of a repertoire of plainchant.[53] This editorial practice is clear already in the first prints of Attaingnant and Susato from the 1530s and 1540s, where pieces in D, E, F, and G are placed together and editors found logical spots to squeeze in pieces in C and A.[54]

Attaingnant and Susato called no attention to the modal ordering of their prints, but it was a defining feature of the commercial musical press circa 1540. We should see modal order as a habit of the printshop, and modes as a kind of in-house filing system for music editors. Functioning like unannounced chapters, modal pigeonholes helped sort small pieces into larger groupings, but some slots were regularly overstuffed and others empty. Chanson composers strongly favored pieces in G and F in flat systems, whereas pieces in E and C were very unusual and pieces in D and A fall somewhere in between. In Arcadelt's output of 126 chansons, for example, 76 are in G or F with a flat in the signature. Such imbalances created modally uneven anthologies that show up the irregularities of the repertoire and doubtless also the preferences of composers, singers, and instrumentalists.

Like these earlier chansonniers, Costeley's *Musique* is loosely organized according to the eight church modes, and it too shows the overwhelming preponderance of pieces in G and F with flat signatures typical of the repertoire as a whole. It has very much the look of an anthology compiled by editors, and there is no strong reason to ascribe the order of pieces to Costeley himself, let alone to suggest that he entertained any precompositional plans to make a book of his scattered music. Further exacerbating its incoherence as a bibliographic object is the fact that it is a miscellany: the proverbs of Solomon, *chansons spirituelles,* and a noel stand cheek by jowl with the filthy patter song "Grosse garce noire & tendre," classic expressions of *fin amour* such as "Pourquoy amour n'a il plus de flambeau," and a series of pieces best described as "fight songs" that may have been used for the musical instruction of Charles IX, whom Costeley likely taught from the age of ten.[55] Other chansons are more securely linked to events in the young sovereign's life, such as the six-section *Prise du Havre* on the recovery of Le Havre from the English following their acquisition of it at the Treaty of Hampton Court in September 1562. This song, like Janequin's *La Guerre,* plays out the progress of a battle with a noisy central section setting the text "fiffres sifflez, cornetz enflez, sonnez clerons, tonez canons, entrons soldatz les murs sont bas, la tour est esbranlée, prenons ces loupz, tuon les tous, tuon les tous, ilz sont à nous, leur gloyre est escoulée" (whistle fifes, puff cornets, sound clarions, fire cannons, soldiers go in, the walls are down, the tower is burned, take these wolves, kill them all, kill them all, they are ours, their glory is past).[56] Of a similar ilk is the four-section *Prise du Calais* celebrating the retaking of the port city from the English in 1564. These occasional chansons addressed to the "jeune Roy debonnaire" illustrate the organic evolution of the print over the course of a decade as Costeley added pieces to his portfolio. Thus, the *Musique* was pulled together like any other anthology that gathered up of a flurry of chansons written over an expanse of time for untold performances and only later made them into a book. In this respect, it is thoroughly a product of the lyric culture in which Costeley, La Grotte, and Clereau all worked, one appreciative of Pléiade verse, but unmindful of the holistic nature of the books and poems from which composers tore stanzas for musical setting. With the *Musique*, chansonniers graduated to a grander scale and received the seal of royal authority, but the book still originated in the ferment of the *musique de la chambre*, which required songs for the education and pleasure of the young king, for entertainment at affairs of state, and for simple amusement.

Of a completely different nature are the musical sonnet cycles that began to be published in Paris shortly thereafter, all in the larger format used for Costeley's *Musique* and most with dedications or panegyrics (see table 4).[57]

In title, the prints by Philippe de Monte, Guillaume Boni, Anthoine de Bertrand, and Jean de Maletty all suggest themselves more or less as musical renditions of Ronsard's *Les Amours*, but in reality, they vary quite significantly in the degree to which they concentrate on Ronsard's verse.[58] Here it is relevant to remember that *Les Amours* was a fairly coherent cycle of sonnets describing Ronsard's love for his mistress, Cassandra. Despite some significant chronological inconsistencies and the deliberately fragmentary form of all sonnet cycles, a loose sequence of events can be read into the progression of Ronsard's poems, and this narrative explains the grouping of sonnets and the subjects they treat: the first sight of the beloved, her beauty, jealousy, the pain of separation, and recollection.[59] In short, the poems articulate the phases of love and desire in an archetypal and ultimately unhappy courtly love affair. Written as a book, Ronsard's cycle allows the sonnets to accumulate meaning when read contiguously, though they could also easily be appreciated as individual works.[60] Indeed, Petrarch may have been so idolized during the first age of print precisely because his sonnets were so suited to replication both as coherent books and as scattered rhyme. The standardized nature of the Petrarchan sonnet made it perfect for high-volume production, repackaging expressions of unrequited love in fourteen lines, using favorite oxymorons and regular formulas that satisfied readers who craved novelty but in familiar forms.

TABLE 4. Chansonniers Based on the Sonnets of Pierre de Ronsard

---

1575 *Sonetz de P. de Ronsard, mis en Musique a 5. 6. et 7. parties par M. Phil. de Monte*
Paris: Le Roy & Ballard
(in quarto oblong, 165 x 215, 20 fol., ded. from Jacques Anthoine de la Chapelle to the duc d'Alençon)

1575 *Sonetz de P. de Ronsard, mis en Musique a 5. 6. et 7. parties par M. Phil. de Monte*
Louvain: Pierre Phalèse, and Antwerp: Jean Bellère
(in quarto oblong, 165 x 215, 20 fol., ded. from Jacques Antoine de La Chapelle to the duc d'Alençon)

1576 *Sonets de P. de Ronsard Mis en Musique à quatre parties, par Guillaume Boni, reveus et corrigés par Henry Chandor*
Paris: Nicolas Du Chemin
(in quarto oblong, 172 x 230, 20 fol., ded. from Boni to Henry III)

1576 *Les Amours de P. de Ronsard, mises en musique a quatre parties par Anthoine de Bertrand*
Paris: Le Roy & Ballard
(in quarto oblong, 171 x 230, 30 fol., 10 liminary sonnets, royal coat of arms, preface "au lecteur debonaire," reprinted 1578, 1587)

1576 *Sonetz de P. de Ronsard mis en musique a. IIII. parties par G. Boni, Premier livre*
Paris: Le Roy & Ballard
(in quarto oblong, 171 x 230, 24 fol., two liminary sonnets and Latin verse by Jean Dorat, royal coat of arms, reprinted 1577, 1579, 1584, 1593, 1597, 1608, 1624)

1576 *Sonetz de P. de Ronsard mis en musique a. IIII. parties par G. Boni, Second livre*
Paris: Le Roy & Ballard
(in quarto oblong, 171 x 230, 24 fol., Latin verse by Jean Dorat, one liminary sonnet, reprinted 1579, 1584, 1594, 1607)

1576 *Chansons, odes, et sonetz de Pierre Ronsard, mises en musique a quatre, a cinq et huit parties par Jean de Castro*
Louvain: Pierre Phalèse, and Antwerp: Jean Bellère
(in quarto oblong, 150 x 198, 22 fol., ded. to François Le Fort)

1578 *Second livre des Amours de P. de Ronsard. mis en musique à IIII. parties par Anthoine de Bertrand*
Paris: Le Roy & Ballard
(in quarto oblong, 168 x 210, 24 fol., 5 liminary sonnets, two further poems by Bertrand, reprinted 1587)

1578 *Les Amours de P. de Ronsard, mises en musique a quatre parties par Jehan de Maletty*
Paris: Le Roy & Ballard
(in quarto oblong, 178 x 228, 24 fol., one liminary sonnet)

In a boldly economic analysis of French sonnet cycles, Cécile Alduy argues that the Pléiade's proliferation of sonnets itself relied on "a remarkable economy of means" achieved through the recycling of metaphors, tropes, and forms.[61] The sonnet cycle, she maintains, "can be read as a cost-efficient system that addressed the economic anxiety of a generation of poets caught between the aspiration to impose the autonomy of their art and their social dependence on a patron."[62] To readers, sonnet cycles offered a stock of poems that could be read in any order, like those in *recueils de chansons*. For French authors, in Alduy's analysis, sonnet sequences were a principal genre by which they established the book as a "marketplace" where they could negotiate relationships with patrons.

Les Amours opens with a group of sonnets exploring two conceits that particularly appealed to chanson composers: first, the initial enchantment of love, and second, the mistress as poetic muse for the creation of the sonnet cycle itself. Composers setting *Les Amours* often chose texts from among the first sonnets of the cycle to open their chansonniers, translating Ronsard's powerful association of love's desire with the creative act directly into song in a tradition going back at least as far as Horace's odes. The opening chanson of Jean de Maletty's collection, "Amour, Amour, donne moy paix ou trève," sets sonnet 11 from *Les Amours*, a text that depicts the poet in the first throes of love. Ronsard recounts the lover's plight that drives him to lyric creation, and Maletty, by choosing this text for the opening of his chansonnier, invokes the moment of first love as inspiration for his song collection.[63] Philippe de Monte chose similarly in his *Sonetz de P. de Ronsard*. Here, too, the opening sonnet is drawn from early in one of Ronsard's cycles, the *Continuation des Amours* (1555). In the text, "Que me servent mes vers, & les sons de ma lyre" (sonnet 14), Ronsard beautifully elaborates the heartache at the source of his poetic creation—"I cry, I moan, I torture myself, I write a thousand sonnets"—and wonders "what good to me are my verse and the sounds of my lyre?"[64] Monte scores the first line for a single voice in a highly madrigalistic turn elsewhere absent from the collection, which is primarily cast in the abstract imitative polyphony characteristic of Netherlandish chansons.[65] Indeed, the "northern" style of Monte's writing may have prompted the knockoff edition printed by Phalèse and Bellère the same year.[66] Inasmuch as we can judge from the two surviving partbooks, Maletty, too, steers clear of madrigalistic effects, though with a lighter, more homophonic style typical for French chansons.

Maletty and Monte borrowed only the initial conceits of Ronsard's *Amours* to launch their collections: in what followed, Monte mixed sonnets from Ronsard with those of others with little concern for reproducing Ronsard's books in musical form, though most of the sonnets are drawn from *Les Amours*. A *Second livre* came out the same year with even fewer texts by Ronsard, leaving us to suppose that if Monte had ever set out to produce a version of *Les Amours* in music, the project unraveled before he could even fill the twenty-four folios of his first book, a grab bag of poems including Marot's "Lorsque je voy en ordre la brunette" and some anonymous verse already set by other composers ("Comme la Tourterelle," "Reviens vers moy"). All in all, little more than half of Monte's chansons are "sonetz de Ronsard."[67]

Strikingly different are the chansonniers of Guillaume Boni and Anthoine de Bertrand, who deliberately aimed to recreate the formal and narrative structures of Ronsard's sonnet cycle in their settings. In the first instance, all four prints consist entirely of Ronsard's sonnets, making them fairly titled "*Les Amours . . . set to music.*" Bertrand's first book, *Les Amours de P. de Ronsard, mises en musique a quatre parties*, offers the most compelling example of a coherently organized chansonnier. As Jeanice Brooks has demonstrated, Bertrand carefully chose his texts to create a condensed version of the lyric narrative underlying Ronsard's *Les Amours*: the chanson texts follow the order in which they appeared in *Les Amours*, beginning with six of Ronsard's first seven sonnets, retracing the development of Ronsard's affair with Cassandra step by step, and ending with two sonnets appended to *Les Amours* in 1567 that describe the sacrifice of the poet's heart to a hopeless love and his subsequent death.[68] Bertrand clearly thumbed through an edition of Ronsard's *Œuvres* from 1567, 1571, or 1572, page by page, as he chose thirty-five sonnets to set. This number of sonnets roughly corresponds to the amount of music that would fit nicely into a thirty-two-folio quarto partbook (thirty sonnets would have produced a more spacious result, with one chanson per page and a couple of folios left for the title page, preface, and liminary sonnets). Arguably, Bertrand began by taking into account the material form of the book and the amount of music that would fit on each folio if he produced settings of forty to fifty breves, choosing enough sonnets to fill the eight sheets of paper comprising each partbook.

Having established his cycle of texts, Bertrand then set about composing music for them by grouping the sonnets together in sets. He wrote music for each group in the same tonal configuration. He could have chosen to begin the book in D and work his way through the musical alphabet, to E, F, and G—this scheme would have followed the modal orders used by editors of chanson anthologies. But editors, who worked with stacks of songs from here and there, devised their books after the music was written, and modal ordering came after the fact of composition. Bertrand, by contrast, was thinking in terms of modal organization from the moment he sat down to compose. Having first compiled a "book" of chanson texts with thematically delineated "chapters," he then also decided to play with the tonal types he would use for each group. Rather than proceeding in standard "alphabetical" or "numerical" order (D, E, F, G, or what would have been considered modes 1 through 8 in the system of church modes), he devised a different order that he felt better suited the affective evolution of the poems.

An outline of the print derived from the research of Jeanice Brooks is given as table 5, in which the textual and tonal order of the pieces is shown in a short form that makes clear the interlocking cycles of poetry and music.[69] The second column shows how Bertrand condensed Ronsard's cycle by choosing sonnets from across the whole of *Les Amours* and retaining the overall order in his own musical cycle. Reading across to the third column, one quickly sees that Bertrand has set groups of contiguous sonnets in like modal categories. Readers skilled in music theory should note that the modal classifications given in column three have been determined based on each song's configuration of system, ambitus, and final following the nomenclature developed by Harold Powers.[70] These modal "assignments" reflect the modal categories as interpreted by early modern editors.[71] Such designations are far from absolute. For instance, pieces in C with high clefs and a natural signature (nos. 28–30 in Bertrand's print) were considered mode 6 transposed in France and Flanders, whereas many Italians would have understood them as transpositions of mode 7, and in the Venetian circles of Gioseffo Zarlino they would have been categorized as mode 1.[72] Despite the fallibility of such modal assignations, though, a pattern emerges in table 5 showing that groups of chansons setting fairly coherent runs of sonnets from *Les Amours* are set in the same mode.

Normally the music historian should doubt the intentions of a sixteenth-century composer when it comes to the question of "mode" and hold fast to the practice of describing a piece "in D" or a piece "in G with high clefs and a flat in the signature" in blank terms rather than making the leap to declare them pieces in mode 1 (or mode 1 transposed, as the flat would indicate in the G piece). So too, labels such as "Dorian" should be approached with caution. But here is an instance in which one can rightfully use the term "mode," for it appears that Bertrand determined the tonal configurations for each group of texts with modal affects in mind.

TABLE 5. Interlocking Textual and Tonal Cycles in Anthoine de Bertrand's *Premier livre des Amours*

Number in Bertrand, Les Amours, (1576)	Number in Ronsard Les Amours[1]	Modal Classification
1–8	1–3, 5–7, 11, 64	4
9	50	4 transposed
10–12	23–24, 34	1 transposed
13–16	39, 41, 45–46	2 transposed
17–19	92–93, 208	2 transposed, D final
20–27	104–6, 110, 124, 126–28	6
28–30	38, 131, 134	6 transposed
31	47	7
32	143	6 transposed, G final
33	213	7
34–35	220, 242	8

[1]Text as numbered in the 1567 edition of the *Oeuvres* of Ronsard.

He and many of his contemporaries believed that modal melodies produced particular responses in listeners, and musical humanists in France were enthralled with the idea of recreating music that would produce ethic effects in listeners, even if the exact nature of the Dorian, Phrygian, and other Greek modes described by Plato remained unclear.[73] Pontus de Tyard dedicated his musical treatise *Solitaire second* (1555) almost exclusively to an explication of the Greek modes; the academy of Jean-Antoine de Baïf and Joachim Thibault de Courville explicitly set out to revive ancient Greek music in order to infuse the souls of listeners with moral passions; and in addition to his continual references to the ravishing qualities of song, Ronsard specifically recalled the legendary effects of Phrygian, Dorian, and Lydian music in his preface to the 1560 *Livre de meslanges*.[74] In his own prefaces, Bertrand tackled the more experimental subject of how music written in the diatonic genera could be extended into chromatic and enharmonic forms (here he shows his devotion to the theories of Nicola Vicentino), but given that the diatonic modes were the starting place for experiments in musical rapture, it seems safe to assume that when he says even the diatonic genera can produce "de merveilleux effectz" he is speaking of the sorts of modal affects backing the conception of his own book.[75]

Pinning down the exact nature of Bertrand's affective scheme is difficult, but at the very least, one should be struck by the extraordinary number of pieces in mode 4 that open the collection. They suggest the calming effect of the Hypo-Phrygian—a remedy to violent passions and curative for inappropriate sexual desires.[76] In these sonnets of first love, Ronsard concentrates vividly on the sight of Cassandre, Love's venomous arrow, the loss of his soul, and of the very divinity of his *déesse*. To interpret the significance of any modal choice too absolutely is always a mistake, but it seems plausible that Bertrand matched Ronsard's love-struck deification of his mistress with the gentle intoxification of the *Sousphrygienne,* said to soften bad tempers and set the bellicose world of the Phrygian to rights. If nothing else, the plagal modes employed across the whole of the *Premier livre* arguably produce a dark and serious affect in performance with their low vocal ranges. By contrast, Bertrand's *Second livre* is full of lighter poems in the style Ronsard called "plus bas et populaire," ones set to music in the brighter authentic modes in a collection avoiding the Phrygian and Hypo-Phrygian altogether.[77]

Bertrand's modal scheme would not have been very evident outside the context of his book—singers might not have noticed it, and in any case, they likely would have been used to picking and choosing songs from anthologies, not singing straight through books of music. The idea of elaborating a large-scale plan to heighten the affect of a cycle of song texts is far from the hurly-burly of performing and the requests and obligations directing the output of professional composers, and it brings us close to the space of the *estude* or study, full of books of poetry and perhaps a writing desk. Bertrand's extraordinary project is of the highest interest because it shows a composer co-opting an editorial strategy of the book trade in order to add an extra level of codicological unity to his chansonnier, giving it extra heft and a more strongly determined textuality. In the late sixteenth century, modal order became a point of intersection between the world of books and the world of music making, a way to create a book-length musical structure from song-length pieces. Bertrand was not the first composer to execute such a project, but they are rare in the secular repertoire.[78] Planning a series of compositions based on the eight church modes came more naturally to composers working in sacred genres. Unsurprisingly, given his dealings with printers and involvement in the book trade, Lassus produced a few such cyclic works, most notably his Seven Penitential Psalms (written in 1560, and printed in Munich in 1584) and the *Lagrime di San Pietro* (Munich, 1595), which set a cycle of spiritual madrigals by Luigi Tansillo. Doubtless relevant in this regard is the stipulation in Lassus's printing privilege from Henry III that printers were to issue his pieces "en tel ordre qu'il adviseroit" (in such order as he should advise).[79] Such careful cyclic planning is likewise implied in other late sixteenth-century collections, such as Palestrina's settings of eight poems from Petrarch's *Vergine* cycle in modes 1 through 8, which were printed at the head of his *Madrigali a 5* of 1581, and, from France, Claude Le Jeune's famous exemplifications of Zarlino's twelve-mode system in the *Dodecacorde* (1598) and *Octonaires* (1606).[80] Even while it is arguable that the modal ordering of these cycles projected the piety encouraged at that time by both Protestant and Catholic reformers, I would add that in their afterlives as printed books, these cyclic projects nicely supported the authorial ambitions of their composers.[81] Bertrand's project in particular is entirely secular, and in it we can see most clearly a love of books and the desire to capture for his songs the order, regulation, and completeness available in bibliographic forms.

A CULTURE OF MUSIC BOOKS

Here we should recall that Bertrand was a gentleman-composer, his estates apparently affording a life of relative leisure unencumbered by the need for benefices or salaried appointment, one that would have brought with it the luxury of contemplation.[82] The liminary poems in Bertrand's prints by Jacques Salomon, Louis du Pin, Jean de Rangouse, Robert Garnier, Jacques Grévin, Gabriel de Minut, Pierre de Brach, and other poets from Toulouse imply that Bertrand frequented gatherings of the Collège de Science et Art de Rhétorique there (later known as the Académie des Jeux Floraux), a unique institution combining civic humanism with a lyric tradition that reached its most spectacular expression each year with poetic contests and the awarding of prizes in poetry.[83] Bertrand's attention to Ronsard, moreover, is consonant with Ronsard's importance in Toulouse, for Grévin and Garnier considered themselves to be Ronsard's disciples. Bertrand's *Troisiesme livre* contains a few *jeux* by Grévin and Ronsard, poetic exchanges that give us some sense of the trials of the Jeux Floraux and Bertrand's participation in the Académie and its contests. The sphere of educated amateurs in which Bertrand composed is further suggested by the musical activities of the poet-parliamentarian Rangouse (who also set the verses of Ronsard to music) and the administrator Gabriel de Minut (who wrote "un livre de la musique" according to the sixteenth-century bibliographer La Croix du Maine), two other gentlemen-composers who were evidently friends of Bertrand.[84] It is also possible that the large number

of Ronsard settings coming out of Toulouse reflects the tastes of the cardinal Georges d'Armagnac, a generous patron of artists, authors, and scholars, dedicatee of Jean Yssandon's *Traité de musique pratique* (Paris, 1582),
and an individual whom scholars have long presumed welcomed both Bertrand and Boni into his circle in Toulouse.[85]

The Ronsardian cast of literary salons in Toulouse and the musical in-
clinations of the city's jurists, clerics, and aristocrats make themselves felt
in Bertrand's poetic choices, but in other senses as well, Bertrand's *Amours
de P. de Ronsard* owed a debt to the culture of books in the city. The very
integrity of Bertrand's *Premier livre* evinces the bibliophilia of d'Armagnac,
who collected rare editions and manuscripts for himself and for the royal
library of Fontainebleau during his Italian sojourns as ambassador to Venice and Rome, where he was made cardinal in 1544. Over the years, his
familia included his lifelong friend and secretary, the humanist Guillaume Philandrier (whom Titian portrayed at the cardinal's side in a painting now in the Louvre), the royal historiographer Pierre de Paschal, the
poets Olivier de Magny and Joachim Du Bellay, and François Rabelais.
The contents of Armagnac's extensive library surely served the men of
letters in his circles, just as their dedications imply their contributions to
it; the collection was so renowned for its manuscripts that Ercole d'Este
asked to borrow a number of the cardinal's Greek codices for copying in
1560.[86] So strong was the culture of erudition in his household and so influential his politics of supporting intellectuals with prebends and canon-
ates that recent scholarship has credited him with sustaining a unique
flourishing of humanism in the Midi.[87] The partial inventory of Armagnac's holdings prepared in 1561 just after his elevation to Archbishop of
Toulouse shows that he owned copies of Tyard's *Solitaire premier* and
Ronsard's *Quatre premiers livres des Odes*, vernacular books that verify
the cardinal's taste for neo-Platonic poetics and Pléiade verse and establish
a context for books of music such as Bertrand's *Les Amours*.[88]

The bibliophilia operative in Bertrand's "bookish" books of Ronsard
settings becomes even clearer when we compare them to the prints of
Guillaume Boni, a comparison that likewise shows the contrasting compositional habits of the bibliophilic gentleman versus the professional musician. Boni was master of the choirboys at Toulouse Cathedral and was
Bertrand's almost exact contemporary. The two certainly knew each other,
for Boni wrote one of the liminary sonnets for Bertrand's *Premier livre*.
Indeed, they may even have planned a joint edition of Ronsard settings,
for between them they set twelve of the first thirteen sonnets of *Les*

Amours, with no duplications (see table 6). The first ten chansons (sonnets 1–9 and 11), moreover, are set by both composers in the same—unusual—tonal types (♮–A–c1) and (♮–E–c1); Boni then set sonnets 12 and 13 in G with a flat signature and high clefs, the same tonal type used by Bertrand for his next group of chansons setting Ronsard's texts 24, 23, and 34. The two books thus interlock in an extraordinary way reminiscent of the *Cantiones* of William Byrd and Thomas Tallis (1575), in which sets of three motets by each composer are paired according to tonality. Indeed, the interlocking settings imply that at some stage—perhaps as early as 1565, when we know King Charles IX heard some of Boni's "chansons of Ronsard" (the "nuper Ronsardicis carminibus" mentioned in the preface to Boni's 1573 print of motets)—Boni and Bertrand determined to set at least part of *Les Amours* as a coherent cycle, divvying up the sonnets between them and deciding together on some basic features.[89] Had it been completed, in literary leanings it would have resembled later competitive collaborations in which composers set series of madrigal texts with matching refrains, as in *Il trionfo di Dori* (Venice: Angelo Gardano, 1592) and the *Triumphes of Oriana* (London: Thomas East, 1601) curated by Thomas Morley. For one extraordinary Italian anthology, *L'amorosa Ero* (1588), eighteen of the country's most notable composers even agreed to devise settings of the same text in the same mode, mode 1.[90] All of these projects sought to immortalize artistic networks in collectively composed editions.

Boni and Bertrand published their Ronsard settings the same year, but independently, and whereas Bertrand's first book presents the sonnets as a unified poetic cycle matched with a significant sequence of modes, Boni's more scattered poetic choices are arranged in the typical fashion, with the tonal types representing modes 1 through 8 in simple numerical order. This standard pattern of organization would have been familiar to readers used to looking through anthologies to find pieces in good signatures for their instruments and good ranges for their voices, and in this respect, the shape of Boni's book results from the performance practices of the day. Nonetheless, it is also likely that Boni set out with a book of some sort in mind, since a number of sonnets found next to each other in Ronsard's cycle are printed side by side in Boni's collection, having been composed in the same tonal configuration. In the first book, for example, nine pairs or sets of contiguous poems from Ronsard's collection were set in like tonal types and printed together in the chansonnier, possibly for performance in little sets.[91]

TABLE 6. Sonnet Settings by Anthoine de Bertrand and Guillaume Boni from the Opening of Pierre de Ronsard's *Les Amours*

Number in Ronsard's Les Amours[1]	Incipit of Setting	Composer	Tonal Type
1	Qui voudra voir	Bertrand	♮–A–c1
2	Nature ornant la dame	Bertrand	♮–E–c1
3	Dans le serein	Bertrand	♮–A–c1
4	Je ne suis point	Boni	♮–A–c1
5	Je parangonne au soleil	Bertrand	♮–A–c1
6	Ces liens d'or	Bertrand	♮–A–c1
7	Bien qu'à grand tort	Bertrand	♮–E–c1
8	Lors que mon oeil	Boni	♮–A–c1
9	Le plus toffu	Boni	♮–A–c1
10	—	—	—
11	Amour, amour donne moy	Bertrand	♮–A–c1
12	J'espere et crain	Boni	♭–G–g2
13	Pour estre en vain	Boni	♭–G–g2
—	—	—	—
24	Tes yeux divins	Bertrand	♭–G–g2
25	Ces deux yeux bruns	Bertrand	♭–G–g2
34	Las! je me plains	Bertrand	♭–G–g2

[1]Order as in the 1552 edition, which—for numbers 1 through 39—was retained in subsequent editions. Some of the opening lines were revised. See Ronsard, *Oeuvres complètes*, ed. Céard, Ménager, and Simonin, 1:1219–33 for a critical commentary.

In its first edition, from the presses of Du Chemin, Boni dedicated the *Sonets de P. de Ronsard* to Henry III, saying:

> Je me suis enhardy (non sans grand crainte & timidité) de vous présenter tres-humblement quelques Sonets de Ronsard (& non un tas de chansons folles & lascives) que j'ay mariés et joints à ma musique, le moins mal dont je me suis peu adviser.[92]

> > [I am emboldened (not without great fear and timidity) to offer you very humbly some sonnets by Ronsard (and not a pile of silly and lascivious songs), which I have married and joined to my music as best I can.]

Boni makes a point to distinguish his sonnet settings from the "mad and lascivious songs" so often published in chansonniers, possibly just rehearsing a moral commonplace, but a distance he may even have emphasized by choosing sonnets full of classical references (as in "Je ne suis point") and severe imagery (as, for instance, in "Lors que mon oeil" and "Le plus tofu"). In musical style, too, Boni's approach is generally sober and not unlike his moralizing *Quatrains du Sieur de Pybrac* of 1582 with a style of word painting that—when it is used at all—is grounded in effective declamation, careful employment of silences, and strategic repetition of words and phrases.[93]

Given their conventionality, perhaps the most arresting aspect of these chansons is the sheer beauty of their presentation in the editions of Le Roy & Ballard, in large quarto with initials cut in the style of Jean Cousin. The luxuriousness of the printing denied the likeness of this music to the "sacks of chansons" that really did exist at the time, sacks such as those filled with the music owned by Hans Heinrich Herwart and appraised in an inventory of 1586 as "nichts werth."[94] Whereas so many partbooks ended up stacked in trunks, thrown into bags, or piled on shelves unbound where mice could chew at their pages—to quote from one of the liminary poems in Bertrand's *Second livre*—the very material form of Boni's *Sonetz* and Bertrand's *Les Amours* presupposed that they would be met with greater care than the chansonniers in the diminutive octavo format used by Le Roy & Ballard in those same years for their *Livre de chansons* series and even La Grotte's *Chansons de P. de Ronsard, Ph. Desportes, et autres, mises en Musique* (1569) and Fabrice Marin Caietain's *Airs mis en musique . . . sur les poësies de P. de Ronsard & autres* (1576).[95] Song per song, the typography in the prints of Boni and Bertrand required almost twice as much paper as that in the run-of-the-mill chansonnier from the same press. The large initials, which are ornamented with mythological figures such as Diana, nymphs, and satyrs and beasts such as griffins, monkeys, snakes, crabs, lions, and dolphins, frequently occupy three staves, and they are employed as often as possible without forcing parts to run over onto the next page (see figure 13).

Confronted with the silent beauty of their pages, the expansive margins, the graceful arabesques and illustrations in the large initials, and the many liminary poems, panegyrics, and dedicatory texts in svelte italics, the modern historian used to working with the plainer little prints of the day like those from Attaingnant or Petrucci's *Misse Josquin* cannot fail to be impressed with the sheer triumph of letterpress printing. Viewed, moreover, in light of the coherence of their contents, the books of Boni and Bertrand establish a new kind of material presence for composers of chansons, one even more pronounced than that advanced by Le Roy & Ballard's *Mellange d'Orlande de Lassus* or *Musique de Guillaume Costeley.*

Figure 13.   Anthoine de Bertrand, *Premier livre des Amours de P. de Ronsard* (Paris: Le Roy & Ballard, 1578), bassus partbook, fol. 28v. By permission of the Jean Gray Hargrove Music Library, University of California, Berkeley.

In 1530, Attaingnant was issuing chansonniers in gothic black-letter type with minimal ornament, multiple authors, and titles announcing sheer numbers: "twenty-six new songs," "thirty-two new songs," and so forth. One chansonnier was like the next and deliberately so, given a publishing strategy that encouraged buyers to collect an entire series. Attaingnant had three series going simultaneously at one point, and across his career he issued over one hundred editions in series that, like the *Sixiesme livre contenant xxvij chansons nouvelles* of 1539 (shown in figure 2), subordinated authorship to the primary values of serial marketing and quantity. As in the world of popular music in 1960s America before albums became a significant medium for marketers, artists, and listeners, every song was a "single," and the ephemerality of 45 rpm records a desideratum. Attaingnant is selling compilations in which the individual authors of the contents matter little and the material form of the book itself aims to provide maximum enjoyment through volume, not packaging. In the years that intervened between 1539 and 1576, the year in which Le Roy & Ballard published the Ronsard chansonniers of Boni and Bertrand,

Parisian printers experienced and advanced several revolutions, in book design, typography, and—as we have seen—in authorship.[96] These changes did not happen in isolation, nor strictly though production-end strategizing. Rather, shifts in graphic technology and the possibilities available to poets and musicians depended on the broader cultures of reception and consumption feeding back into them. These books issued into a discursive environment where authors' portraits, liminary verse, dedications, airy typesetting, large margins, ornamented initial letters, and oversized paper imparted meaning, enough to give a carefully produced chansonnier stand-alone cultural cachet in the materialistic world of books, whether they were sung from or not.[97]

BOOKS, *BIBLIOTHÈQUES*, AND BIBLIOGRAPHIES

One strong affirmation of the material authority conveyed by these music prints is their healthy pattern of survival. Bertrand's prints offer a good case study, since the series ultimately ran to three books. The first book from 1576 was reprinted in 1578 with two sequels, the *Second livre des Amours de P. de Ronsard* and the *Troisiesme livre de chansons*. The *Second* and *Troisiesme livre* show none of the cyclic ordering of text and tonality evident in the *Premier livre*, and whereas the *Premier livre* consisted entirely of sonnets from *Les Amours*, the *Second livre* mixed sonnets drawn from a number of Ronsard's publications along with a few of his *chansons*. In the *Troisiesme livre* all unifying poetic structures break down entirely and we are left with a mix of poems—only three of which are by Ronsard—not unlike the sequel to *Les Amours de P. de Ronsard* that Jean de Maletty brought out, a second book setting a range of texts by Ronsard, Desportes, and other unidentified poets.[98] Despite the fact that the tight organizational forms we see in Bertrand's *Premier livre* come apart by the *Troisiesme livre* (which no longer includes Ronsard's name in the title), the three books were numbered as a set and apparently marketed that way in 1578 and in a second edition in 1587. We have no idea what the print runs were for these editions, so it is impossible to know whether copies from them survive in good numbers because more were printed or because their larger format, extensive paratexts, and more beautiful typography added to their collectiblity. But based on the extant copies, I believe that one factor was the bookish size of the series, and in this case I mean not the dimensions of the format (large quarto), but the number of folios when all three books were bound together by voice type. At around seventy-six folios, each set of parts made a nice tract volume on its own, and it is striking how many copies survive in sixteenth-century bindings in exactly this form, as bound sets of Bertrand's *Premier* to *Troisiesme livre*. At this size, they just top Costeley's *Musique*, the *Mellange d'Orlande de Lassus*, and the rival *Meslanges de maistre Pierre Certon* printed by Du Chemin in 1570, which was eighty folios long.[99]

Most of the copies of the Bertrand prints that survive come down to us in sixteenth-century tract volumes, and of them, four contain the whole series of Bertrand titles and only these titles (see table 7).[100] The "bookishness" of the series and the way it encouraged collectors to have the prints bound in this way helped guarantee the survival of Bertrand's music and the material evidence of his authorship, which would have been far more fragile than, for instance, that for Boni, who lived and worked for an institution with its own archives and music library, the Cathedral of St. Etienne. In their very material form, Bertrand's books helped ensure that I can write about him today. Certainly there were other single-author chanson series that encouraged buyers to bind their sheet music into books. The chansonniers and "meslanges" or miscellanies by Lassus issued by Le Roy & Ballard in the 1570s and 1580s, also in the large format and elegant typography used for the Costeley *Musique* and the Bertrand and Boni prints, are a good example. But the Lassus chansonniers were never issued in a numbered series, only with suggestive titles—the *Mellange d'Orlande de Lassus* (1570, 1576, 1586), *Chansons nouvelles d'Orlande de Lassus* (1571, 1576, 1581) and the *Continuation du Mellange d'Orlande de Lassus* (1584, 1596, 1597)—and they were reprinted on a sort of haphazard schedule that suggests Le Roy & Ballard liked to have them in stock, but not necessarily that they were thought of as a coherent set meant to go together in a particular order. We find all of these prints by Lassus, Costeley, Boni, and Bertrand appearing together in various constellations in some of the larger tract volumes that survive from the period, such as the tenor and bassus volumes at the Bibliothèque de l'Arsenal and two complete sets at the New York Public Library, Music Reserve *MN P534 and *MN C696, the first of which is listed in table 7. The Arsenal volumes belonged to the Collège d'Harcourt in Paris (now the lycée Saint-Louis), and judging from the close range of dates, the prints they contain were probably purchased, bound, and went into the music collection of the college right around 1577.[101] Though limited chronologically to a fairly restricted period of time and containing only prints from Le Roy & Ballard, whose shop was, after all, only five streets away from the college, in the rue Jean de Beauvais, the set contains a substantial range and mix of repertoire, with motets for four to twelve voices, chansons for four

TABLE 7. Volumes in Sixteenth-Century Bindings Containing
Anthoine de Bertrand's *Les Amours de P. de Ronsard*, books 1–2.

Berkeley, Jean Gray Hargrove Music Library, M1584.B46.A6P case X
Superius partbook, bound in parchment (olim Bibl. Alfred Cortot)
   Bertrand, *Les Amours de P. de Ronsard*, 1576

Berkeley, Jean Gray Hargrove Music Library, M1584.B46.A6P case X
Bassus partbook, bound in parchment (olim Bibl. Alfred Cortot)
   Bertrand, *Premier livre des Amours de P. de Ronsard*, 1578
   Bertrand, *Second livre des Amours de P. de Ronsard*, 1578

Blois, Bibliothèque Abbé Grégoire, L164
Superius partbook, bound in parchment, ties worn away
Ex libris "F. Louys Chevrier" (sixteenth century)[1]
Ex libris "Monastery St Launoman Blesensis" (seventeenth century)
   Bertrand, *Premier livre des Amours de P. de Ronsard*, 1587
   Bertrand, *Second livre des Amours de P. de Ronsard*, 1587
   Bertrand, *Troisiesme livre de chansons*, 1587

New York, New York Public Library, Music Reserve *MN P534
SCTB partbooks, bound in white vellum stamped in gold with gold edges,
   gauffering, and peach silk ties
   Premier livre des chansons (Louvain: Phalèse, 1563)
   Second livre des chansons (Louvain: Phalèse, 1561)
   Tiers livre des chansons (Louvain: Phalèse, 1563)
   Quatriesme livre des chansons (Louvain: Phalèse, 1564)
   Cincquiesme livre des chansons (Louvain: Phalèse, 1564)
   Sixiesme livre des chansons (Louvain: Phalèse, 1563)
   Septiesme livre des chansons (Louvain: Phalèse, 1567)
   Bertrand, *Premier livre des Amours de P. de Ronsard*, 1578
   Bertrand, *Second livre des Amours de P. de Ronsard*, 1578
   Bertrand, *Troisiesme livre de chansons*, 1578
   Boni, *Sonets chrestiens mis en musique* (Lyon: [Charles Pesnot], 1579)
   Boni, *Sonets chrestiens . . . second livre* (Lyon: [Charles Pesnot], 1579)

Paris, Bibliothèque de l'Arsenal rés N.F. 55073
Tenor and bassus partbooks, bound in parchment
Ex libris "pro Collegio harcuriano"
   Lassus, *Liber primus modulorum, quinis vocibus*, 1571
   Lassus, *Secundus liber modulorum, quinis vocibus*, 1571
   Lassus, *Tertius liber modulorum quinis vocibus*, 1573
   Lassus, *Moduli quinis vocibus nunquam hactenus editi*, 1571
   Lassus, *Moduli quatuor et octo vocum*, 1572
   Lassus, *Moduli sex septem et duodecim vocum*, 1573
   Lassus, *Moduli quatuor 5. 6. 7. 8. et novem vocum*, 1577

(continued)

TABLE 7. *(continued)*

Lassus, *Novem quiritationes divi Job,* 1572
Lassus, *Chansons nouvelles a cinc parties avec deux dialogues a huict,* 1576
Boni, *Sonetz de P. de Ronsard, Premier livre,* 1576 (T), 1577 (B)
Bertrand, *Les Amours de P. de Ronsard,* 1576
Costeley, *Musique,* 1570

Paris, Bibliothèque nationale rés. Vm7 247(1), 247 (3), 248 (2)
Superius partbook, bound in parchment, ties worn away
    Bertrand, *Premier livre des Amours de P. de Ronsard,* 1578
    Bertrand, *Second livre des Amours de P. de Ronsard,* 1587
    Bertrand, *Troisiesme livre de chansons,* 1587

Paris, Bibliothèque nationale rés. Vmd 79 (olim Bibl. G. Thibault)
Superius partbook, bound in brown leather with gold stamping
Ex libris: Andreve de Pelletier
    Bertrand, *Premier livre des Amours de P. de Ronsard,* 1578
    Bertrand, *Second livre des Amours de P. de Ronsard,* 1578
    Bertrand, *Troisiesme livre de chansons,* 1578

Paris, Bibliothèque nationale rés. Vm7 247(1), 247 (2), 248
Tenor partbook, bound in parchment (no ties)
    Bertrand, *Premier livre des Amours de P. de Ronsard,* 1578
    Bertrand, *Second livre des Amours de P. de Ronsard,* 1578
    Bertrand, *Troisiesme livre de chansons,* 1578

SOURCE: All printed by Le Roy & Ballard unless otherwise indicated.
  [1]Louys Chevrier was, in the late sixteenth century, a cleric at Notre-Dame de Mamers, a priory attached to the Abbey of Saint-Laumer de Blois, to which his book subsequently went. See Gabriel Fleury, "Le Prieuré et l'église de Notre-Dame de Mamers," *Revue historique et archéologique du Maine* 38 (1895): 142–74, at 156–57.

to six voices, and a couple of dialogues *à 8*. At approximately 336 folios per volume, just this single set of tract volumes could have constituted a substantial portion of the music library for the college. The volumes, moreover, were evidently used a considerable amount. Not only are the pages well thumbed (and by no means is this always the case with volumes of sixteenth-century music), the bassus partbook includes a number of solfège exercises added by hand on blank staves here and there.

In the Harcourt volumes, Bertrand's first book, in the first edition from 1576, is stuck on its own between Boni's *Premier livre* and Costeley's *Musique* in a group of "other" chansonniers at the end of books dominated by the motets of Lassus.[102] If, as seems likely, the college purchased and had the prints bound in 1577, books 2 and 3 of Bertrand's series would not yet have come out, and one wonders whether by that time Boni's second book, which is also missing, was out of print, since the Harcourt parts for Boni's *Premier livre* are a mongrel set of editions from 1576 and 1577. Altogether more coherent are the large tract volumes now in the New York Public Library, beautifully bound in white vellum with gold goffered edges and clearly part of a larger music library if the matching bindings on Music Reserve *MN P534 and *MN C696 and the sixteenth-century shelf marks on the spines are any indication (6.21.A, 6.21.B, and so forth, which probably located the books by bookcase, shelf, and partbook, "ABCD" standing for SCTB). Here the Bertrand series is present in full, bound with other chansonniers, including spiritualized versions of Boni's *Sonetz*.

The New York volumes and those from Harcourt are substantial preservation-minded "library" books, objects destined for the bibliophile's shelf or a college music room. They show no outward concern for authorship, since they anthologize Bertrand's single-composer prints in larger books. By now, my point should already be clear, that the other tract volumes listed in table 7 present Bertrand's works more coherently. In them, authorship aligns directly with the codicological unit of the book. Yet even here, we see how strongly the chanson resisted the practices of naming that in other sorts of books had become a determining factor of identity, cataloging, and bibliography. The superius partbook with the shelf mark Vm7 247 says simply "superius" on its vellum cover. So, too, the bassus partbook in Berkeley has no inscriptions on what is left of the cover. The most beautiful binder's volume on the list, F-Pn réserve Vmd 79, includes the name of the owner on the covers, "Andreve de . . . Pelletier," but no mention of Bertrand. Only the tenor partbook F-Pn réserve Vm7 247 says "Bertrand" on the cover and the spine (which says "Boni" as well).

While the evidence of the bindings is noteworthy, I do not think that their lack of names denies the significance of the Ronsard chansonniers as markers of a shift in the authorial status of chanson composers. Such a shift is apparent in the prints themselves. The bindings express a different set of pressures, those of the music collections in which the books found homes and the styles of bindings preferred by individual bibliophiles. The seventeenth-century definition of authorship advanced by Furetière's *Dictionnaire universel*—"those who have had a book or books printed"—is certainly on its way.[103] Indeed, the fundamental presumption that books make authors seems already to have been operable for the first generation of great bibliographers working in France, namely, François de La Croix du Maine and Antoine Du Verdier.[104]

As announced in its lengthy title, the *Bibliotheque* of François de la Croix du Maine (Paris, 1584) compiled over three thousand entries of books in the French language, both printed and manuscript, some over five hundred years old.[105] The bibliography was designed to aid the king in stocking his library, and whereas subsequent bibliographers often excluded music from their catalogs—Gabriel Naudé is one proximate example—La Croix du Maine had taken the music-loving Anton Francesco Doni's *Libraria* (Venice, 1550) as a model, seeking to achieve for French vernacular literature what Doni initiated for Italian.[106] Doni had cataloged music in a separate section at the end of his book, where he included a number of anthologies, but La Croix du Maine organized his bibliography according to author and alphabetized composers and their books right alongside authors of verbal texts. Egalitarian on the one hand, the *Bibliotheque* nonetheless ends up discriminating against music, for La Croix du Maine's attention to authorship led him to exclude anthologies and hence to neglect mention of many chanson composers; since the bibliography covered only vernacular works, prints of sacred music such as Masses and motets were excluded as well, which meant that the Latin-texted genres in which composers generally preferred to establish their careers in print had no place in the *Bibliotheque*. The same was true for the extensive bibliography of Antoine Du Verdier that came out the following year.[107] Claudin de Sermisy and Pierre Certon—among the most prominent composers in royal service—receive no mention, and this is not a matter of historical distance, since Du Verdier, who had obviously seen one of the Machaut manuscripts ("un livre de ses amours . . . escrit en main sur parchemin"), includes an entry for him.[108] Machaut's obsession with preserving his oeuvre guaranteed his place in author-centric histories already in the sixteenth century. By contrast, also missing from the bibliographies of Du Verdier and La Croix du Maine is Jacques Arcadelt, whose chansons dominated the catalog of Le Roy & Ballard in the 1560s and whose name was used in titles of their anthologies. Lassus fares a little better: Du Verdier includes a long entry for him with the opening stanzas of a panegyric by Estienne Jodelle, but La Croix du Maine leaves him out entirely, despite the fact that Le Roy & Ballard printed far more chansons by Lassus than by any French composer during the decade before Du Verdier and La Croix du Maine published their bibliographies, and in splendid single-author editions.

The composers who do appear in both bibliographies are Anthoine de Bertrand, Guillaume Boni, Guillaume Costeley, Nicolas de La Grotte, Clément Janequin, Didier Lupi, and Jean de Maletty. The entry for Boni from La Croix du Maine is a fairly typical example, with most of the information taken directly from the title page of the music print:

GABRIEL BONI OU DE BONI, natif de Sainct Flour en Auvergne, maistre des enfans de choeur de S. Estienne de Tolose,&c.

    Il a mis en musique les Sonnets de Ronsard, imprimez à Paris l'an 1576. auquel temps il florissoit, & estoit estimé tresexcellent en sa profession de Musique.[109]

> [He set the Sonnets of Ronsard to music, which were printed in Paris in 1576, at which time he flourished, and was esteemed to be most excellent in his profession of music.]

This list of composers fairly much speaks for itself—Janequin's prominence was strongly established by the many prints and reprints of his chansons in single-composer editions beginning as early as 1528; Costeley's *Musique* obviously secured a reputation for him in print; Lupi set a collection of *Chansons spirituelles* on texts by Guillaume Guéroult; and all the rest—Bertrand, Boni, La Grotte, and Maletty—composed books of Ronsard settings. In the vernacular, there seems no question that books made composers authors more assuredly than did individual works, which could be lost in the shuffle of anthologies. Though I have not discussed La Grotte's *Chansons de P. de Ronsard, Ph. Desportes, et autres* at much length, it might have been the most popular Ronsard chansonnier of all: printed in small quarto in 1569 and 1570, it was one of the first chansonniers to name Ronsard in its title and proved to be of enduring appeal, with reprints in octavo in 1572, 1573, 1575, and 1580. These eighteen brief and simple *voix de villes* printed on just twenty folios earned La Grotte a place in both La Croix du Maine and Du Verdier, thanks to the fact that Le Roy & Ballard printed them as a set with La Grotte's name on the title page alongside the names of Ronsard and Desportes.

    The bibliographies of La Croix du Maine and Du Verdier helped establish a discourse privileging authors that musicologists still operate within today, and strikingly, their lists are not so far from today's. We have no major study of Arcadelt's chansons, for instance, of which there are 126 scattered throughout anthologies, and this despite their stylistic significance in the repertoire of the 1550s and 1560s and notwithstanding the fact that Arcadelt spent the last seventeen years of his life in France in the service of the politically influential and highly musical cardinal of Lorraine. The negative example of Arcadelt's poor fortunes should cast in even brighter relief the dramatic success of a provincial unknown like Bertrand, whose works found historical mooring in the weight of authors' names and the books to which they were attached. I do not fault Du Verdier or La Croix du Maine for missing Arcadelt, for proper names still organize scholarship today. Authorship, even in its bluntest bibliographic form—author, title, publisher, date—is the first principal organizing materials in bibliographies and catalogs. The findability of names channels the paths of research, distinguishing one group of songs from another, adding profile to histories, positioning work in a field. Now liberated from the simplistic organizational schemes of the "Author," "Title," and "Subject" card catalogs still in evidence in some research libraries, bibliography is defining new codes for locating and navigating the world of texts, ones that make smaller items like poems and chansons searchable alongside books, yet the grip of the Foucauldian author-function inherited from Romantic literary discourse is still with us, and with it the siren song of author-centric, genius-bound cults of individuality and personal style. More than just a name, "Ronsard" was the name of an author, the signature of a poet who presciently discerned that it was not the Muses, but the talents of copperplate engravers, typesetters, and hand letterpress printers who could confer laurels on his *Amours* and secure his place on Mount Parnassus. A hybridized rose was named for him in 1987.

5. Resisting the Press: Performance

It would be tidy to end here. The Petrarchan books of Ronsard settings discussed in the preceding chapter seem to trumpet the coming sovereignty of the author and a new importance for books of music. They witness French chanson composers turning to the Ronsardian book as the model for a form of lyric publication entrusted not to the voice, but to the codex. Whereas in the 1550s and 1560s singers and composers had resisted Ronsard's sonnets and instead chosen his *chansons* and strophic odes for their songs, when the sonnet did finally arrive in printed chansonniers, it was in conjunction with a new attitude toward the book as a mode of publication, almost as if through ink and paper and lead type the voice might be cast in more enduring forms. Ronsard's poetics of lyric eternity and his turn to Horace and Petrarch may have been prompted by the onset of deafness in his youth, but by the 1570s print publication had clearly gained such credibility for poets that even some composers began to conceive of their oeuvres in the form of quarto partbooks. Bertrand, whose *Amours . . . mises en musique* of 1576 is the most bookish of all of the sonnet prints, described his chansons as "mes labeurs tracez sus un papier" (my labors traced on paper), a phrase exquisitely turned toward the solitude of the writing desk, the contemplative quality of Ronsard's *Amours*, and the intellectual work of composing counterpoint, but also charged with the physical act of inscribing, of entextualizing his music.

And even so, despite Bertrand's ample investment in his own writing, in Ronsard's writerly sonnets, in collecting liminary verse from local poets, and in working up extensive neo-Platonic prefaces that showed his familiarity with the microtonal experiments of Vicentino, despite this textual self-fashioning, the elaborate presentation of these relatively straightforward musical settings shows signs of strain. It evinces the dissatisfaction of an armchair amateur longing after the bustle of workaday music making. In the preface to *Les Amours . . . mises en musique,* Bertrand praises "sense" over "mathematics" and "pleasure" over "une difficulté subtillement recherché" (a subtly refined complexity) as though highly conscious of the oppositions between notes on the page and the sometimes surprising realities of performance. He explains, oddly, how he finds it more satisfying to enjoy his songs written down on paper, since delight at hearing his works "animated by the voice" comes but seldom: "something that I would only achieve rarely in the places where I would give my difficult songs to be handled and sung."[1] Whereas Boni could enlist his charges in the choir at St. Etienne to sing his compositions, Bertrand apparently had no such luck, lacking as he did an appointment to a cathedral, chapel, or court and probably also the musical formation of a professional chorister or polyphonist. His distress (at the ineptitude of the local singers he was usually able to round up?) plays strangely against the fineness of the prints—which, after all, came from far-off Paris, not Toulouse—and it emphasizes his exclusion from the very coteries to which the books beg entry with the come-hither arabesques of their lettering and large inviting pages.

Scholars such as Elizabeth Eisenstein and those following in her wake have argued that the dissemination of texts in print bridged the intellectual divides enforced by geography, creating a "revolution in communication" and eventually giving rise to a Republic of Letters that was geographically dispersed but nonetheless coherent.[2] We have seen this sort of literary republic in formation in the projects of Anton Francesco Doni, François de La Croix du Maine, and Antoine Du Verdier, who produced some of the first bibliographies to include books of music. These early modern scholars used print as a tool to take control of the burgeoning number of books in the world, and they reinvented the *biblioteca,* *bibliothèque,* and *libraria* as a virtual library without walls, universal and comprehensive.[3] La Croix du Maine, who was born and lived in Le Mans after studies in Paris, amassed a huge library of his own as a resource for the *Premier volume de la bibliotheque du sieur de la Croix du Maine* (Paris, 1584), but clearly his ambitions extended beyond publishing a list of his own books. In 1579 he issued a flier, printed in Le Mans, asking men of letters in France and elsewhere to contribute information to his catalog, sending out his request along the distribution networks by which print reached its multiple publics and thanks to their responses adding the libraries of others to his own.[4]

In the case of music, however, print could not replace performance and the cultural geography built up through oral dissemination. The history of musical authorship—bookish, eternalizing, and inky—stands not alone, but in counterpoise to the large but fragilely documented history of sounding music. We have already explored the performative side of this evidentiary divide at various turns, most often when biography offered up a context in which to understand how, when, or why a particular work came out in print. Sometimes a negative–positive relationship characterized those insights: Carpentras wrote most of his sacred music and had it printed only after developing tinnitus; Costeley issued his *Musique* just when semi-retiring from the musical establishment at court; and some highly esteemed chapelmasters like Josquin apparently never pursued careers in print. To be sure, there are entirely positive cases as well, in which printing and music making neatly coincide. These come particularly from later in the sixteenth century: Palestrina and Lassus actively poured personal resources and energy into securing printed legacies that effectively benefit their status in music histories to this day. In the last pages of this study, though, in fairness to the broad world of music making that is sometimes badly represented in print, let us circle outward from books and composers in order to test what music history can become when one works beyond the limits imposed by the cultures (and cults) of authorship. What follows contests the history of authorship triumphant presented in the previous chapter, using the success of the *Amours* chansonniers as the foil for a counterhistory of the performances against which that success might also be measured. Rather than seeing print as reflective of music making, this approach concentrates on what musical prints cannot or do not represent. Here I follow the lead of Tim Carter, whose insightful essay on the first prints of Italian monody from around 1600 explored the complexities performers encountered when they decided to enter into print.[5] For a star soloist like Giulio Caccini, print offered the professional gain of staking his claim as an innovator of the new, flamboyant style of singing that he presents in his *Le nuove musiche* of 1602. Full of coloratura and requiring an entirely new typographic range of note values to set them to the page, Caccini's "new songs" delight the eye, appealing to connoisseurs who could afford the folio editions. But despite their notational intricacies, which promise readers (then and now) direct access to the legendary embellishments of Caccini, Jacopo Peri, Francesco Rasi, and other luminaries of the age, prefaces to these prints of "professional" music often assert that to really appreciate the style, one had to hear it performed by a singer in the know. Such remarks establish a gap between text and realization, between purchased sheet music and the performer's trade secrets. Carter's essay shows how uncertain the benefits of print appeared to the professional singer-composers who developed the new style and how their anxieties over becoming authors produced scores that hide as much as they expose of the singer's art. These tensions surrounding print recall the publications of other "secret" repertories like the *Madrigali* Luzzasco Luzzaschi wrote for the singing ladies of Ferrara, and they inspire this last, brief chapter, in which we consider an authority that has haunted this study from the start but has not been addressed directly: the performer.

It is significant that none of the composers who published whole books of Ronsard settings were ever associated with the French court. Boni and Bertrand lived in Toulouse, Philippe de Monte worked at the imperial court, and Jean de Maletty was probably living in Provence at the time he wrote his sonnet settings.[6] Their music was printed in Paris even though each of them lived no less than a six-week journey away. It may be that Ronsard's strong presence in the textual forms of *Les Amours* attracted composers who were too distant to fashion or maintain a reputation in performance; in Bertrand's case it seems to have prompted a tendency to vest meaning in inaudible features such as paratextual elements, the physical beauty of the print, and modal and poetic cycles that performers could easily have disregarded if they recognized them at all.

The prints of Bertrand and Boni have been taken as monuments of French song production in the last third of the sixteenth century. Already in 1926–27, Henry Expert edited Bertrand's three *livres* for the series *Monuments de la Musique française au Temps de la Renaissance,* and the prefaces to the *Premier* and *Second livre des Amours,* in particular, have prompted critical study.[7] Boni, too, has dominated recent investigation into secular music in late sixteenth-century France, with critical editions of his *Sonetz de P. de Ronsard* and *Quatrains du Sieur de Pybrac* coming out in 1987 and 2000, respectively.[8] An anomaly born of writing, printing, and the simple fact that music historians rely primarily on documentary evidence, these works cast such a long shadow that by comparison even secular music at the French court remains a relative mystery. Yet the fact that the origins of these prints encircle Paris at such a great distance suggests that while some aspects of authorship were only available in print, this material form of authority held less appeal for musicians in Paris, whose lives must have been filled with endless performing seasons of church services, fetes, and balls, and continual demands for concerts and occasional music. In 1575, the *musique de la chambre* of Henry III included some seventeen singers and twenty instrumentalists, mostly keyboard players, lutenists, violinists, and probably a harpist, all in salaried positions; the *chapelle de musique* (singers of sacred polyphony) comprised around thirty singers, most of whom served two quarters a year.[9] The Queen Mother, Catherine de' Medici, had her own Italian violin band numbering six to eight players, as did Queen Elisabeth d'Autriche, the widow of Charles IX. Catherine also maintained an expanding *chapelle* modeled on the king's that by the mid-1580s was nearly as large, and in 1568, Charles's seventeen-year-old brother, the future Henry III, already had eight musicians in his own *musique de la chambre* including a lutenist, a singer-violinist, a viol player, and the spinet player Nicolas de La Grotte, who seems to have been in Henry's exclusive employ. The princes of Lorraine and their cousins the Guises retained analogous bands of musicians, as did other satellite courts such as that of the Maréchal de Retz, whose wife, Catherine de Clermont, was lady-in-waiting to Catherine de' Medici and a woman of considerable erudition who knew Latin and Greek, wrote poetry, played the lute, and held a salon frequented by Guillaume Costeley and Adrian Le Roy.[10] And this is to say nothing of the singers staffing Notre Dame, the music making at churches, cloisters, and *collèges*, and the goings-on at private academies like that of Jacques Mauduit, the humanist who taught himself music "from books" (according to Marin Mersenne) and who is said to have transferred the Académie de la poésie et de la musique to his own home after Jean-Antoine de Baïf's death in 1589.[11] Musical life in aristocratic circles was rich enough that Carnival seasons peaked with weeks of music in the form of masquerades, tourneys announced with allegorical songs, banquets punctuated by instrumental concerts, and lavishly staged quasi-theatrical events hosted at a succession of noble estates. Singing sirens floated across water to greet Charles IX at Fontainebleau in 1564, a rocky Mount Parnassus staffed with nymphs and Muses made repeat appearances in fetes and ballets across the years, and Estienne Le Roy, the legendary castrato and *maistre des petitz chantres de la chambre*, played everything from Mercury to satyrs in court spectacles. In the 1572 *Paradis d'amour* staged in the Salle de Bourbon, Le Roy descended from heaven singing the verse of Ronsard, who—like the violinist Balthasar de Beaujoyeulx and so many other top musicians at court—must have had to hustle when such entertainments were requested.[12]

The sheer concentration of these institutions and activities implies that professional musicians such as Costeley were too busy performing to arrange for the printed publication of their works, something confirmed by the timing of Costeley's *Musique*, which came off the press in the months just before he moved to Evreux, where he eventually became a tax collector, *conseilleur du roi*, and president of the society of Saint Cecilia.[13] Indeed, there is hardly any correlation between the registers of musicians receiving salaries or even one-time gifts from the royal households and the composers being published by Le Roy & Ballard: in addition to Costeley's *Musique* (1570) and La Grotte's *Chansons de P. de Ronsard, Ph. Desportes, et autres, mises en Musique* (1569), the only other prints of polyphonic music coming out of court in the decades between 1569 and 1596 were the *Balet comique de la Royne ... par Baltasar de Beaujoyeulx* (1582), La Grotte's *Premier livre d'airs et chansons à 3, 4, 5, 6 parties* (Paris: Leon Cavellat, 1583), and Pierre Bonnet's *Premier livre d'airs* (1585); we could add Jacques Mauduit's *Chansonnettes mesurées de Jan-Antoine de Baïf* (1586) to this list, but Mauduit was a gentleman-composer and royal secretary, not a career musician.[14] Such inverse relationships between printed production and court life seem to have worked in the other direction as well, since after Ronsard became *aumônier du roi*, the coherence of his books of verse unraveled, and we find his poetry jumbled together in "mélanges" of occasional verse such as the *Elegies, Mascarades, et Bergerie* (1565), almost as though performance had a deconstructive effect.[15]

The relative dearth of printed polyphony directly associable with the French court presents an even more extreme possibility: that music making in the innermost circles of French society was dominated by poets, singers, and instrumentalists whose performances required only the flimsiest textual supports if anything at all. If the nature of their appointments is any indication, the most highly rewarded musicians garnered such riches from performing music, not writing it. First among them was the castrato Estienne Le Roy, Abbé de Saint Laurent and a royal almoner like Saint-Gelais, Ronsard, and Philippe Desportes, a very high position that brought with it revenues from ecclesiastical benefices; other prized musicians were named as *valets de chambre*, a step down in the hierarchy, but still a post resulting from royal favor: Guillaume Le Boulanger, sieur de Vaumesnil (lute), Mathurin Dugué (lute), and Beaujoyeulx (violin), all instrumentalists.[16] Two of the best-kept musicians at court were a husband–wife team of singer-lutenists: Girard de Beaulieu, who sang the virtuoso bass part of Glaucus in the *Balet comique* and his wife Yolande Doria, who sang the role of Thetys in the same production.[17] So renowned was Beaulieu that emperor Rudolph II sent agents to engage him following the assassination of Henry III in 1589. Superstars of their own time, we have only the shadowiest record of the lives these musicians led behind the closed doors of royal chambers, the daily performances at the *lever* and *coucher* of the king, for table blessings at meals, and so forth.[18] There is certainly no evidence that all of these highly paid musicians composed, and who knows how much they dealt with written part music at all. Indeed, even for those musicians who did stop at some point to write down a little music that later came out in print—Nicolas de La Grotte and Guillaume Costeley—we have virtually no materials from which to reconstruct their own performances as instrumentalists. According to the rambling panegyric in La Croix du Maine, La Grotte was famed as one of the most sublime organists of the century, yet only one keyboard fantasy of his survives; likewise, we know almost nothing of Costeley's work as *organiste ordinaire du roi,* the only trace of which is the garbled fragment of a fantasy in F-Pn fr. 9152.[19]

The seclusion of *musique de la chambre,* the oral-traditional nature of entertainment in the noble retreats at the heart of the court, and the privileging of performance as an object of patronage all compromised the preeminence of written polyphony, limiting the cultural significance of compositional fame and musical authorship in the most elite circles of French society.[20] And this suggests a significant conclusion for all historians of early modern texts, whether literary, theatrical, or musical, for here music nicely exemplifies the role of embodied renderings in the transmission of all sorts of genres. In the very same noble salons animated by the *musique de la chambre,* when aristocrats, princes, and their familiars engaged with books, they most often listened to them read aloud. Many courts institutionalized the post of official "reader," a scholar-secretary whose responsibilities might include reading and excerpting classics, interpreting texts on political themes, and advising their employers, in addition to providing enjoyable hours from the pages of books such as *Orlando Furioso, Gargantua,* or *Don Quixote.* Queen Elizabeth had a "reader to her majesty"; François Ier, his "lecteur ordinaire du roi"; and Louis XIV, by all indications, preferred to relish literature as something heard, whether on the stage or in the salon.[21] Indeed, so commonplace was the practice of reading epic and chivalric romances aloud that Torquato Tasso's *Gerusalemme liberata* was criticized in the 1580s for being so difficult to understand that it required silent reading.[22] The proliferation of books in print by no means silenced literary authors; rather, print supported traditional pastimes with new materials from which to sing and tell stories. Not only were literary texts inflected by the aural hooks and vocal formulations of an age in which writing was heard as soon as read, authors still published their works in person, through song, reading aloud, acting, and directing lyric contributions to everything from court ballets and dinnertime music to royal entries.

Unlike the polyphonic chansons of Boni, Bertrand, Monte, and Maletty, many of the settings of Ronsard's poetry that survive from court circles channel the improvised style of performance used for musical theater and smaller entertainments given by singers of the *musique de la chambre*. We know that Beaulieu, Doria, Vaumesnil, and Joachim Thibault de Courville all sang and played the lute or "lyre" (probably the *lirone*, a bass version of the *lira da braccio*), and that Estienne Le Roy often entertained Charles IX for whole evenings with performances of Ronsard's verse.[23] While histories tend to count Courville as a "composer" and the others as "chantres et joueurs de luth," it seems clear that in the *musique de la chambre*, composition and improvisation coincided to produce accompanied song in the style that came to be known as *air de cour*.[24]

Strophic, homophonic, easily reducible to lute songs or rendered with instruments on lower parts, airs have their roots in Ronsard's anti-Petrarchan poetics, the *chanson*, and the textual netherworld of solo singing by musicians such as Saint-Gelais, Courville, and Estienne Le Roy. The settings of Saint-Gelais's "Laissez la verde couleur" discussed in chapter 3 are, in effect, proto-airs, a homophonic type of chanson *à 4* or guitar song that some printers called *voix de ville* in titles from the 1550s and Adrian Le Roy renamed *air de cour* in 1571.[25] Most printed airs are set for three or four voices, in this way fitting (or being made to fit) into partbooks, the industry's standard form for vocal music, even though the performance practice behind these harmonized versions seems to have been accompanied solo song. One central source witnessing this scoring is Adrian Le Roy's *Livre d'airs de cour miz sur le luth* of 1571, the first print to bear the generic title *air de cour* and one of the few prints of the century to combine lute tablature with a solo vocal line in white mensural notation, a sort of fake book scoring with just the textual basics of tune and tab, but one demanding design skills that required a printer's determination to produce.

Though unassuming on the page, it is not far fetched to imagine Saint-Gelais drawing tears with "Laissez la verde couleur" as he sang of the grief-stricken goddess Venus kneeling over the body of her dying lover.[26] Across forty stanzas and the twelve to fifteen minutes it takes to declaim the entire poem, "Laissez la verde couleur" blossoms into a stunning set piece as its heartwrenching tableau and symbolic language of roses and tears saturate the senses largely thanks to the song's intoxicating circular melody. In performance, it makes an impression reminiscent of George

Frideric Handel's "Lascia ch'io pianga," justly renowned for its repeating and perfectly balanced eight-measure melody, or Dido's Lament from Henry Purcell's *Dido and Aeneas,* with its timeless ground bass. Like these more famous arias, "Laissez la verde couleur" and, indeed, many *airs de cour* made ideal vehicles for great singers precisely owing to their direct musical language and light scoring, which gave soloists latitude. Liberated from the coordination mandated by polyphonic chansons—even those cast in a polyphony as light handed as "Jouyssance vous donneray"—singers of airs could strum a chord and sing freely, savoring a word here and there, adding an ornament, rushing forward for effect, or settling into the groove of a great dance song, as they wished.

The appeal of airs makes sense when we factor the expressive range of star singer-lutenists into the analysis, and the question of poetic forms and their constraints on performance brings us back to an observeration made early in the preceding chapter, that despite the many sonnet cycles published by Pléiade poets at mid-century, composers long avoided sonnets. Performers may have too: As a genre, airs squarely exclude the sonnet, something already remarked about the poetic choices evident in La Grotte's enduringly popular *Chansons de P. de Ronsard, Ph. Desportes, et autres* and Clereau's *Odes de Ronsard ... à troys parties,* and something likewise true of the Ronsard settings in Adrian Le Roy's *Livre d'airs de cour miz sur le luth* of 1571. In the hothouse environment of the court and the salons of aristocrats such as the Guises and the Countess of Retz (to whom Adrian Le Roy dedicated the *Livre d'airs de cour*), singer-lutenists triumphed, with strophic *airs de cour* as their vehicle. Indeed, polyphonic chansons in the post-Sermisy style of Boni and Bertrand may have been passé even as they came off the press, for when Costeley helped establish an annual musical competition for the society of Saint Cecilia in Evreux in 1576, the secular genres judged by the Puy were the chanson *à 5,* the air *à 4,* and the chanson "légère-facescieuse" *à 4.* The prize for the last sort of chanson—light works *à 4*—was only awarded twice and then dropped from the competition, with airs *à 4* carrying the day. So too, in the 1594 edition of Boni's *Sonetz de P. de Ronsard ... Second livre,* Boni asked readers to excuse the continued publication of these youthful songs of his, ignorant as he had been at the time of the "learned" style of those with greater "art and experience."[27]

I like to read Boni's apology for his aging sonnet settings as a reference to the *air de cour* and the *musique mesurée* of the neo-Platonic academy begun by Jean-Antoine de Baïf and Courville in 1570, music he might not have known when composing the *Sonetz,* and two related genres firmly centered at the French court. Few courtly airs had been issued in print by 1575, and none of the rhythmically innovative "measured" airs of the Académie de la poésie et de la musique, for its statutes explicitly secured all of its poetry and music under virtual lock and key, with the musicians sworn not to borrow or copy it; members had to show a special medallion to gain entry to the concerts, could not bring guests unannounced, and were required to remain silent during songs and to stay away from the cordoned-off stage.[28] *Musique mesurée* is aptly described as *musica reservata*. But by the time of Boni's writing in 1594, airs had gained a strong presence in print through a series of affordable octavo chansonniers issued by Le Roy & Ballard: an anthology edited by Caietain (1576), Didier Le Blanc's arrangements of *Airs de plusieurs musiciens* (2 volumes, 1579), and the *Vingtquatrieme livre d'airs et chansons* (1583), which contained the first settings of Baïf's secret *chansonnettes mesurées* to come into print.

Unassuming in their material form and giving away little from their titles, these anthologies nonetheless bear the pulse of music from the inner circles of the court. Of Le Blanc's sources, we know nothing, but in the other prints we find airs by a number of musicians working for and near the Valois, namely, Caietain, Beaulieu, Courville, Le Jeune, La Grotte, Adrian Le Roy, Jean Planson, and Jacques Salmon.[29] Caietain was an Italian organist in the service of the Guises, one of the most powerful families in France; Planson was organist at the royal parish church of Saint-Germain-l'Auxerrois just across from the Louvre; Jacques Salmon sang in the *musique de la chambre* and—among other things—collaborated with Balthasar de Beaujoyeulx on the *Balet comique de la Royne*.[30] In 1578 Caietain reported in the dedication of his *Second livre d'airs* that airs, chansons, and villanelles were daily fare at the Hôtel de Guise in the Marais, and we can suppose that Beaulieu, Vaumesnil, and Courville occasionally graced those gatherings.[31] In Caietain's first book of *Airs mis en musique . . . sur les poësies de P. de Ronsard* (1576), he recounts how he frequented the "school" of Courville and Beaulieu, one the Orpheus and the other the Arion of France and both accomplished at "lyre songs" ("recits de la Lyre").[32] He also stresses the neo-Platonic origins of airs, "which the Greeks call Melopoeia" or the art of composing melodies, hinting that this is the first public release of the closed-door experiments conducted at the Académie de la poésie et de la musique, where academicians aimed to recreate the affective power of ancient Greek music with carefully designed rhythms. It is somewhat ironic that thanks to the wordy exposés of his dedications, we know more about the wannabe Caietain than about the royal musicians he so admired, but it also owes entirely to his printing enterprise that any airs of Beaulieu and Courville come down to us at all.

If printed redactions of these airs are meant to reveal the secrets of high-caliber performers in the *musique de la chambre*, the notation divulges little, since it shoehorns rhythmically sophisticated melodies into rigid mensural schemes and matches them with pro forma harmonizations *à 4*. Indeed, perhaps the most revealing air of all is the most formulaic one—the lone little sonnet setting Caietain stuck at the end of the *Airs mis en musique . . . sur les poësies de P. de Ronsard*: "He Dieu du ciel je n'eusse pas pensé" (see example 4). Subtitled "air pour chanter tous sonets," the song is a throwback to the anonymous "Modo di cantar sonetti" in Petrucci's fourth book of *Frottole* [1505] and Certon's homophonic timbre for "J'espere et crains" in the 1552 *Supplément* of *Les Amours*—all are polyphonic settings of a stock poetic form meant to serve for multiple texts (for the Certon, see example 3).[33] Caietain provides a setting in one of Ronsard's favorite patterns of alternating masculine and feminine rhymes (mffm mffm ffm ffm), thus guaranteeing its usefulness, though given that the second tercet of this particular sonnet rhymes fmf, presumably performers could make the minor adjustments required to sing virtually any sonnet in decasyllabic lines to this music, no matter what the alternation of masculine and feminine endings. For the most part, Caietain's rhythms respect the flow of each line of poetry, many of them marked by Ronsard with those predictable caesuras after the fourth syllable: "He Dieu du ciel . . . Qu'un seul depart . . . Je n'ay sur moy . . . Ains du tout mort . . . Mon pauvre cœur, . . ." and so forth, the lines read almost like a series of incipits from the table of an Attaingnant chansonnier. Finally, the melody in the superius stays within the very narrow range of a sixth around its G final, with mostly conjunct motion and numerous repeated notes (especially in the first two lines). Chromatic inflections from F♯s and B♭s, when paired with the shift out of triple time in the second half of the quatrain, provide the tune with enough interest to bear hearing again for the second quatrain and, rhythmically modified yet again, for the two tercets (printed separately with the heading "Reste du sonnet"). Patches of triplets crop up throughout the tercets, suggesting the subtlety with which Beaulieu and Courville declaimed Ronsard's poetry to the lute or *lirone*, the variety of pacing and delivery that could be wrung out of a tune as simple as this one, and the inadequacy of mensural notation to capture the more exquisite details of timing, as hard as this representation tries.

Example 4.   Fabrice Marin Caietain, "Air pour chanter tous sonets." In *Airs mis en musique . . . sur les poësies de P. de Ronsard* (Paris: Le Roy & Ballard, 1576), fol. 39. From *The Sixteenth-Century Chanson*, ed. Jane A. Bernstein, 30 vols. (New York: Garland, 1987–1995), 4: 96–99.

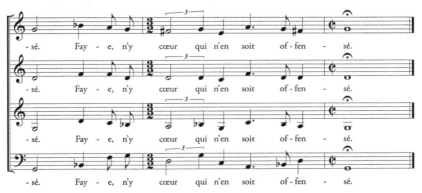

- sé. Fay - e, n'y cœur qui n'en soit of - fen - sé.

Helas! je suis à-demy trespassé,
Ains du tout mort, las! ma douce inhumaine,
Avecques elle, en s'en allant, emmaine
Mon pauvre cœur de ses beaux yeux blessé.

Reste du sonet

Que pleust à Dieu ne l'a - voir ja-mais veü - e! Son œil si beau ne

5

m'eust la flam - me es - meu - e Par qui me faut un tour-ment

Tel, que ma main m'occiroit à c'este heure,
Sans un penser que j'ay dela revoir,
Et ce penser garde que je ne meure.

The extemporized performances suggested in the rhythms of Caietain's setting emerge with even fuller force in its harmonization of the melody, where Caietain rotely transcribes the old fauxbourdon routine for improvising four parts from one. The tenor moves a sixth below the superius with octaves at the beginning and ends of lines; the bassus moves in alternating thirds and fifths below the tenor with octaves at the beginning and ends of lines; and finally, the contratenor moves in alternating thirds and fourths above the tenor, beginning and ending each line with a fifth (see table 8 for a chart of these interval patterns). The result is a series of root position chords with no errors in counterpoint, hardly something for a polyphonist to put his name to, but a good bit of filler at the end of this book of airs and a sure way to sing nicely in four parts—a genuine "modo di cantar sonetti." In sum, the more closely we read between the lines, the more completely this song slips from our grasp, receding into the murk of unwritten practices by which *improvvisatori* sang Petrarch's sonnets before they were remade into madrigals in the sixteenth century by Franco-Flemish polyphonists working south of the Alps.

Caietain's "air pour chanter tous sonets" projects no compositional ambitions whatsoever, it stakes no claims to authorship. Almost stenographic in nature, it sits right at the limits of textuality in that space that editors, arrangers, social climbers, voyeurs, and—eventually—professional writers increasingly filled with printed matter as the sixteenth century wore on. It seems to let us in on music people made but did not usually write

TABLE 8. Chart of Intervals in Fabrice Marin Caietain, "Air pour chanter tous sonets," mm. 1–18, intervals relative to the tenor

---

S

6 6 5|6 6|6 6|6 6|6|6 6 6|6|6 6 6|6 8|6 6|6 6 6|6 6 6 8|6 6 6 6|

C

3 3 3|4 4|4 4|4 4|3|4 4 4|4|4 4 4|3 4|4 4|4 4 4|3 4 4 4|4 4 4 4|

T

3 3 8|5 5|5 5|5 5|3|5 5 5|5|5 5 5|3 3|5 5|5 5 5|3 5 5 3|5 3 5 5|

B

S

6 66 6 6|6 6 6 6|8 6 66|6 6 6 6 6 6|8 ‖

C

3 43 4 3|4 4 3 4|5 3 43|4 3 4 4 3 5|5 ‖

T

3 53 5 3|5 3 8 5|8 3 53|5 3 5 3 8 3|8 ‖

B

---

down, trafficking a great tune, one Caietain may have devised himself or picked up from Vaumesnil, Courville, or Beaulieu. Caietain here appears to join the ranks of admitted transcribers of airs like Jean Chardavoine, Didier Le Blanc, and Adrian Le Roy. Unsurprisingly, most of the scholarly interest generated by Caietain's output has focused on his two revealing dedications to the duke of Guise, which have been mined many times over for what they can tell us about the early *air de cour* and those musicians who apparently did not bother to write down what they did, let alone to write about it.[34] Is this the way we should think of some other "composers" of chansons—as scribes hovering around performers? Were some chanson composers simply the rare singer or instrumentalist with a knack for "bookkeeping" and writing things down? We find the same fauxbourdon formula, for instance, written out note for note in Pierre Sandrin's setting of Mellin de Saint-Gelais's "Puisque vivre en servitude," a chanson with an already troubled attribution history that in this light seems no longer worth attributing at all.[35] So, too, Boni recalls the fauxbourdon formula almost verbatim at the opening of his *Quatrains du Sieur de Pybrac* for the gloss of the ten commandments: "Dieu tout premier, puis Pere et Mere honore," using it to lead students toward musical literacy from the catechistic world of rote memorization, singing canons at the unison, harmonizing psalm tones, and, we can suppose, singing in parts by employing these ancient formulas.

Author-centric histories run dry in the face of habits, practices, ways of doing things, and airs (a generic term that, after all, also a means a way of being, an expression). Caietain's "air pour chanter tous sonets" is but a slip of a song to pit against the textual monuments produced by Bertrand and Boni, so much so that readers may wish I had ended this book a chapter ago with the attainment of authorship so neatly manifest in those sonnet settings from Toulouse. As a "work," Caietain's air poses no challenge to, say, the intensity of Bertrand's creative process, the care with which he selected his texts, chose the modes in which he composed, and elaborated his madrigalisms. Moreover, as a text, Caietain's air is utterly unremarkable, stuck modestly at the end of some very small partbooks that are stock and unadorned save for the extra folios occupied by the dedication in each book. It is from a different world, one contiguous with writing and print culture, but not wholly of it.

Frustrated, we could revise this discussion and promote performers as authors, according to them the authority of the "scriptural" traditions in which Bertrand worked, asserting the triumph of performance, even in print, as airs outlived the popularity of other sorts of polyphonic chansons. Yet out of fairness to performers and performance—and here I speak as a professional orchestral musician, not as a writer of academic books—I want to resist this urge to replace authors with performers, since this sleight of hand presupposes that performances were understood as some sort of "work," analogous to a written composition. The Romantic work concept that still organizes much scholarship according to "life and works" narratives hardly pertained to most polyphonic music in the sixteenth century, let alone to performances. To assimilate performers to the world of writing and textuality would be to capture them in an eternal purgatory, committing them to something other than the effervescent sensual beauties of sounding music, the thrill of delighting the listeners around them (listeners now gone), and receiving the adoration of their living contemporaries. They told their musical jokes with no intention that we would still be laughing at their wit centuries later, happy to sing and play with no thought to recordings, replication, or preservation.

Notes

INTRODUCTION

1. "Memini summum quendam virum dicere, Josquinum iam vita defunctum, plures cantilenas aedere, quam dum vita superstes esset," *Selectissimarum mutetarum . . . tomus primus* (Nuremberg: Petreius, 1540), fol. 2r. On the Forster preface, see Stephanie P. Schlagel, "A Credible (Mis)Attribution to Josquin in Hans Ott's *Novum et insigne opus musicum*: Contemporary Perceptions, Modern Conceptions, and the Case of *Veni sancte Spiritus*," *Tijdschrift van de Koninklijke Vereniging voor Nederlandse Muziekgeschiedenis* 56 (2006): 97–126, at 101.

2. The prints by Ott that kicked off the trend were *Novum et insigne opus musicum* (Nuremberg, 1537) and *Secundus tomus novi operis musici* (Nuremberg, 1538).

3. On the history of Josquin's chansons in print and the ways in which his authorship was configured in vernacular repertoires, see Kate van Orden, "Josquin, Renaissance Historiography, and the Cultures of Print," in *The Oxford Handbook to the New Cultural History of Music*, ed. Jane Fair Fulcher (New York: Oxford University Press, 2011), 354–80.

4. See Stanley Boorman, *Ottaviano Petrucci: A Catalogue Raisonné* (New York: Oxford University Press, 2006), 274–76, 477–84.

5. See the definition in Antoine Furetière, *Dictionnaire universel*, 3 vols. (The Hague and Rotterdam: Arnout and Reinier Leers, 1690), 1:fol. V3r. Also see Roger Chartier, "Figures of the Author," in *The Order of Books: Readers, Authors, and Libraries in Europe between the Fourteenth and Eighteenth Centuries*, trans. Lydia G. Cochrane (Stanford, CA: Stanford University Press, 1994), 25–59.

6. Other single-composer books of music have not have survived. But see the fascinating reconstruction of two such manuscripts in Alejandro Enrique Planchart, "The Books that Guillaume Du Fay Left to the Chapel of Saint Stephen," in *Sine Musica Nulla Disciplina . . . Studi in Onore de Giulio*

Cattin, ed. Franco Bernabei and Antonio Lovato (Padua: Il poligrafo, 2006), 175–212.

7. For an analysis of what constituted a "book" of music in an age when most music was printed in parts and virtually all printed books were sold unbound, see Kate van Orden, *Materialities: Books, Readers, and the Chanson in Sixteenth-Century Europe* (forthcoming).

8. Martha Feldman, "Authors and Anonyms: Recovering the Anonymous Subject in *Cinquecento* Vernacular Objects," in *Music and the Cultures of Print*, ed. Kate van Orden with an afterword by Roger Chartier (New York: Garland, 2000), 163–99. Honey Meconi raises a similar point in her "Petrucci's Mass Prints and the Naming of Things," in *Venezia 1501: Petrucci e la stampa musicale*, ed. Giulio Cattin and Patrizia Dalla Vecchia (Venice: Fondazione Levi, 2005), 397–414, at 397–98: "because musicology has been largely composer-oriented, we tend to ignore the vast quantities of anonymous music coming from this period, focusing instead on pieces by named composers and sometimes forgetting that many attributed works have but a single ascription."

9. Feldman, "Authors and Anonyms, 168–69.

10. An excellent anthology of central texts on the cultural study of books as been compiled by David Finkelstein and Alistair McCleery, eds., *The Book History Reader* (London and New York: Routledge, 2002). The most definitive publications of the 1980s include Henri-Jean Martin and Roger Chartier, eds, *Histoire de l'édition française*, 4 vols. (Paris: Promodis, 1982–86); D. F. McKenzie, *Bibliography and the Sociology of Texts*, The Panizzi Lectures 1985 (London: British Library, 1986); and Roger Chartier, *The Cultural Uses of Print in Early Modern France*, trans. Lydia G. Cochrane (Princeton, NJ: Princeton University Press, 1987).

11. Michel Foucault, "What Is an Author?" in *Language, Counter-Memory, Practice: Selected Essays and Interviews*, ed. Donald F. Bouchard, trans. Donald F. Bouchard and Sherry Simon (Ithaca, NY: Cornell University Press, 1977), 113–38.

12. Ibid., 123.

13. For the specific references, see David Fallows, *Josquin*, Collection "Épitome Musical" (Turnhout: Brepols, 2009), 392 and 394, respectively. For a reading of Glarean that is highly sensitive to the range of music books with which he worked, see Cristle Collins Judd, *Reading Renaissance Music Theory: Hearing with the Eyes* (Cambridge: Cambridge University Press, 2000).

14. Baldassare Castiglione, *The Courtier*, trans. George Bull (London: Penguin Classics, 1976), 145.

15. Furetière, *Dictionnaire universel*, 1:fol. V3 recto, "en fait de Litterature, se dit de tous ceux qui ont mis en lumiere quelque livre. Maintenant on ne le dit que de ceux qui en ont fait imprimer." The much briefer definition in the *Vocabolario degli accademici della Crusca* (Venice: Giovanni Alberti, 1612) gives a good idea of contemporary priorities; note that there is no mention of print: "Inventore di che che si sia, o quegli dal quale alcuna cosa trae la sua prima origine, e, per lo più, si dice degli scrittori" (99).

16. Gary Tomlinson, "Musicology, Anthropology, History," in *The Cultural Study of Music: A Critical Introduction,* ed. Martin Clayton, Trevor Herbert, and Richard Middleton (New York and London: Routledge, 2003), 31–44, at 39.

17. The notion of the musical "work" did exist in some form by 1500. Many scholars have cited Johannes Tinctoris as a primary witness, who already around 1480 could list a canon of composers whose "immortal fame" rested on the written circulation of their music "throughout the whole world." Here notation and its ability to transcend the ephemerality of performance promised writing musicians far-reaching glory of a sort that seems to concur with twentieth-century, text-based definitions of compositional authority. For the passage from Tinctoris just quoted and a savvy reading of it, see Rob C. Wegman, "From Maker to Composer: Improvisation and Musical Authorship in the Low Countries, 1450–1500," *Journal of the American Musicological Society* 49 (1996): 409–79, at 461. Also see discussions of the "work" of music before 1500 in Reinhard Strohm, *The Rise of European Music, 1380–1500* (Oxford: Oxford University Press, 1993), 1–5, 412–88 ("France and the Low Countries: The Invention of the Masterwork"); Lydia Goehr, *The Imaginary Museum of Musical Works: An Essay in the Philosophy of Music* (Oxford: Oxford University Press, 1994); and Anthony Newcomb, "Notions of Notation and the Concept of the Work" (paper presented at the Sixty-Ninth Annual Meeting of the American Musicological Society, Houston, Texas, November 2003). A smart analysis of the difficulties historians have had dating the work concept, with particular relevance to the early modern period, is given in John Butt, "The Seventeenth-Century Musical 'Work,'" in *The Cambridge History of Seventeenth-Century Music,* ed. Tim Carter and John Butt (Cambridge: Cambridge University Press, 2005), 27–54. My object-based approach largely brackets the philosophical conundrums surrounding the "work" by concentrating instead on the material configuration of compositional authority.

18. See Newcomb, "Notions of Notation and the Concept of the Work."

19. "Ne fa apertissima profession et esponele cose sue partite a tutti per indurli a merviglia dell' arte sua." On Gesualdo, see Anthony Newcomb, "Carlo Gesualdo and a Musical Correspondence of 1594," *Musical Quarterly* 54 (1968): 409–36, with this quote and translation given at 413–14.

20. Musicological contributions to the history of reading are surprisingly few, despite general interest in the humanities in reading as "active," "embodied," "performative," and so forth—all aspects thrown into bright relief by musical texts. For a notable exception, see Richard Wistreich, "Music Books and Sociability," *Il Saggiatore musicale* 18 (2011): 230–44. Wistreich is especially attentive to the group readings structured by the material forms of partbooks.

21. On the forms in which music circulated and the readerships implied by them, see van Orden, *Materialities: Books, Readers, and the Chanson.*

22. See Philippe Canguilhem, "Le projet FABRICA: Oralité et écriture dans les pratiques polyphoniques du chant ecclésiastique (XVIᵉ–XXᵉ siècles),"

Journal of the Alamire Foundation 2 (2010): 272–81; and Canguilhem, "Les sources écrites du faux-bourdon au 16ᵉ siècle: un cas-limite de 'composition' à la Renaissance" (paper presented at the session "Music between *extempore* performance and *opus perfectum et absolutum*," at the Nineteenth Congress of the International Musicological Society, Rome, Italy, July 2012).

23. See Wegman, "From Maker to Composer," an exemplary study in which Wegman is careful to juxtapose writing with other highly valued polyphonic practices that did not rely on texts.

24. See Fallows, *Josquin*, 353–82, for a list of documents pertaining to Josquin.

25. The anecdote comes from Johannes Manlius, *Locorum communium collectanea* (Basel, 1562) and is cited along with a number of others by Rob C. Wegman, " 'And Josquin Laughed . . .' Josquin and the Composer's Anecdote in the Sixteenth Century," *Journal of Musicology* 17 (1999): 319–57, at 322. For a complete list of references to Josquin to 1777, see Fallows, *Josquin*, 383–409.

26. See Wegman, " 'And Josquin Laughed,' " 321.

27. Fallows, *Josquin*, 349.

28. In this respect, Rob C. Wegman's study "From Maker to Composer" has been a useful model, for in it Wegman takes care to trace the development of musical authorship in the late fifteenth century against a cultural background that includes the improvisatory practices of the age.

29. See especially Chartier, "Figures of the Author."

30. See James Haar, "Orlando di Lasso, Composer and Print Entrepreneur," in van Orden, ed., *Music and the Cultures of Print*, 125–51, with information about the privileges at 135 and 140.

31. Anton Francesco Doni, *Dialogo della musica* (Venice: Girolamo Scotto, 1544); Anton Francesco Doni, *La libraria del Doni fiorentino. Nella quale sono scritti tutti gl'autori vulgari con cento discorsi sopra quelli. Tutte le traditioni fatte dall'altre lingue, nella nostra & una tavola generalmente come si costuma fra librari* (Venice: Gabriel Giolito de Ferrari, 1550).

32. The passage from Martin Luther is cited in Elizabeth L. Eisenstein, *The Printing Press as an Agent of Change: Communications and Cultural Transformations in Early Modern Europe*, 2 vols. in 1 (Cambridge and New York: Cambridge University Press, 1979), 304. For the Rabelais see François Rabelais, *Pantagruel*, ed. V. L. Saulnier (Geneva: Droz, 1965), 44.

33. Adrian Johns, *The Nature of the Book: Print and Knowledge in the Making* (Chicago: University of Chicago Press, 1998). A synopsis of the debate can be found in an *American Historical Review* Forum organized and introduced by Anthony Grafton: "How Revolutionary Was the Print Revolution?" *American Historical Review* 107 (2002): 84–86; followed by Adrian Johns, "How to Acknowledge a Revolution," *American Historical Review* 107 (2002): 106–25; and Elizabeth L. Eisenstein, "An Unacknowledged Revolution Revisited," *American Historical Review* 107 (2002): 87–105, 126–28.

34. Johns, *The Nature of the Book*, 31. For a complete history of piracy, see Adrian Johns, *Piracy: The Intellectual Property Wars from Gutenberg to Gates* (Chicago: University of Chicago Press, 2009).

35. Johns, *The Nature of the Book*, 182.

36. Darnton's essay originally appeared in *The Kiss of Lamourette: Reflections in Cultural History*, rev. ed. (New York: Norton, 1990), 107–36.

37. Chartier, *The Order of Books*, 55.

38. Ibid., 28. Also see McKenzie, *Bibliography and the Sociology of Texts*.

39. To cite only a few book-length studies: for Handel, see Winton Dean, *Handel's Operas, 1726–1741* (Woodbridge, UK, and Rochester, NY: Boydell Press, 2006), the long-awaited sequel to Winton Dean and John Merrill Knapp, *Handel's Operas, 1704–1726* (Oxford and New York: Clarendon Press, 1987); for Verdi, see Philip Gossett, *Divas and Scholars: Performing Italian Opera* (Chicago: University of Chicago Press, 2006); and Roger Parker, *Remaking the Song: Operatic Visions and Revisions from Handel to Berio* (Berkeley and Los Angeles: University of California Press, 2006).

1. THE WORLD OF BOOKS

1. See Stanley Boorman, *Ottaviano Petrucci: Catalogue Raisonné* (New York: Oxford University Press, 2006), with an account of Petrucci's double- (or possibly triple-) impression method at 160–64 and his materials at 109–48. Petrucci's main competitor in the first decades of the sixteenth century, Andrea Antico, avoided music type entirely and printed from painstakingly cut woodblocks, which only affirms how resistant polyphony was to the technological formulas that accelerated the production of alphabetic texts.

2. On Attaingnant and the single-impression method, see Daniel Heartz, *Pierre Attaingnant, Royal Printer of Music: A Historical Study and Bibliographical Catalogue* (Berkeley and Los Angeles: University of California Press, 1969), 43–52. Single-impression printing was likely invented in England. See A. Hyatt King, "The Significance of John Rastell in Early Music Printing," *Library*, 5th series, vol. 26 (1971): 197–214.

3. This figure was compiled principally by consulting the following catalogs: Jane A. Bernstein, *Music Printing in Renaissance Venice: The Scotto Press, 1539–1572* (New York: Oxford University Press, 1998); Boorman, *Ottaviano Petrucci*; Laurent Guillo, *Les éditions musicales de la renaissance lyonnaise* (Paris: Klincksieck, 1991); Heartz, *Pierre Attaingnant*; François Lesure and Geneviève Thibault, "Bibliographie des éditions musicales publiées par Nicolas du Chemin (1549–1576)" *Annales musicologiques* 1 (1953): 269–373; Mary S. Lewis, *Antonio Gardano, Venetian Music Printer, 1538–1569: A Descriptive Bibliography and Historical Study*, 3 vols. (New York: Garland, 1988–2005), vol. 1; Samuel F. Pogue, *Jacques Moderne: Lyons Music Printer of the Sixteenth Century* (Geneva: Droz, 1969); and RISM (*Répertoire international des sources musicales*), Series B/I *Recueils imprimés du XVIᵉ siècle* (Munich: G. Henle Verlag, 1960).

4. Of Attaingnant's production of 174 editions cataloged by Heartz in *Pierre Attaingnant*, 79 are chansonniers or lute intabulations of chansons. Of the 319 editions cataloged by François Lesure and Geneviève Thibault in *Bibliographie des éditions d'Adrian Le Roy et Robert Ballard (1551–1598)* (Paris: Société Française de Musicologie, 1955), 187 are of chansons or airs, and this figure—which accounts for 58 percent of their known editions—does not include intabulations. For a synthetic analysis of editorial strategies in Paris across the century, see Audrey Boucaut-Graille, "Les éditeurs de musique parisiens et leurs publics: 1528–1598" (Ph.D. diss., Tours, Centre d'Études Supérieures de la Renaissance, 2007).

5. Of Du Chemin's ninety-six polyphonic editions cataloged by Lesure and Thibault in "Bibliographie des éditions musicales publiées par Nicolas du Chemin," forty-five are chansonniers; see Richard Freedman and Philippe Vendrix, directors, *Les livres de chansons nouvelles de Nicolas Duchemin, 1549–1568,* http://ricercar.cesr.univ-tours.fr/3-programmes/EMN/Duchemin/; and Audrey Boucaut-Graille, "L'imprimeur et son conseiller musical: les stratégies éditoriales de Nicolas du Chemin (1549–1555)," *Revue de musicologie* 91 (2005): 5–25. Of the sixty-eight editions from Susato cataloged by Ute Meissner in *Der Antwerpener Notendrucker Tylman Susato: Eine bibliographische Studie zur niederländischen Chansonpublikation in der ersten Hälfte des 16 Jahrhunderts,* 2 vols., Berliner Studien zur Musikwissenschaft 11 (Berlin: Verlag Merseburger, 1967), twenty-eight are French chansonniers, three are chansonniers in Flemish, and eight are Souterliedekens (in Flemish). On the importance of chanson anthologies to Susato's printing venture, see Kate van Orden, "Tielman Susato, Music, and the Cultures of Print," in *Tielman Susato and the Music of His Time,* ed. Keith Polk (Stuyvesant, NY: Pendragon Press, 2005), 143–63. Samuel F. Pogue has cataloged fifty-three surviving polyphonic editions from the presses of Jacques Moderne in Lyon (Pogue, *Jacques Moderne*), of which twenty-one are chansonniers.

6. See Geneviève Thibault, "De la vogue de quelques livres français à Venise," *Bibliothèque d'Humanisme et Renaissance* 2(1935): 61–65.

7. On the commercial interest in duos and trios, see Daniel Heartz, " 'Au pres de vous': Claudin's Chanson and the Commerce of Publishers' Arrangements," *Journal of the American Musicological Society* 24 (1971): 193–225.

8. See, respectively, Howard Mayer Brown, ed., *A Florentine Chansonnier from the Time of Lorenzo the Magnificent: Florence, Biblioteca Nazionale Centrale, MS Banco Rari 229,* Monuments of Renaissance Music 7, 2 vols. (Chicago: University of Chicago Press, 1983); Allan W. Atlas, *The Cappella Giulia Chansonnier (Rome, Biblioteca Apostolica Vaticana, C.G.XIII.27),* 2 vols. (Brooklyn: Institute of Mediaeval Music, 1975–76); Howard Mayer Brown, "A 'New' Chansonnier of the Early Sixteenth Century in the University Library of Uppsala: A Preliminary Report," *Musica Disciplina* 37 (1983): 171–233; Martin Picker, ed., *The Chanson Albums of Marguerite of Austria: MSS 228 and 11239 of the Bibliothèque royale de Belgique, Brussels* (Berkeley: University of California Press, 1965); and Peter Woetmann Christoffersen, *French*

Music in the Early Sixteenth Century: Studies in the Music Collection of a Copyist of Lyons; The Manuscript 'Ny kgl. Samling 1848 2° in the Royal Library, Copenhagen, 3 vols. (Denmark: Museum Tusculanum Press, University of Copenhagen, 1994).

9. On Petrucci's attribution practices, see Boorman, *Ottaviano Petrucci,* 251–53; and Honey Meconi, "Petrucci's Mass Prints and the Naming of Things," in *Venezia 1501: Petrucci e la stampa musicale,* ed. Giulio Cattin and Patrizia Dalla Vecchia (Venice: Fondazione Levi, 2005), 397–414, in which she demonstrates precisely how attentive Petrucci was to naming Masses and composers by comparison with attribution practices evident in manuscripts of the time.

10. See Heartz, *Pierre Attaingnant,* catalog nos. 2, 5–10.

11. On the problems of anonymity and composite authorship, see especially Nancy J. Vickers, "The Unauthored 1539 Volume in Which Is Printed the *Hectamophile, The Flowers of French Poetry,* and *Other Soothing Things,* in *Subject and Object in Renaissance Culture,* ed. Margreta De Grazia, Maureen Quilligan, and Peter Stallybrass (Cambridge: Cambridge University Press, 1996), 166–88, and Martha Feldman, "Authors and Anonyms: Recovering the Anonymous Subject in *Cinquecento* Vernacular Objects," in *Music and the Cultures of Print,* ed. Kate van Orden with an afterword by Roger Chartier (New York: Garland, 2000), 163–99. For one example of a printer contracting for material, see Claude Dalbanne, "Robert Granjon, imprimeur de musique," *Gutenberg Jahrbuch* 14 (1939): 226–232.

12. See Jean-Pierre Babelon, *Paris au XVIe siècle* (Paris: Hachette, 1986), 159–66.

13. For a summary of the attributions in various editions of Arcadelt's *Secondo libro a 4,* see, for instance, Bernstein, *Music Printing in Renaissance Venice,* 167–68, 223. Martha Feldman explores the culture of authorship in Venice in "Authors and Anonyms."

14. The literature on the publication history of the Arcadelt books is extensive. See especially Thomas W. Bridges, "The Publishing of Arcadelt's First Book of Madrigals," 2 vols. (Ph.D. diss., Harvard University, 1982), 1:87–89; Bernstein, *Music Printing in Renaissance Venice,* 167–70, 223; Catherine Weeks Chapman, "Andrea Antico" (Ph.D. diss., Harvard University, 1964), 352–62; Iain Fenlon and James Haar, *The Italian Madrigal in the Early Sixteenth Century: Sources and Interpretation* (Cambridge: Cambridge University Press, 1988), 245–51; Lewis, *Antonio Gardano,* 1:208–9.

15. Richard J. Agee, "The Venetian Privilege and Music-Printing in the Sixteenth Century," *Early Music History* 3 (1983): 1–42. On unidentified privileges from the decade, see ibid., 3.

16. On the Milanese edition and Gardane's reaction to it, see Bridges, "The Publishing of Arcadelt's First Book of Madrigals," 1:67–68; Fenlon and Haar, *The Italian Madrigal,* 240–41 (including the dedication); and Bernstein, *Music Printing in Renaissance Venice,* 168.

17. See Bernstein, *Music Printing in Renaissance Venice,* 365–66, 363–64, 315, and 248.

18. The print of Rore's *Di Cipriano Rore et di altri eccellentissimi musici il terzo libro di madrigali a cinque voce* (Venice: Scotto, 1548) included a dedication signed by Paolo Vergelli, a flautist from Padua. On the dedication of the Rore print (really an anthology) and the public–private dichotomies in Venice, see Martha Feldman, *City Culture and the Madrigal at Venice* (Berkeley and Los Angeles: University of California Press, 1995), 61 and chap. 7, respectively.

19. See James Haar, "Notes on the 'Dialogo della Musica' of Antonfrancesco Doni," *Music & Letters* 47 (1966): 198–224, at 208–9.

20. See the excellent analysis of the printing of Shakespeare's plays and his lack of involvement with printed publication in David Scott Kastan, *Shakespeare and the Book* (Cambridge: Cambridge University Press, 2001), esp. chap. 1. The statistic comes from pp. 20–21.

21. Roger Chartier, *Publishing Drama in Early Modern Europe*, The Panizzi Lectures 1998 (London: British Library, 1999), 52.

22. Stephen Orgel, "What Is an Editor?" *Shakespeare Studies* 24 (1996): 23–29, at 23.

23. See Roger Chartier, "Copied Onely by the Eare," in Chartier, *Publishing Drama*, chap. 2.

24. The line comes from John Marston's preface to *The Malcontent* (London: Printed by V. S. for William Aspley, 1604), fol. A2r and is analyzed in Chartier, *Publishing Drama*, 51.

25. Kastan, *Shakespeare and the Book*, 17.

26. Richard Wistreich, "Introduction, Musical Materials and Musical Spaces," in *Renaissance Studies* 26 (2012): 1–12, at 1. Wistreich's pathbreaking contributions to the history of reading are a welcome addition to a field that has lacked much input from musicologists, despite interest in recent decades in the performative quality of reading (as "active," "embodied," and so forth—aspects thrown into bright relief by musical texts). Also see Wistreich, "Music Books and Sociability," *Il Saggiatore musicale* 18 (2011): 230–44.

27. Francesco Corteccia, *Libro primo de madrigali a quattro voci* (Venice: Scotto, 1544), fol. 1v. The dedication is given and discussed in Bernstein, *Music Printing in Renaissance Venice*, 300–301, 151.

28. Bernstein, *Music Printing in Renaissance Venice*, 85, 115.

29. Jacquet Berchem, *Madrigali a cinque voci . . . libro primo* (Venice: Gardane, 1546), ii. See Haar, "Notes on the 'Dialogo della Musica' of Antonfrancesco Doni," 208n44. The dedication is reproduced in Lewis, *Antonio Gardano*, 1:509.

30. Despite assumptions that it was Gardane who printed the *Primo libro di madrigali a cinque voci*, it was probably printed in Rome by Antonio Barrè. See James Haar, "The Early Madrigals of Lassus," *Revue belge de Musicologie / Belgisch Tijdschrift voor Muziekwetenschap* 39–40 (1985–86): 17–32, at 32. For an analysis of the contents that suggests the collection was designed with Venetian tastes in mind, see Sarah M. Stoycos, "Making an Initial Impression: Lassus's First Book of Five-Part Madrigals," *Music & Letters* 86 (2005): 537–59. On Lassus's Italian prints overall, including his supervision of print-

ing of the *Libro quarto de madrigali a cinque voci* of 1567 and his presentation of the dedicated volume to the duke of Ferrara, see Bernstein, *Music Printing in Renaissance Venice*, 204–6.

31. See the impressive bibliographic and historical study of Kristine K. Forney, "Orlando di Lasso's 'Opus 1': The Making and Marketing of a Renaissance Music Book," *Revue belge de Musicologie / Belgisch Tijdschrift voor Muziekwetenschap* 39–40 (1985–86): 33–60.

32. For an overview of Lassus's career in print, see James Haar, "Orlando di Lasso, Composer and Print Entrepreneur," in van Orden, ed., *Music and the Cultures of Print*, 125–51.

33. The privileges are discussed and reproduced in Richard Freedman, "Who Owned Lasso's Chansons?" *Yearbook of the Alamire Foundation* 6 (2008): 159–76.

34. See Agee, "The Venetian Privilege and Music–Printing"; and Freedman, "Who Owned Lasso's Chansons?" 166–67.

35. Rebecca Wagner Oettinger, "Berg v. Gerlach: Printing and Lasso's Imperial Privilege of 1582," *Fontes Artis Musicae* 51(2004): 111–34.

36. Pierre de Ronsard, *Le Bocage de P. de Ronsard, Vandomoys, dedié a P. de Paschal, du bas païs de Languedoc* (Paris: Veuve Maurice de la Porte, 1554), fols. Aii^r-Aiiii^v, at Aii^v. See Freedman, "Who Owned Lasso's Chansons?" 167, with excerpt and translation on 174–76.

37. The privilege is printed in Guillaume Boni, *Sonetz de Pierre de Ronsard mis en musique a quatre parties* (Paris: Le Roy & Ballard, 1576), fol. 24v in the tenor partbook. See E. (Eugénie) Droz, "G. Boni, musicien de Ronsard," in *Mélanges offerts à M. Abel Lefranc* (Paris: Droz, 1936), 270–81, with the privilege given at 275–76. The privilege refers to the author's need to correct errors in a prior edition, most likely Boni's *Sonets de P. De Ronsard* (Paris: Nicolas Du Chemin, 1576), which had been edited by Henry Chandor.

38. See Roger Chartier, "Property and Privilege in the Republic of Letters," trans. Arthur Goldhammer, *Daedalus* 131 (2002): 60–66.

39. "Diderot's Letter on the Book Trade, Paris (1763)," in *Primary Sources on Copyright (1450–1900)*, ed. L. Bently and M. Kretschmer, www.copyright history.org, p. 16 (accessed October 19, 2012).

2. MUSIC BOOKS AND THEIR AUTHORS

1. On Antico's title page, see Iain Fenlon, *Music, Print, and Culture in Sixteenth-Century Italy*. The Panizzi Lectures 1994 (London: British Library, 1995), 29–33, and on dedicatory scenes in general see Roger Chartier, "Princely Patronage and the Economy of Dedication," in *Forms and Meanings: Texts, Performances, and Audiences from Codex to Computer* (Philadelphia: University of Pennsylvania Press, 1995), 25–42, at 29–31.

2. See André Pirro, "Leo X and Music," *Musical Quarterly* 21 (1935): 1–16.

3. See Cynthia J. Brown, "Text, Image, and Authorial Self-Consciousness in Late Medieval Paris," in *Printing the Written Word: The Social History of*

Books, circa 1450–1520, ed. Sandra L. Hindman (Ithaca, NY, and London: Cornell University Press, 1991), 103–42.

4. For a transcription of the privilege, see Claudio Sartori, *Bibliografia delle opere musicali stampate da Ottaviano Petrucci,* Biblioteca di bibliografia italiana 18 (Florence: L. S. Olschki, 1948), 22–23; the privilege is translated in Catherine Weeks Chapman, "Andrea Antico" (Ph.D. diss., Harvard University, 1964), 447–48.

5. Paper sizes were standardized in the fourteenth century. See Jane A. Bernstein, *Print Culture and Music in Sixteenth-Century Venice* (Oxford: Oxford University Press, 2001), 34–35.

6. Elizabeth Armstrong, *Before Copyright: The French Book-Privilege System, 1498–1526.* Cambridge Studies in Publishing and Printing History (Cambridge: Cambridge University Press, 1990), 11–12.

7. On the competition between the two publishers implied by the wording of Antico's privileges, see Stanley Boorman, *Ottaviano Petrucci: Catalogue Raisonné* (New York: Oxford University Press), 99–100.

8. See *Canzoni novi con alcune scelte de varij libri di canto* (Rome: Antico, 1510), the first volume in the series, and *Canzoni, sonetti, strambotti e frottole libro tertio* (Rome: Antico, 1513), the third book. Presumably a *libro secondo* was printed in the same years.

9. See Brian Richardson, *Printing, Writers, and Readers in Renaissance Italy* (Cambridge and New York: Cambridge University Press, 1999), 69–76.

10. Translation from Chapman, "Andrea Antico," 446–47, with the original given as Plate 7

11. Reproduced in Sartori, *Petrucci,* 23–24; translated in Chapman, "Andrea Antico," 452–53.

12. On the two title pages see Stanley Boorman, "Early Music Printing: An Indirect Contact with the Raphael Circle," in *Renaissance Studies in Honor of Craig Hugh Smyth,* ed. Andrew Morrogh, 2 vols. (Florence: Barbèra, 1985), 1:533–50. Also see Fenlon, *Music, Print, and Culture,* 29–33. On the title page of the *Frottole intabulate,* see Knud Jeppesen, *Die italienische Orgelmusik am Anfang des Cinquecento,* 2 vols. (Copenhagen: Hansen, 1960), 1:49–50. For a fuller exploration of the hypothesis suggested by Jeppesen—that the monkey refers to Petrucci—see Hiroyuki Minamino, "A Monkey Business: Petrucci, Antico, and the Frottola Intabulation," *Journal of the Lute Society of America* 26–27 (1993–94): 96–106.

13. See Boorman, "Early Music Printing," 1:546; and Knud Jeppesen, *La frottola,* 3 vols. (Aarhus: Universitetsforlaget i Aarhus, 1968–70) 1:51, who guessed that the figure was a stock image of Apollo.

14. Antico's papal privilege of 1513 praises the accuracy and craftsmanship evident in Antico's books of frottole—no doubt the woodcut on the title page of the 1510 *Canzoni nove* was a plus in advertising his technical skills. The privileges are reproduced in plates and translated in Chapman, "Andrea Antico," 445–46, 447–48, and 452–53.

15. See Armstrong, *Before Copyright*, 11–13. Also see Frederick John Norton, *Italian Printers, 1501–1520: An Annotated List with an Introduction,* Cambridge Bibliographical Society Monographs 3 (Cambridge: Bowes and Bowes, 1958), xxvii–xxviii. On papal privileges and music, see Boorman, *Ottaviano Petrucci,* 97–101.

16. See Armstrong, *Before Copyright*, 6–7; H. F. Brown, *The Venetian Printing Press 1469–1600* (London: J. C. Nimmo, 1891); and especially Richard J. Agee, "The Venetian Privilege and Music-Printing in the Sixteenth Century," *Early Music History* 3 (1983): 1–42.

17. Armstrong, *Before Copyright*, 118–25.

18. Ibid., 13. For a sense of relative cost, consider that Scotto advanced Antico 604 ducats and 59½ bolendini to finance the publication of the *Liber quindecim missarum.*

19. See Daniel Heartz, *Pierre Attaingnant, Royal Printer of Music: A Historical Study and Bibliographical Catalogue* (Berkeley and Los Angeles: University of California Press, 1969), 113.

20. According to Elizabeth Armstrong (*Before Copyright*, 158–59), books printed in France with only the words "Cum privilegio" or "Cum gratia et privilegio" were rarely specious in their claims. For a counterexample from Italy, see Agee, "The Venetian Privilege and Music-Printing," 18.

21. See the dedication to the *Liber lamentationum Hieremiae prophetae Carpentras,* in Carpentras, *Eliziarii Geneti (Carpentras) Opera Omnia,* ed. Albert Seay, Corpus Mensurabilis Musicae 58, 5 vols. ([N.p.]: American Institute of Musicology, 1972–73), 2:xii, xiv.

22. Antico's privileges were sought only after work was under way (surely the case for the *Liber quindecim missarum,* for which the privilege was granted only fifteen weeks before the title page was printed; likewise, the *Frottole intabulate* came off the press less than three weeks after its privilege was secured). One well-documented series of struggles to secure a papal privilege and defend a Venetian one is recounted in Anthony Newcomb, "Editions of Willaert's 'Musica Nova': New Evidence, New Speculations," *Journal of the American Musicological Society* 26 (1973): 132–45.

23. Paper costs varied, but could represent from 60 percent to 75 percent of the cost of the finished product. Prices fluctuated greatly according to supply and difficulties of transporting the paper. Venetian printers enjoyed a healthy supply from paper mills in the Veneto, but in Antwerp, for instance, Christopher Plantin had to import paper from France and Germany, since what little paper that was manufactured in the Netherlands was not of very high quality. See Leon Voet, *The Golden Compasses: A History and Evaluation of the Printing and Publishing Activities of the Officina Plantiniana at Antwerp,* 2 vols. (Amsterdam: Vangendt, 1972), 2:19; Fenlon, *Music, Print, and Culture,* 29; and Bernstein, *Print Culture and Music,* 34–35.

24. On the financial arrangements, see Chapman "Andrea Antico," 54–61; and Bernstein, *Print Culture and Music,* 75.

25. Bernstein, *Print Culture and Music,* 86–87.

26. See most recently, William Pettas, *A History & Bibliography of the Giunti (Junta) Printing Family in Spain 1514–1628* (New Castle, DE: Oak Knoll Press, 2005); and William Pettas, *A Sixteenth-Century Spanish Bookstore: The Inventory of Juan de Junta* (Philadelphia: American Philosophical Society, 1995).

27. See Mary Kay Duggan, *Italian Music Incunabula: Printers and Type* (Berkeley: University of California Press, 1992), 129–42, 201, and 207–8. Antonio Giunta's great uncle, Luc'Antonio, was responsible for editing the volumes, which were printed by Johann Emerich of Speyer. The copies in the Jean Hargrove Music Library at the University of California, Berkeley, measure 555 × 385 mm.

28. Chapman, "Andrea Antico," 69–75.

29. Samuel Pogue, *Jacques Moderne, Lyons Music Printer of the Sixteenth Century* (Geneva: Droz, 1969), 34–44.

30. Heartz, *Pierre Attaingnant*, 91.

31. See François Lesure and Geneviève Thibault, "Bibliographie des éditions musicales publiées par Nicolas du Chemin (1549–1576)," *Annales musicologiques* 1 (1953): 269–373, at 274.

32. Ibid., 274–77.

33. By my calculations, approximately thirty books of tablature were printed in Paris between Granjon's introduction of his new font in 1551 and 1558. Most were intabulations of chansons and dances already printed by Attaingnant. See Daniel Heartz, "Parisian Music Publishing under Henry II: A Propos of Four Recently Discovered Guitar Books," *Musical Quarterly* 46 (1960): 448–67; and Kate van Orden, "Robert Granjon and Music during the Golden Age of Typography," in *Music in Print and Beyond: Hildegard von Bingen to The Beatles*, a festschrift for Jane A. Bernstein, ed. Roberta M. Marvin and Craig A. Monson, Eastman Studies in Music (Rochester, NY: University of Rochester Press, 2013).

34. Richard Sherr, *Papal Music Manuscripts in the Late Fifteenth and Early Sixteenth Centuries*, Renaissance Manuscript Studies 5 (N.p.: American Institute of Musicology, 1996), 1–2.

35. On bad copies at the Vatican, see the complaint in Carpentras, *Eliziarii Geneti (Carpentras) Opera Omnia*, 2:xii, xiv.

36. See Lesure and Thibault, "Bibliographie des éditions musicales publiées par Nicolas du Chemin," catalog nos. 26, 34, 35, 47–58, 60–63, and 88–91; Masses printed in sets include catalog nos. 33 and 36.

37. *Missarum musicalium certa vocum, varietate, secundum varios quos referunt modulos distinctarum, liber primus, ex diversis ijsdemque peritissimis auctoribus collectus* (Paris: Nicolas Du Chemin, 1568); and *Missarum musicalium certa vocum, varietate, secundum varios quos referunt modulos & cantiones distinctarum, liber secundus, ex diversis iisdemque peritissimis auctoribus collectus* (Paris: Nicolas Du Chemin, 1568). See Lesure and Thibault, "Bibliographie des éditions musicales publiées par Nicolas du Chemin," catalog nos. 92 and 93.

38. There might be a case to be made for motets having been the preferred genre of status for composers at the French court under François Ier. See John T. Brobeck, "Musical Patronage in the Royal Chapel of France under Francis I (r. 1515–1547)," *Journal of the American Musicological Society* 48 (1995): 187–239. This taste at court may arguably be reflected in the unusual set of large-format, single-composer motet prints by Claudin de Sermisy, Pierre Certon, and Johannes Lupi that Attaingnant issued in 1542. See Heartz, *Pierre Attaingnant*, 317–19.

39. For a collection of references to Josquin up to 1777, see David Fallows, *Josquin*, Collection "Épitome Musical" (Turnhout: Brepols, 2009), 383–409.

40. Bonnie J. Blackburn has identified two important likely sources of Petrucci's music. One was Petrus Castellanus, Petrucci's editor, *maestro di cappella* at SS Giovanni e Paolo in Venice, and a collector of music. See Bonnie J. Blackburn, "Petrucci's Venetian Editor: Petrus Castellanus and His Musical Garden," *Musica Disciplina* 49 (1995): 15–45. The other source was Girolamo Donato, the Venetian ambassador of Lorenzo de' Medici, a music lover and dedicatee of the *Odhecaton*. Donato likely heard Josquin's music and quite possibly met the composer. See Bonnie J. Blackburn, "A Lost Isaac Manuscript," in *Musica Franca: Essays in Honor of Frank A. D'Accone*, ed. Irene Alm, Alyson McLamore, and Colleen Reardon, Festschrift Series 18 (Stuyvesant, NY: Pendragon Press, 1996), 19–44. Also see Boorman, *Ottaviano Petrucci*, chap. 9.

41. See Boorman, *Ottaviano Petrucci*, 150–51.

42. Ibid., 479.

43. See the entries in Boorman, *Ottaviano Petrucci*, catalog nos. 4, 22, 30, 54, 59, and 62. Of the sixty-two parts that survive (in full or incomplete sets of partbooks), only three include Josquin's name on the covers of the binding, all listed under Cat. No. 62: D-B, Mus.ant.pract.D227, S, T, B have "MI JOSQUIN" on the back board; A-Wn, S.A.77.C.19, once belonging to Raymond Fugger, bears his binding, with "MISSE IOSQUIN" on the superius only; and GB-CW, an altus volume containing Masses of Josquin, Mouton, La Rue, Agricola, and Févin, was inscribed "Missae Josquin quattuor vocibus," despite its inclusion of other composers' works.

44. Boorman, *Ottaviano Petrucci*, 274–78.

45. Ibid., 276.

46. Ibid., 275.

47. Ibid.

48. See Brian Richardson, *Printing, Writers, and Readers in Renaissance Italy*, 80–99.

49. Jane A. Bernstein, *Music Printing in Renaissance Venice: The Scotto Press, 1539–1572* (New York: Oxford University Press, 1998), 83.

50. For a history of this tendency, see Andrew Kirkman, "The Invention of the Cyclic Mass," *Journal of the American Musicological Society* 54 (2001): 1–47.

51. A notable exception is presented by the two manuscripts of his compositions owned by Guillaume Dufay. See Alejandro Enrique Planchart, "The

Books that Guillaume Du Fay Left to the Chapel of Saint Stephen," in *Sine Musica Nulla Disciplina ... Studi in Onore de Giulio Cattin*, ed. Franco Bernabei and Antonio Lovato (Padua: Il poligrafo, 2006), 175–212.

52. For a complete description of the manuscript, see Herbert Kellman, "The Origins of the Chigi Codex: The Date, Provenance, and Original Ownership of Rome, Biblioteca Vaticana, Chigiana, C. VIII. 234," *Journal of the American Musicologocial Society* 11 (1958): 6–19. For the facsimile see Herbert Kellman, ed., *Vatican City, Biblioteca apostolica vaticana, MS Chigi C VIII 234*, Renaissance Music in Facsimile 22 (New York: Garland, 1987).

53. The principal manuscripts are Dijon, Bibliothèque Municipale, 517; Copenhagen, Kongelige Bibliotek, Thott 291, 8°; Washington, DC, Library of Congress, M2.1 L25 Case (the Laborde Chansonnier); and Wolfenbüttel, Herzog August Bibliothek, Guelf. 287 Extravagantium. See Jane Alden, *Songs, Scribes, and Society: The History and Reception of the Loire Valley Chansonniers* (New York: Oxford University Press, 2010). Of the 273 chansons contained in this complex of five related manuscripts copied in the Loire Valley in the 1460s and 1470s, the authors of 148 still have not been identified, despite the best efforts of scholars.

54. On Florence Biblioteca Nazionale Centrale, Banco Rari 229, see Howard Mayer Brown, ed., *A Florentine Chansonnier from the Time of Lorenzo the Magnificent: Florence, Biblioteca Nazionale Centrale, MS Banco Rari 229*, Monuments of Renaissance Music 7, 2 vols. (Chicago: University of Chicago Press, 1983); and on Berlin, Staatliche Museen Preussischer Kulturbesitz, Kupferstichkabinett 78.C. 28, see Sean Gallagher, "The Berlin Chansonnier and French Song in Florence, 1450–1490: A New Dating and Its Implications," *Journal of Musicology* 24 (2007): 339–64.

55. See Sylvia Huot, *From Song to Book: The Poetics of Writing in Old French Lyric and Lyrical Narrative Poetry* (Ithaca, NY: Cornell University Press, 1987); and Ardis Butterfield, *Poetry and Music in Medieval France: From Jean Renart to Guillaume de Machaut* (Cambridge: Cambridge University Press, 2002). On authorship and the book in the Middle Ages, see Alastair J. Minnis, *Medieval Theory of Authorship: Scholastic Literary Attitudes in the Later Middle Ages* (London: Scolar Press, 1984); and Ardis Butterfield, "Articulating the Author: Gower and the French Vernacular Codex," *Yearbook of English Studies* 33 (2003): 80–96. An important foil to the examples of Machaut and de la Halle are two recent musicological studies that establish the primacy of scribes as "authors" of manuscripts: see Alden, *Songs, Scribes, and Society;* and Emma Dillon, *Medieval Music-Making and the* Roman de Fauvel (Cambridge and New York: Cambridge University Press, 2002).

56. "Ma tres-souveraine dame, je vous eusse porté mon livre pour vous esbattre, où toutes les choses sont que je fis onques: mais il est en plus de .xx. pieces; car je l'ay fait faire pour aucun de mes seigneurs; si que je le fais noter, et pour ce il convient que il soit par pieces. Et quant il sera notés, je le vous porteray ou envoieray, s'il plaist à Dieu." For the evidence of Machaut's involvement in the manuscript publication of his works and a chronology of the

sources see Sarah Jane Williams, "An Author's Role in Fourteenth-Century Book Production: Guillaume de Machaut's 'livre où je met toutes mes choses," *Romania* 90 (1969): 433–54, this quote from the *Voir Dit* at 442. Also see Lawrence Earp, "Machaut's Role in the Production of Manuscripts of His Works," *Journal of the American Musicological Society* 42 (1989): 461–503.

57. On "Toute Belle" (Péronne d'Armentières) and lyrics attributed to her in the *dit*, see Sarah Jane Williams, "The Lady, the Lyrics, and the Letters," *Early Music* 5 (1977): 462–68.

58. Cited and translated in Earp, "Machaut's Role," 472.

59. The principal manuscripts whose production could be said in some sense to have been supervised by Machaut are MS "C" : F-Pn f. fr. 1586 (ca. 1350–56); MS "Vg": GB-Cccc (illustrated ca. 1371–75); and MS "A": F-Pn f. fr. 1584 (ca. 1372–77). MS "F-G": F-Pn f. fr. 22545–46 (illustrated ca. 1390, but possibly begun in Machaut's lifetime) also appears to have been copied from Machaut's exemplar. The other Machaut manuscripts under discussion here are MS "B": F-Pn f. fr. 1585; and MS "E": F-Pn f. fr. 9221. See Earp, "Machaut's Role."

60. The Mass and some other works do not appear in the relatively early manuscript "C."

61. Thus, they are not autograph manuscripts, but this is not so surprising, for Lawrence Earp has estimated that a manuscript of the size of "A" would have taken one and a half to two years to manufacture ("Machaut's Role," 488n46); in the next century there is evidence that Christine de Pisan was the scribe of her own manuscripts, and some scholars believe that Lassus copied out the manuscript of the Sibylline Prophesies now in Vienna, but the preparation of manuscripts was generally a separate profession. On Pisan, see Earp, "Machaut's Role," 480.

62. See Robert K. Root, "Publication before Printing," *Proceedings of the Modern Language Association* 28 (1913): 417–31; Armando Petrucci, *Writers and Readers in Medieval Italy: Studies in the History of Written Culture,* ed. and trans. Charles M. Radding (New Haven, CT, and London: Yale University Press, 1995), 145–68; Lucien Febvre and Henri-Jean Martin, *The Coming of the Book: The Impact of Printing, 1450–1800,* trans. David Gerard, 2nd ed. (London and New York: Verso, 1997); Richardson, *Printing, Writers, and Readers in Renaissance Italy,* 49–53; and Pascale Bourgain, "L'édition des manuscrits," in *Histoire de l'édition française,* ed. Henri-Jean Martin and Roger Chartier, 4 vols. (Paris: Promodis, 1982–86), 1:49–75.

63. Root, "Publication before Printing," 418–19.

64. See Earp, "Machaut's Role," 476–79; and Margaret Bent, "The Machaut Manuscripts *Vg, B,* and *E,*" *Musica Disciplina* 37 (1983): 53–82.

65. Jean Destrez, *La "Pecia" dans les manuscrits universitaires du XIIIe et du XIVe siècle* (Paris: Éditions Jacques Vautrain, 1935). On the use of fascicles by music scribes, see Charles Hamm, "Manuscript Structure in the Dufay Era," *Acta Musicologica* 34 (1962): 166–84; and Alden, *Songs, Scribes, and Society,* chap. 4.

66. Earp, "Machaut's Role," 477.

67. Ibid.

68. Root, "Publication before Printing," 420–21.

69. Reprinted and translated in Carpentras, *Eliziarii Geneti (Carpentras) Opera Omnia*, 2:xi, xiii. "The book of the Lamentations of the Prophet Jeremiah by Carpentras, recently enriched by him, and more accurately revised, because they not so long ago came into the hands of many and a part of them had been, perchance, copied without the author's consent; (and even the final touches not yet made)."

70. Earp, "Machaut's Role," 467–68.

71. On the dating of the manuscript, see Mark Everist, "The Polyphonic *Rondeau c.* 1300, Repertory and Context," *Early Music History* 15 (1996): 59–96, at 59–60.

72. See Armando Petrucci, "Minute, Autograph, Author's Book," in *Writers and Readers*, 145–168.

73. For a detailed examination of this shift in career patterns, see Christopher Reynolds, "Musical Careers, Ecclesiastical Benefices, and the Example of Johannes Brunet," *Journal of the American Musicological Society* 37 (1984): 49–97.

74. Nino Pirrotta, "Music and Cultural Tendencies in 15th-Century Italy," *Journal of the American Musicological Society* 19 (1966): 127–61.

75. We do know, though, that Dufay bequeathed two books of his own music to Cambrai Cathedral; the rest of his music collection he gave to the duke of Burgandy. See Planchart, "The Books that Guillaume Du Fay Left to the Chapel of Saint Stephen."

76. On presentation manuscripts produced by the Alamire workshop, see Herbert Kellman, ed. *The Treasury of Petrus Alamire: Music and Art in Flemish Court Manuscripts, 1500–1535* (Ghent and Amsterdam: Ludion, 1999).

77. Henry is said to have composed two Masses as well, though they do not survive. See David Fallows, "Henry VIII as a Composer," in *Sundry Sorts of Music Books: Essays on the British Library Collections Presented to O.W. Neighbour on His 70th Birthday*, ed. C. Banks, A. Searle and M. Turner (London: British Library, 1993), 27–39.

78. James P. Carley, ed., *The Libraries of King Henry VIII*, Corpus of British Medieval Library Catalogues 7 (London: British Library and British Academy, 2000).

79. Erasmus, for instance, seems to have given Henry VIII volumes of his works in at least two specially dedicated copies, one manuscript and the other print. See Cecil H. Clough, "A Presentation Volume for Henry VIII: The Charlecote Park Copy of Erasmus's *Institutio principis Christiani*," *Journal of the Warburg and Courtauld Institutes* 44 (1981): 199–202.

80. Cited in Pirro, "Leo X and Music," 8. On salaries, see Reynolds, "Musical Careers," 88–90.

81. Pirro, "Leo X and Music," 8–9.

82. For this and the story of Josquin writing a motet to remind Louis XII of a benefice that he had promised to the composer, see Fallows, *Josquin*, 87–93, who assesses their validity.

83. See Martha Farahat, "Villanescas of the Virtuosi: Lasso and the *Commedia dell'arte*," *Performance Practice Review* 3 (1990): 121–37.

84. Huot, *From Song to Book*.

85. Examples of music prints in this size abound—I am thinking here of the chanson series issued by Phalèse and Le Roy & Ballard in the 1550s and Antico's Mass and motet series from 1521. On canards, see Jean-Pierre Seguin, *L'information en France avant le périodique: 517 canards imprimés entre 1529 et 1631* (Paris: G-P Maisonneuve et Larose, 1964).

86. See Carpentras, *Eliziarii Geneti (Carpentras) Opera Omnia*, 2:xi–xv.

87. The other examples are four Alamire manuscripts containing the Masses of La Rue from the second decade of the century that were likely political gifts from the court of the Netherlands or luxury transmissions of repertoire, and a book of Masses by Heinrich Isaac owned by the court in Munich.

88. Carpentras, *Eliziarii Geneti (Carpentras) Opera Omnia*, 1:xi–xiv.

89. Although they are anthologies, two folio choirbooks deserve mention here as luxury prints that evince many of the ambitions seen in Antico's *Liber quindecim missarum*: the *Liber selectarum cantionum* (Augsburg: Grimm and Wirsung, 1520); and the *Viginti missarum musicalium* (Paris: Attaingnant, 1532). See Martin Picker, *"Liber selectarum cantionum* (Augsburg: Grimm und Wyrsung, 1520): A Neglected Monument of Renaissance Music and Music Printing," in *Gestalt und Entstehung musikalischer Quellen im 15. und 16. Jahrhundert*, ed. Martin Staehelin (Wiesbaden: Harrassowitz, 1998), 149–67; and Heartz, *Pierre Attaingnant*, 78–86, who investigates the significance of Attaingnant's title woodcut of the court at Mass, the dedication of the print, and the way it positioned Attaingnant to receive the title of Royal Printer of Music in 1537.

90. "Opere di musica, cioè messe, mottetj, madrigali, basse, contraponti, lamentation, et qualunque delle composition sue." See Agee, "The Venetian Privilege and Music-Printing," 28. The "basse" may refer to the cantus firmus La Spagna and the counterpoints Festa apparently wrote on it. See Iain Fenlon and James Haar, *The Italian Madrigal in the Early Sixteenth Century: Sources and Interpretation* (Cambridge: Cambridge University Press, 1988), 74n17.

91. See Mitchell P. Brauner, "The Parvus Manuscripts: A Study of Vatican Polyphony, ca. 1535 to 1580" (Ph.D. diss., Brandeis University, 1982).

92. Agee, "The Venetian Privilege and Music-Printing," 27–28.

93. These sorts of shifts that take place in manuscript and printed book production at nearly the same time suggest that for this period, study of both bibliographic forms is essential. See David McKitterick, *Print, Manuscript, and the Search for Order, 1450–1830* (Cambridge: Cambridge University Press, 2003).

94. The table's restriction to books in folio is slightly artificial and intended as a way to exclude partbooks. It also excludes tablatures, which witness parallel developments and certainly merit study; technically, it also excludes fifteenth-century sources in smaller formats, but in fact, there are no surviving single-composer manuscripts between those of Machaut and the La Rue Masses listed in table 1, so the overview is a fair account of the history of this particular sort of "authored" musical codex.

95. Rome C.S. 36 and likely C.S. 34 went to Leo X; Vienna N.B. 15496 went to Charles, Archduke of Austria; and Montserrat 773 perhaps to Margaret of Austria. Kellman, ed., *The Treasury of Petrus Alamire*.

96. Giovanni Pierluigi da Palestrina, *Missarum liber primus: Roma 1554*, ed. Giancarlo Rostirolla (Palestrina: Fondazione Giovanni Pierluigi da Palestrina, 1975). On the circumstances surrounding the publication of the volume, see the introduction to this facsimile edition.

97. For a synopsis of the events and an analysis of how Palestrina financed his publishing career, see Jane A. Bernstein, "Publish or Perish? Palestrina and Print Culture in 16th-Century Italy," *Early Music* 35 (2007): 225–35.

98. The historical self-consciousness that modern scholars have attributed to composers of cyclic Mass Ordinary settings was by no means as complete around 1500 as is often claimed. See Kirkman, "The Invention of the Cyclic Mass."

99. See Suzanne G. Cusick, *Valerio Dorico: Music Printer in Sixteenth-Century Rome* (Ann Arbor, MI: UMI Research Press, 1981), esp. 67–72 and plate 18.

100. See the descriptions in Pogue, *Jacques Moderne*, 41–44, 191–94, and 201–3.

101. Cusick, *Valerio Dorico*, 72.

102. For the estimate of the relative cost to Palestrina of the edition, see Bernstein, "Publish or Perish?" 226. Her calculations are based on the contract for a similar publication drawn up between Morales and Dorico, on which see Cusick, *Valerio Dorico*, 95–101. As an additional note, according to the contracts between Dorico and the bookseller-publishers Antonio Salamanca and Giovanni della Gatta, Morales was to have taken out privileges for Naples, Venice, and the Papal States. See Richardson, *Printing, Writers, and Readers in Renaissance Italy*, 61–62.

103. For the contract and its implications, see Cusick, *Valerio Dorico*, 95–101.

104. Bernstein, "Publish or Perish?"

105. See Jane A. Bernstein, "Made to Order: Choirbook Publications in Cinquecento Rome," in Uno gentile et subtile ingenio: *Studies in Renaissance Music in Honour of Bonnie J. Blackburn*, ed. Jennifer Bloxam, Gioia Fiolcamo, and Leofranc Holford-Strevens. Collection "Épitome Musical" (Turnhout: Brepols, 2009), 669–76, at 675. She goes on to add that "nearly all of Philippe de Monte's thirty-four madrigal books were printed in Venice, but of his forty Masses that survive in manuscript, only nine of them were published."

106. For a catalog of prints made during the composer's lifetime, see Horst Leuchtmann and Bernhold Schmid, *Orlando di Lasso: seine Werke in zeitgenössischen Drucken, 1555–1687* (Kassel and New York: Bärenreiter, 2001).

107. See Horst Leuchtmann, vol. 1: *Orlando di Lasso: sein Leben,* and vol. 2: *Briefe* (Wiesbaden: Breitkopf und Härtel, 1976–1977), 1:163–66.

108. For a list of the entire series, which ran to twelve titles (some of them too short to be included in table 2), see *Grove's Dictionary of Music and Musicians,* ed. J. A. Fuller Maitland, 5 vols. (New York and London: Macmillan, 1904), 1:307. I am deeply grateful to David Crook for helping me clarify the publishing history of the series.

109. Leuchtmann, *Orlando di Lasso,* 1:164.

110. On Guerrero's career in print, I paraphrase Robert Stevenson, "Francisco Guerrero (1528–1599): Seville's Sixteenth Century-Cynosure," *Inter-American Music Review* 13 (1992): 21–98, at 60–71.

111. For two instances of Tomás Luis de Victoria having gifts of his partbooks refused, see Bernstein, *Music Printing in Renaissance Venice,* 142, 150.

112. A. Ducrot, "Histoire de la Cappella Giulia au XVIᵉ siècle depuis sa fondation par Jules II (1513) jusqu'à sa restauration par Grégoire XIII (1578)," *Mélanges d'archéologie et d'histoire* 75 (1963): 179–240, 467–559, at 514–15.

113. See the newly discovered letters in Valerio Morucci, "Cardinal's Patronage and the Era of Tridentine Reforms: Giulio Feltro della Rovere as Sponsor of Sacred Music," *Journal of Musicology* 29 (2012): 262–91.

114. See Robert Lindell and Brian Mann, "Monte, Philippe de," in Grove Music Online, www.oxfordmusiconline.com (accessed April 21, 2011).

115. See Jean-Auguste Stellfeld, *Bibliographie des éditions musicales plantiniennes,* Académie royale de Belgique, Classe des beaux-arts, Mémoires, ser. 2, vol. 5, fasc. 3 (Brussels: Palais des Académies, 1949), 74–77.

116. The situation is recounted in ibid., 12–15. For a fuller sense of the scope of Plantin's publishing projects and the relatively small amount of music coming off his presses, see Voet, *The Golden Compasses.*

117. Stellfeld, *Bibliographie des éditions musicales plantiniennes,* 14–15.

118. Ibid., 94–100.

3. AUTHORS OF LYRIC

1. Letter printed in facsimile and transcribed in François Lesure and Geneviève Thibault, *Bibliographie des éditions d'Adrian Le Roy et Robert Ballard (1551–1598)* (Paris: Société Française de Musicologie, 1955), 36–37.

2. See Richard Freedman, "From Munich to Paris: Orlando di Lasso, Adrian Le Roy, and Listeners at the Royal Court of France," in *Die Münchner Hofkapelle des 16. Jahrhunderts im europäischen Kontext,* ed. Theodor Göllner, Bernhold Schmid, and Severin Putz (Munich: Bayerische Akademie der Wissenschaften, 2006), 143–59; and on the privilege, see Richard Freedman, "Who Owned Lasso's Chansons?" *Yearbook of the Alamire Foundation* 6 (2008): 159–76.

3. See Jessie Ann Owens, ed., *Vienna Österreichisches Nationalbibliothek, Musiksammlung, Mus. Hs. 18.744,* Renaissance Music in Facsimile 25 (New York and London: Garland, 1986).

4. Peter Bergquist, "The Poems of Orlando di Lasso's 'Prophetiae Sibyllarum' and Their Sources," *Journal of the American Musicological Society* 32 (1979): 516–38, at 516–20.

5. The literature on *musica reservata* is extensive; on the *Prophetiae Sibyllarum* in this context, see Freedman, "From Munich to Paris"; for the Quickelberg quote, see Wolfgang Boetticher, *Orlando di Lasso und seine Zeit, 1532–1594: Repertoire-Untersuchungen zur Musik der Spätrenaissance,* Quellenkataloge zur Musikgeschichte 27, 2 vols. (Kassel: Bärenreiter, 1958; repr. Wilhelmshaven: Florian Noetzel, Heinrichshofen, 1999), 1:250.

6. See Ignace Bossuyt, "The Copyist Jan Pollet and the Theft in 1563 of Orlandus Lassus' 'Secret' Penitential Psalms," in *From Ciconia to Sweelinck: Donum natalicium Willem Elders,* ed. Albert Clement and Eric Jas (Amsterdam: Rodopi, 1994), 261–67.

7. See, respectively, Martha Feldman, *City Culture and the Madrigal at Venice* (Berkeley and Los Angeles: University of California Press, 1995), chap. 7; Anthony Newcomb, *The Madrigal at Ferrara, 1579–1597,* 2 vols. (Princeton, NJ: Princeton University Press, 1980), 1:7–67; and Isabelle His, *Claude Le Jeune (v. 1530–1600): un compositeur entre Renaissance et Baroque* (Arles: Actes Sud, 2000), chap. 4.

8. In addition to the example of Guerrero traveling to Rome to check proofs of the *Missarum liber secundus,* the correspondence between Monte and Plantin concerning the *Liber I missarum* shows that proofs were being sent back and forth. See Jean-Auguste Stellfeld, *Bibliographie des éditions musicales plantiniennes,* Académie royale de Belgique, Classe des beaux-arts, Mémoires, series 2, vol. 5, fasc. 3 (Brussels: Palais des Académies, 1949), 96–98. Printing contracts often stipulate that the composer will see proofs.

9. See Kristine K. Forney, "Orlando di Lasso's 'Opus 1': The Making and Marketing of a Renaissance Music Book," *Revue belge de Musicologie / Belgisch Tijdschrift voor Muziekwetenschap,* 39–40 (1985–86): 33–60. Also see Donna G. Cardamone and David L. Jackson, "Multiple Formes and Vertical Setting in Susato's First Edition of Lassus's 'Opus 1,'" *Music Library Association Notes,* 2nd Ser., 46 (1989): 7–24.

10. On Moderne's editions of Morales see Samuel F. Pogue, *Jacques Moderne: Lyons Music Printer of the Sixteenth Century* (Geneva: Droz, 1969), 41–44, 191–94, and 201–3; on Jambe de Fer, see Frank Dobbins, *Music in Renaissance Lyons* (Oxford: Clarendon Press, 1992), 197–98; on Corteccia, see the dedication to the *Libro primo de madrigali a quattro voci* (Venice: Scotto, 1544) in Jane A. Bernstein, *Music Printing in Renaissance Venice: The Scotto Press, 1539–1572* (New York: Oxford University Press, 1998), 301.

11. See the dedications reproduced in Lesure and Thibault, *Bibliographie des éditions d'Adrian Le Roy et Robert Ballard,* 27–50, particularly the evocative dedications by Fabrice Marin Caietain (p. 36) and Jean Yssandon (p. 43).

12. For Lassus's exchange with the emperor, in which he complains about the bad editions of his music, see Horst Leuchtmann, "Ein neugefundener Lasso-Brief," in *Festschrift Rudolf Elvers zum 60. Geburtstag*, ed. Ernst Hert-trich and Hans Schneider (Tutzing: Hans Schneider, 1985), 349–57; and Henri Vanhulst, "Lasso et ses éditeurs: remarques à propos de deux lettres peu con-nues," *Revue belge de Musicologie / Belgisch Tijdschrift voor Muziekweten-schap* 39–40 (1985–86): 80–100; and for the privilege, see Hansjörg Pohlmann, *Die Frühgeschichte des musikalischen Urheberrechts (ca. 1400–1800)* (Kassel: Bärenreiter, 1962), 271. On Lassus's career in print, see James Haar, "Orlando di Lasso, Composer and Print Entrepreneur," in *Music and the Cultures of Print*, ed. Kate van Orden with an afterword by Roger Chartier (New York: Garland, 2000), 125–51.

13. For a wide-ranging look at the problem with special consideration of Haydn, see John Spitzer, "Authorship and Attribution in Western Art Music" (Ph.D. diss., Cornell University, 1983).

14. "Praeterea multi ex illis, quorum mentionem feci, audent etiam Com-ponistarum titulum sibi arrogare, cumq[ue] intra spacium dimidij anni multo sudore qualemcumq[ue] cantiunculam, quae vix tres concordantias habeat, fabricarunt, statim typis illam excudi curant, quo etiam ipsorum magnum & gloriosum nomen in universa terra notum fiat." Hermann Finck, *Prac-tica musica* (Wittenberg,1556), facsimile ed. (Bologna: Forni Editore, 1969), fol. Ooiii^v. Cited in Jane A. Bernstein, "Financial Arrangements and the Role of Printer and Composer in Sixteenth-Century Italian Music Print-ing." *Acta Musicologica* 63 (1991): 39–56, at 48, from which this translation is drawn.

15. See Margaret McGowan, *Ideal Forms in the Age of Ronsard* (Berkeley: University of California Press, 1985), 114–9; and Brian Jeffery, "The Idea of Music in Ronsard's Poetry," in *Ronsard the Poet*, ed. Terence Cave (London: Methuen, 1973), 209–39. The language equating writing with the "lyre" was one well-developed in Italy by this time.

16. Pierre de Ronsard, *Oeuvres complètes*, ed. Jean Céard, Daniel Ménager, and Michel Simonin, 2 vols. (Paris: Gallimard, 1993–94), 1:676–78.

17. See Terence Cave, *The Cornucopian Text: Problems of Writing in the French Renaissance* (Oxford: Clarendon Press, 1979), 226, 232.

18. Margaret W. Ferguson's study of Du Bellay's *Deffence* brings out the theme of French ascendance particularly well. See her "The Exile's Defense: Du Bellay's *La Deffence et illustration de la langue françoyse*," *Publications of the Modern Language Association* 93 (1978): 275–89.

19. See Thomas W. Bridges, "The Publishing of Arcadelt's First Book of Madrigals," 2 vols. (Ph.D. diss., Harvard University, 1982).

20. See James Haar, "Notes on the 'Dialogo della Musica' of Antonfran-cesco Doni," *Music & Letters* 47 (1966): 198–224, at 215–16.

21. See Daniel Heartz, *Pierre Attaingnant, Royal Printer of Music: A Historical Study and Bibliographical Catalogue* (Berkeley and Los Angeles: University of California Press, 1969), catalog nos. 4, 40, 75, 90, 91, and 155.

22. On Janequin's career and that of his chansons in print, see Richard Freedman, "Clément Janequin, Pierre Attaingnant, and the Changing Image of French Music, ca. 1540," in *Charting Change in France around 1540*, ed. Marian Rothstein (Selinsgrove: Susquehanna University Press, 2006), 63–94, at 78–80.

23. See Heartz, *Pierre Attaingnant*, 91, catalog no. 166; and Lawrence F. Bernstein, "Claude Gervaise as Chanson Composer," *Journal of the American Musicological Society* 18 (1965): 359–81.

24. See Heartz, *Pierre Attaingnant*, 91–95.

25. See Isabelle Cazeaux and John T. Brobeck, "Sermisy, Claudin de," in Grove Music Online, www.oxfordmusiconline.com (accessed April 27, 2011); and Barthélemy Aneau, *Quintil Horatian*, as cited in Joachim Du Bellay, *La deffence et illustration de la langue françoyse* (Paris, 1549), ed. Henri Chamard, Société des Textes Français Modernes (Paris: Didier, 1970), 112n4.

26. Indeed, so one-sided was the exchange that Daniel Heartz was hard-pressed to explain it, going so far as to suggest halfheartedly that Sermisy received financial remuneration from the printer. See Heartz, *Pierre Attaingnant*, 93.

27. On the institutions at court and Claudin's roles there, see Christelle Cazaux, *La musique à la cour de François Ier* (Paris: École nationale des Chartes, and Tours: Centre d'Études Supérieures de la Renaissance, 2002).

28. For the works list, see Cazeaux and Brobeck, "Sermisy, Claudin de." On "Tant que vivray," see Heartz, *Pierre Attaingnant*, catalog nos. 2, 9, 32, and 74. For arrangements, see nos. 13 and 23. On the several arrangements of "Aupres de vous," see the landmark article of Daniel Heartz, " 'Au pres de vous': Claudin's Chanson and the Commerce of Publishers' Arrangements," *Journal of the American Musicological Society* 24 (1971): 193–225.

29. See Annie Coeurdevey, *Bibliographie des oeuvres poétiques de Clément Marot mises en musique dans les recueils profanes du XVIe siècle* (Paris: Honoré Champion, 1997), 19–20; and Howard Mayer Brown, *Music in the French Secular Theater, 1400–1550*, 2 vols. (Cambridge, MA: Harvard University Press, 1963), 1:275. On the remarkable publishing history of the *Septiesme livre*, see Henri Vanhulst, "Un succès de l'édition musicale: le 'Septiesme livre des chansons a quatre parties' (1560–1661/3)," *Revue belge de Musicologie / Belgisch Tijdschrift voor Muziekwetenschap* 32–33 (1978–79): 97–120.

30. These attribution patterns are analogous to those explored in Martha Feldman, "Authors and Anonyms: Recovering the Anonymous Subject in *Cinquecento* Vernacular Objects," in van Orden, ed., *Music and the Cultures of Print*, 163–99.

31. On "Resjouissons nous," see Leeman L. Perkins, "Toward a Typology of the 'Renaissance' Chanson," *Journal of Musicology* 4 (1988): 421–47, at 440. A few modern ensembles specializing in this repertoire have taken up the challenge of learning how to improvise polyphony in as many as four or more parts. I would especially note the work of The King's Noyse, David Douglass, director, and Le Poème Harmonique, Vincent Dumestre, director. Both groups

perform entire concerts without music by using a combination of memory and improvisation. Some evidence that sixteenth-century musicians thought about harmony "top-down" can be found in F-Pn Rés. Vmf 13 (1–17), a well-worn volume of superius partbooks originally owned by Louis Cramoisy, royal harpsichordist under Henry II. It contains books 1 through 15 of Le Roy & Ballard's *Livre de chanson* series. Cramoisy seems to have used it on its own for teaching and as a sort of fake book at a time when the *voix de ville* was in fashion.

32. For the poetic and musical sources see Coeurdevey, *Bibliographie des oeuvres poétiques de Clément Marot mises en musique*, 10–12.

33. In this sentence and in other discussions of strophic poetry, I use *"chanson"* in italics to refer to the poetic genre that is characterized by multiple strophes, frequent short line lengths of six or seven syllables, and occasional patterns mixing line lengths.

34. See *La journée des madrigaux*, ed. Emile Colombey (Paris: Aubry, 1856), 18.

35. Text in Coeurdevey, *Bibliographie des oeuvres poétiques de Clément Marot mises en musique*, 10; translation in Jane A. Bernstein, ed., *French Chansons of the Sixteenth Century* (University Park, PA: Pennsylvania State University Press, 1985), 17.

36. The tenor of Claudin's setting is given as a basse danse by Thoinot Arbeau, *Orchésographie. Et traicte en forme de dialogue, par lequel toutes personnes peuvent facilement apprendre & practiquer l'honneste exercice [des] dances* (Langres, 1589), fols. 33v-37r, and paraphrased in the setting of Adrian Willaert. See Brown, *Music in the French Secular Theater*, 1:244–46.

37. For a contemporary explanation of these cadence formulas, see Michel de Menehou, *Nouvelle instruction familiere, en laquelle sont contenus les difficultés de la Musique, avecques le nombre des concordances, & accords: ensemble la maniere d'en user, tant à deux, à trois, à quatre, qu'à cinq parties* (Paris: Nicolas Du Chemin, 1558), fols. Ci^r–Cii^r.

38. On descant, see Rob C. Wegman, "From Maker to Composer: Improvisation and Musical Authorship in the Low Countries, 1450–1500," *Journal of the American Musicological Society* 49 (1996): 409–79. On the kinds of singing prompted by duo arrangements, see Kate van Orden, "The Parisian Chanson: Prints and Readers," in *Imparare, Leggere, Comprare Musica nell'Europa del Cinquecento*, a special issue of *Il Saggiatore Musicale* 18 (2011): 191–208.

39. See the late fifteenth-century treatise of Guilielmus Monachus, *Guilielmi Monachi De Preceptis Artis Musicae*, ed. Albert Seay, Corpus Scriptorum de Musica 11 (N.p.: American Institute of Musicology, 1965). Also see Murray C. Bradshaw, *The Falsobordone. A Study in Renaissance and Baroque Music* (Stuttgart: American Institute of Musicology, 1978), though Bradshaw fails to recognize that this is not just an Italian practice. Philippe Canguilhem has launched an extensive collaborative research project with ensembles that can improvise polyphony in sixteenth-century styles; for a preliminary report of their findings, see Philippe Canguilhem, "Le projet FABRICA: Oralité et écri-

ture dans les pratiques polyphoniques du chant ecclésiastique (XVIe–XXe siècles)," *Journal of the Alamire Foundation* 2 (2010): 272–81; and Canguilhem, "Les sources écrites du faux-bourdon au 16e siècle: un cas-limite de 'composition' à la Renaissance" (paper presented at the session "Music between *extempore* performance and *opus perfectum et absolutum*," at the Nineteenth Congress of the International Musicological Society, Rome, Italy, July 2012).

40. Benedic Macé and Laurens Dandin, *Instruction pour apprendre a chanter a quatre parties, selon le Plainchant, les Pseaumes, & Cantiques* (Caen: Benedic Macé, 1582).

41. For a fascinating study of fauxbourdon techniques in the Spanish song repertoire, see Giuseppe Fiorentino, *"Folía": El origen de los esquemas armónicos entre tradición oral y transmisión escrita*, DeMusica 17 (Kassel: Editions Reichenberger, 2013).

42. See Christopher Simpson, *The Compendium of Practical Musick* (London: printed by William Godbid for Henry Brome, 1667), 128–31. Simpson spells out the process so exactly in his little introduction to fugues that it is worth citing here, despite its late date. In the four-voice example he gives there, he uses a figure outlining a pair of rising thirds that move down stepwise, but goes on to say that fourths and fifths are also good choices and "oftentimes requisite for the better maintaining the Air of the Musick."

43. See John Milsom, "Absorbing Lassus," *Early Music* 33 (2005): 305–20, at 312.

44. See William F. Prizer, "The Frottola and the Unwritten Tradition," *Studi musicali* 15 (1986): 3–37.

45. The quotes come from Howard Mayer Brown and Richard Freedman, "Chanson," §3, "1525 to the mid-16th century," in Grove Music Online, www.grovemusiconline.com (accessed April 28, 2011). Also see Howard Mayer Brown, "The *Chanson rustique*: Popular Elements in the 15th- and 16th-Century Chanson," *Journal of the American Musicological Society* 12 (1959): 16–26; Brown, "The Genesis of a Style: The Parisian Chanson, 1500–1530," in *Chanson and Madrigal, 1480–1530*, ed. James Haar (Cambridge, MA: Harvard University Press, 1964), 1–50; and Perkins, "Toward a Typology of the 'Renaissance' Chanson." For an account of the variety of songs printed by Attaingnant and a critique of the "Parisian chanson" designation, see Lawrence F. Bernstein, "The 'Parisian Chanson': Problems of Style and Terminology," *Journal of the American Musicological Society* 31 (1978): 193–240.

46. A setting of Petrarch's madrigal "Non al suo amante" survives in a version by Jacopo da Bologna, though Petrarch's larger verse forms came into their own as *poesia per musica* only in the late fifteenth century with the petrarchistic songs of Il Chariteo and Serafino dall'Aquilano and the sonnet settings of the frottolists. On Dante, see John Ahern, "Singing the Book: Orality in the Reception of Dante's *Comedy*," in *Dante: Contemporary Perspectives*, ed. Amilcare A. Iannucci (Toronto: University of Toronto Press, 1997), 214–39.

47. Michel Foucault, "What Is an Author?" in *Language, Counter-Memory, Practice: Selected Essays and Interviews,* ed. Donald F. Bouchard, trans. Donald F. Bouchard and Sherry Simon (Ithaca, NY: Cornell University Press, 1977), 113–38, at 124.

48. Ibid., 125.

49. Ibid., 126.

50. A relevant critique can be found in Roger Chartier, *The Order of Books: Readers, Authors, and Libraries in Europe between the Fourteenth and Eighteenth Centuries,* trans. Lydia G. Cochrane (Stanford, CA: Stanford University Press, 1994), 25–59.

51. See, for instance, the conference proceedings published in volume 13 of *Early Music History* (1994), especially the essays by Howard Mayer Brown, Jeanice Brooks, and John O'Brien.

52. Pierre de Ronsard, *Les quatre premiers livres des Odes de Pierre de Ronsard, . . . Ensemble son Bocage . . . - Brève exposition de quelques passages du 1er livre des Odes de Pierre de Ronsard, par I. M. P.* (Paris: G. Cavellart [sic], 1550). These years were a turning point for Ronsard. See Philippe Desan, "The Tribulations of a Young Poet: Ronsard from 1547 to 1552," in *Renaissance Rereadings: Intertext and Context,* ed. Maryanne Cline Horowitz, Anne Cruz, and Wendy Furman (Urbana and Chicago: University of Illinois Press, 1988), 184–202.

53. For the privilege, see Pierre de Ronsard, *Le Bocage de P. de Ronsard, Vandomoys, dedié a P. de Paschal, du bas païs de Languedoc* (Paris: Veuve Maurice de la Porte, 1554), fols. Aii^r–Aiiii^v; and Freedman, "Who Owned Lasso's Chansons?" 174–76.

54. Joachim Du Bellay, *L'Olive et quelques autres oeuvres poeticques. Le contenu de ce livre. Cinquante sonnetz à la louange de l'olive. L'Anterotique de la vieille, & de la jeune amye. Vers lyriques. Par I.D.B.A* (Paris: pour Arnoul L'Angelier, 1549).

55. Pontus de Tyard, *Erreurs amoureuses* (Lyon: Jean de Tournes, 1549); Tyard, *Solitaire premier ou prose des Muses et de la fureur poetique, plus quelques vers lyriques* (Lyon: Jean de Tournes, 1552).

56. Jean-Antoine de Baïf, *Les amours de Jan Antoine de Baif* (Paris: Veuve Maurice de la Porte, 1552) and *Quatre livres de l'amour de Francine* (Paris: André Wechel, 1555).

57. Rémy Belleau, *Les Odes d'Anacreon Teien, traduites de Grec en François . . . par Remi Belleau ensemble quelques petites hymnes de son invention* (Paris: André Wechel, 1556).

58. The literature on poetic imitation in the Renaissance is extensive. See especially Thomas M. Greene, *The Light in Troy: Imitation and Discovery in Renaissance Poetry* (New Haven, CT, and London: Yale University Press, 1982); and Cave, *The Cornucopian Text.* On French Petrarchism in particular, see Joseph Vianey, *Le pétrarquisme en France au XVIe siècle* (Geneva: Slatkine Reprints, 1969), with a discussion of poetic forms on 13–45.

59. The debt to Petrarch is indisputable, but the French tradition of poetic cycles lacks the *Canzoniere*'s religious narrative. Cécile Alduy prefers to distinguish the French genre by giving it the secular label "Amours." For a rich analysis of "Amours" poetic cycles in France, beginning with importations of Petrarch's own sonnet cycle, see Cécile Alduy, *Politique des "amours": poétique et genèse d'un genre français nouveau (1544–1560)*, Travaux d'Humanisme et Renaissance 422 (Geneva: Droz, 2007). One important precursor to Ronsard's *Amours* is Maurice Scève's *Délie* of 1544; Alduy also gives significant attention to books printed in Lyon, many of which issued from the presses of Jean de Tournes, a significant publisher of the works of Saint-Gelais. On pre-Pléiade precedents for sonnets in France, see Marcel Françon 67 "Sur le premier sonnet français publié," *Bibliothèque d'Humanisme et Renaissance* 33 (1971): 365–66; C. A. Mayer, "Le premier sonnet français: Marot, Mellin de Saint-Gelais et J. Bouchet," *Revue d'histoire littéraire de la France* 67 (1967): 481–93; John McClelland, "Sonnet ou quatorzain? Marot et le choix d'une forme poétique," *Revue d'histoire littéraire de la France* 73 (1973): 591–607; Hélène Naïs, "La notion de genre en poésie au XVIe siècle," in *La notion de genre à la Renaissance*, ed. Guy Demerson (Geneva: Slatkine, 1984), 103–27; and for music, Georgie Durosoir, "Les genres de la musique vocale," in Demerson, ed., *La notion de genre*, 245–62.

60. On Petrarch's sublimation of desire for his mistress into poetry worthy of laurel wreaths, see John Freccero, "The Fig Tree and the Laurel: Petrarch's Poetics," *Diacritics* 5 (1975): 34–40; and the introduction to Francesco Petrarca, *Petrarch's Lyric Poems: The* Rime sparse *and Other Lyrics*, ed. and trans. Robert M. Durling (Cambridge, MA: Harvard University Press, 1976).

61. See Roger Chartier "Figures of the Author," in *The Order of Books*.

62. See Carla Zecher, *Sounding Objects: Musical Instruments, Poetry, and Art in Renaissance France* (Toronto: University of Toronto Press, 2007), 36–37.

63. Ronsard, *Les quatre premiers livres des Odes*, fol. Aiiiᵛ, "Je ne fai point de doute que ma Poésie tant varie ne semble facheuse aus oreilles de nos rimeurs, & principalement des courtizans, qui n'admirent qu'un petit sonnet petrarquizé, ou quelque mignardise d'amour qui continue tousjours en son propos."

64. Ibid., fol. Avʳ, "Bien que telles gens [those who have succeeded more by opinion than by reason] foisonnent en honneurs, & qu'ordinerement on les bonnette, pour avoir quelque titre de faveur: si mourront ils sans renom, & reputation, & les doctes folies de poëtes survivront les innombrables siecles avenir, criants la gloire des princes consacrés par eus à l'immortalité." On Ronsard and immortality, see Cathy M. Yandell, *Carpe Corpus: Time and Gender in Early Modern France* (Newark, DE: University of Delaware Press, and London: Associated University Presses, 2000), chap. 2.

65. "On peult comme l'argent trafiquer la louange." The line comes from sonnet 152 in Joachim Du Bellay, *Les regrets, Les antiquités de Rome*, ed. Samuel Silvestre de Sacy (Paris: Gallimard, 1967), 170. See Timothy Hamp-

ton, " 'Trafiquer La Louange': L'économie de la poésie dans les *Regrets*," in *Du Bellay et ses sonnets romains: études sur* Les Regrets *et* Les Antiquitez de Rome, ed. Yvonne Bellenger and Jean Balsamo (Paris: Honoré Champion, 1994), 47–60.

66. See Cynthia J. Brown, *Poets, Patrons, and Printers: Crisis of Authority in Late Medieval France* (Ithaca, NY, and London: Cornell University Press, 1995).

67. Ibid., 2.

68. On Lemaire and La Vigne, see Cynthia J. Brown, "Text, Image, and Authorial Self-Consciousness in Late Medieval Paris," in *Printing the Written Word: The Social History of Books, circa 1450–1520*, ed. Sandra L. Hindman (Ithaca, NY, and London: Cornell University Press, 1991), 103–42. On Gringoire's privilege, see Elizabeth Armstrong, *Before Copyright: The French Book-Privilege System, 1498–1526*, Cambridge Studies in Publishing and Printing History (Cambridge: Cambridge University Press, 1990), 104–5.

69. See Cynthia J. Brown, *The Shaping of History and Poetry in Late Medieval France: Propaganda and Artistic Expression in the Works of the Rhétoriqueurs* (Birmingham, AL: Summa, 1985).

70. See Martin Picker, "Josquin and Jean Lemaire: Four Chansons Re-examined," in *Essays Presented to Myron P. Gilmore*, ed. Sergio Bertelli and Gloria Ramakus, 2 vols. (Florence: La Nuova Italia, 1978), 2:447–56; and Dobbins, *Music in Renaissance Lyons*, 27–31.

71. David Fallows, "Jean Molinet and the Lost Burgundian Court Chansonniers of the 1470s," in *Gestalt und Entstehung musikalischer Quellen im 15. und 16. Jahrhundert*, ed. Martin Staehelin (Wiesbaden: Harrassowitz Verlag, 1998), 35–42.

72. On Molinet's publishing efforts, again, see Brown, *Poets, Patrons, and Printers*.

73. Jean Marot, *Doctrinal des princesses et nobles dames*, given as the first item in *Le recueil Jehan Marot*, itself printed in *L'adolescence clementine ou aultrement les oeuvres de Clement Marot* (Paris: Françoys Regnault, 1536).

74. See Brown, *Poets, Patrons, and Printers*, 52–54, who makes a similar argument in the case of André de La Vigne's lawsuit over the *Vergier d'honneur*, 18.

75. See Michel Simonin, *Vivre de sa plume au XVIe siècle ou la carrière de François de Belleforest* (Geneva: Droz, 1992).

76. On the social condition of the Pléiade poets in comparison to that of the Rhétoriqueurs, see Henri Weber, *La création poétique au XVIe siècle en France de Maurice Scève à Agrippa d'Aubigné* (Paris: Nizet, 1955), 63–106.

77. See Michel Simonin, *Pierre de Ronsard* (Paris: Fayard, 1990), 128–29.

78. Ronsard, *Les quatre premiers livres des Odes*, fol. Aiiii^v, "c'est le vrai but d'un poëte Liriq de celebrer jusques à l'extremité celui qu'il entreprend de louer."

79. Ibid., fol. Av^r.

80. Simonin, *Pierre de Ronsard*, 130.

81. For biographical information on Saint-Gelais, see Mellin de Saint-Gelais, *Oeuvres poétiques françaises,* ed. Donald Stone, 2 vols. (Paris: Société des Textes Français Modernes, 1993–95), 1:ix–xii; and Donald Stone, *Mellin de Saint-Gelais and Literary History* (Lexington, KY: French Forum Press, 1983).

82. Aneau, *Quintil Horatian,* reprinted in Du Bellay, *La deffence,* 123n4.

83. "Mais de telz que luy ne s'en trouve pas treize en la grand douzaine," ibid.

84. Saint-Gelais, *Oeuvres poétiques françaises,* 1:x–xi, xiii–xiv.

85. Ibid., 1:xxiii–xxiv.

86. Octavien was the Bishop of Angoulême, and opinions are divided on whether Mellin was Octavien's bastard son or his nephew; the consensus is that he was probably Octavien's son, but no hard facts support this presumption.

87. "J'ay mon breviaire au poing, je chante quelquefois, (Mais c'est bien rarement car j'ay mauvaise vois)," Ronsard, *Oeuvres complètes,* ed. Céard, Ménager, and Simonin, 2:1056, ll. 541–42. For an assessment of Ronsard's understanding of music, see Jeffery, "The Idea of Music in Ronsard's Poetry," 217. Paul Laumonier, in *Ronsard poète lyrique: étude historique et littéraire* (Geneva: Slatkine Reprints, 1972), substantiates Ronsard's debt to earlier French song by detailing the poet's reliance on the figures of speech, tone, and form of song verse, both authored (esp. by Marot) and anonymous. For an analysis that augments this sort of textual criticism with a consideration of the musical practices that shaped Ronsard's texts (most from a later stage in his career than that under discussion here), see Kate van Orden, "*La chanson vulgaire* and Ronsard's Poetry for Music," in *Poetry and Music in the French Renaissance: Proceedings of the Sixth Cambridge French Renaissance Colloquium, 5–7 July 1999,* ed. Jeanice Brooks, Philip Ford, and Gillian Jondorf (Cambridge: Cambridge French Colloquia, 2001), 79–109.

88. As in the fresco of Apollo atop Mount Parnassus decorating the ceiling of the grand ballroom at Fountainebleau. The frescoes were probably painted between 1550 and 1556.

89. Ronsard, *Les quatre premiers livres des Odes,* fol. Aiiii^v, ". . . & ferai encores revenir (si je puis) l'usage de la lire, aujourdui resuscitée en Italie, laquelle lire seule doit & peut animer les vers, & leur donner le juste poix de leur gravité." On Ronsard's notion of *vers mesurés à la lyre,* see especially Jean-Pierre Ouvrard, "Le sonnet ronsardien en musique: du *Supplément* de 1552 à 1580," *Revue de musicologie* 74 (1988): 149–64.

90. See McGowan, *Ideal Forms in the Age of Ronsard,* 114–19; Jeffery, "The Idea of Music in Ronsard's Poetry"; and Zecher, *Sounding Objects,* chap. 1, and for the debate over the chanson, 74–76. The language equating writing with the "lyre" was well developed in Italy by this time.

91. Du Bellay, *La deffence,* 113–15.

92. See Saint-Gelais, *Oeuvres poétiques françaises,* 1:x–xiv.

93. See Pernette du Guillet, *Louise Labé, Oeuvres poétiques, précédées des Rymes de Pernette du Guillet,* ed. Françoise Charpentier (Paris: Gallimard,

1983), 66 and 179n. The printed poetry of Pernette du Guillet raises the question of how authorship differed for poetesses in a lyric economy dominated by Petrarchan verse and its masculine constructions. See Leah L. Chang, *Into Print: The Production of Female Authorship in Early Modern France* (Newark, DE: University of Delaware Press, 2009), esp. chap. 3 on the lyric poetry of Louise Labé.

94. See Aneau, *Quintil Horatien*, cited in Du Bellay, *La deffence*, 115n1. "Et si elles peuvent estre sonnées à la lyre (comme elles sont), meritent le nom de vers lyriques, myeux que les bayes de ton *Olive* ne la suyte, qui ne furent onque chantées ne sonnées, & à peine estre le pourroient."

95. The kinds of music to which Saint-Gelais likely sang his verse were first explored by Daniel Heartz, "*Voix de ville*: Between Humanist Ideals and Musical Realities," in *Words and Music: The Scholar's View*, ed. Laurence Berman (Cambridge, MA: Harvard University Press, 1972), 115–35. On Conde Claros and the Romanesca bass patterns used for Saint-Gelais's verse, see James Haar, "Arcadelt and the Frottola: The Italianate Chanson c. 1550," in *Res musicae: Essays in Honor of James Worrell Pruett*, ed. Paul Laird and Craig Russell (Warren, MI: Harmonie Park Press, 2001), 97–109. I print tunes for all three *chansons* in van Orden, "*La chanson vulgaire* and Ronsard's Poetry for Music," 84.

96. In short, Du Bellay's text repudiates an *ars poetica* printed just the year before, Thomas Sébillet's *L'art poétique françois* (Paris: Gilles Corrozet, 1548). For the citations see Sébillet, *L'art poétique françois*, ed. Félix Gaiffe and Francis Goyet, 3rd ed. (Paris: Société des Textes Français Modernes, 1988), 38, 148, 150.

97. Sébillet, *L'art poétique françois*, 146–50.

98. Ibid., 148.

99. On the *Deploration de Venus* (Lyon: Jean de Tournes, 1545–61), see Saint-Gelais, *Oeuvres poétiques françaises*, 1:xiii–xiv; and Alfred Cartier and Adolphe Chenevière, "Antoine du Moulin: valet de chambre de la reine de Navarre," *Revue d'histoire littéraire de la France* 3 (1896): 90–106, at 96–105. On *Le discours du voyage de Constantinople* and the *Livre de plusieurs pieces*, see Du Bellay, *La deffence*, 114n3.

100. For a discussion of the many *recueils de chansons* in which "Laissez la verde couleur" was printed, see van Orden, "Female Complaintes: Laments of Venus, Queens, and City Women in Late Sixteenth-Century France," *Renaissance Quarterly* 54 (2001): 801–45, esp. 817.

101. See Heartz, "*Voix de ville*," and the excellent analysis of "Laissez la verde couleur," in Haar, "Arcadelt and the Frottola."

102. See Philippe Desan and Kate van Orden, "De la chanson à l'ode: musique et poésie sous le mécénat du cardinal Charles de Lorraine," in *Le mécénat et l'influence des Guises*, ed. Yvonne Bellenger (Paris: Honoré Champion, 1996), 463–87.

103. See Stone, *Mellin de Saint-Gelais*, 11–58.

104. See Haar, "Arcadelt and the Frottola."

105. On Marot's significant publishing career, see Florian Preisig, *Clément Marot et les métamorphoses de l'auteur à l'aube de la Renaissance* (Geneva: Droz, 2004).

106. Clément Marot, *L'adolescence clementine, autrement, les oeuvres de Clement Marot* (Paris: pour Pierre Roffet, par Geoffroy Tory, 1532), fol. ii^r. "Je ne scay (mes treschers Freres) qui ma plus incite a mettre ces miennes petites jeunesses en lumiere: ou voz continuelles prieres, ou le desplaisir que jay eu den ouyr cryer & publier par les rues une grande partie/toute incorrecte/ mal imprimee/& plus au proffit du Libraire, qua lhonneur de Lauther."

107. See Preisig, *Clément Marot et les métamorphoses de l'auteur,* 50, for the reading of this preface. It is disappointing that Preisig pays little attention to the *recueils* in which Marot's verse was printed and makes no mention of the musical prints containing Marot's poetry, despite the wonderful study of Annie Coeurdevey, *Bibliographie des oeuvres poétiques de Clément Marot mises en musique.*

108. For the musical and literary sources of Marot's work, see Coeurdevey, *Bibliographie des oeuvres poétiques de Clément Marot mises en musique,* 187–218; and Brian Jeffery, *Chanson Verse of the Early Renaissance,* 2 vols. (London: Tecla, 1971–76).

109. See Coeurdevey, *Bibliographie des oeuvres poétiques de Clément Marot mises en musique;* "Jouyssance vous donneray" is as good an example as any, for which see ibid., 10–12.

110. Cited in ibid., 190.

4. THE BOOK OF POETRY BECOMES A BOOK OF MUSIC

1. On the lyric metaphor in Ronsard's verse, see Margaret McGowan, *Ideal Forms in the Age of Ronsard* (Berkeley: University of California Press, 1985), 114–19; and Brian Jeffery, "The Idea of Music in Ronsard's Poetry," in *Ronsard the Poet,* ed. Terence Cave (London: Methuen, 1973), 209–39. On music and French poetry more generally, including Ronsard, see Carla Zecher, *Sounding Objects: Musical Instruments, Poetry, and Art in Renaissance France* (Toronto: University of Toronto Press, 2007), esp. chap. 1, "Of Strings, Trumpets, and the Future of French Poetry," 24–56, with a discussion of this poem at 43–44.

2. On the reaction at court see Henri Longnon, "Les déboires de Ronsard à la cour," *Bibliothèque d'Humanisme et Renaissance* 12 (1950): 60–80.

3. Pierre de Ronsard, *Oeuvres complètes,* ed. Jean Céard, Daniel Ménager, and Michel Simonin, 2 vols. (Paris: Gallimard, 1993–94), 1:678, translation my own.

4. See, for instance, Pierre Clereau, *Premier livre de chansons tant Françoises qu'Italiennes nouvellement composées à trois parties* (Paris: Le Roy & Ballard, 1559), a collection of three-voice chansons that sets six odes of Ronsard, though none in their entirety. Three of the odes are Pindaric; for the Homeric odes, all strophes could be sung, yet because several of the settings

are of isolated inner strophes, it suggests that Cleareau did not intend for the odes to be sung in their entirety. The reedition of this print in 1575 increased the number of odes to thirteen and even included two complete ones. Clereau's four-voice *Dixiesme livre de chansons tant Françoises qu'Italiennes nouvellement composées à quatre parties* of 1559 also included the setting of one strophe from an ode by Ronsard. For a modern edition of the *Premier livre* and a table of Clereau's poetic sources see Clereau, *Les odes de Pierre de Ronsard,* ed. Jane A. Bernstein, The Sixteenth-Century Chanson 7 (New York: Garland, 1988), xiv. For a deft musical analysis, see Jeanice Brooks, "Italy, the Ancient World and the French Musical Inheritance in the Sixteenth Century: Arcadelt and Clereau in the Service of the Guises," *Journal of the Royal Musical Association* 121 (1996): 147–90.

5. The fuller title is *Les Amours de P. de Ronsard, Ensemble le cinquiesme de ses Odes* (Paris: Veuve M. de la Porte, 1552), and the print included the fifth book of Ronsard's odes. *Les Amours* also includes three poems in the strophic form known as the *chanson.*

6. Pierre de Ronsard, *Oeuvres complètes,* ed. Prosper Blanchemain (Paris: P. Jannet, 1857–67); Julien Tiersot, *Ronsard et la musique de son temps* (Leipzig: Breitkopf und Härtel; Paris: Fischbacher, 1903).

7. See Frank Dobbins, "Ronsard, Pierre de," in Grove Music Online, www.oxfordmusiconline.com (accessed May 27, 2011).

8. One musical setting of Ronsard's poetry had already appeared in print, earlier in 1552. See Richard Freedman, "Tradition and Renewal in Du Chemin's *Chansons Nouvelles,*" http://ricercar.cesr.univ-tours.fr/3-programmes/EMN/duchemin/pages/learn.asp (accessed January 23, 2013). For an excellent edition of the *Canzoniere* with English translation, see Francesco Petrarca, *Petrarch's Lyric Poems: The* Rime sparse *and Other Lyrics,* ed. and trans. Robert M. Durling (Cambridge, MA: Harvard University Press, 1976).

9. See Dean Mace, "Pietro Bembo and the Literary Origins of the Italian Madrigal," *Musical Quarterly* 55 (1969): 65–86, which shows the ways in which Bembo's *Prose* acted as a catalyst for the new musical form. Also see Martha Feldman, *City Culture and the Madrigal at Venice* (Berkeley and Los Angeles: University of California Press, 1995), chap. 5 and passim.

10. See Feldman, *City Culture and the Madrigal at Venice,* chaps. 7 and 8.

11. On the very few settings of sonnets in France before this date, see John McClelland, "La mise en musique du sonnet français avant 1552," in *Musique et humanisme à la renaissance* (Paris: Presses de l'École normale supérieure, 1993), 83–100.

12. On the frontispiece to *Les Amours* as a form of "self-coronation" as a poet laureate, see Cécile Alduy, "Lyric Economies: Manufacturing Values in French Petrarchan Collections (1549–1560)," *Renaissance Quarterly* 63 (2010): 721–53, at 737–43.

13. Scotto had experimented with upright quarto for music in 1544 when he printed Anton Francesco Doni's *Dialogo della musica*—another hybrid

book combining music and text—and eventually the Venetian presses would adopt upright quarto for secular music, but always in partbooks.

This was a format and layout Du Chemin used only once more—for the *Chansons spirituelles* of Guillaume Gueroult and Didier Lupi Second, a collection of French psalm translations and other spiritualized songs that would have fit nicely on the shelf next to or bound with a catechism, psalter, or prayer book. Le Roy & Ballard occasionally resorted to upright formats for similar reasons of generic consistency with prayer books, as in Claude Goudimel, *Pseaumes de David* (1562) and *Les Psalmes & Cantiques* (1583) or with Italian prints, as can be seen in the upright formats they used for the villanelle of Lassus (1581), the madrigals of Regolo and Pietro Vecoli (1586 and 1587, respectively), and the madrigals of Marenzio (1598).

It is noteworthy that the copy of *Les Amours* in the British Library is bound together with Nicolas Denisot's *Cantiques du premier aduenement de Iesu-Christ* of 1555, another print that, like *Les Amours*, includes musical notation.

14. Nancy J. Vickers, "The Unauthored 1539 Volume in Which Is Printed the *Hectamophile, The Flowers of French Poetry,* and *Other Soothing Things,* in *Subject and Object in Renaissance Culture,* ed., Margreta De Grazia, Maureen Quilligan, and Peter Stallybrass (Cambridge: Cambridge University Press, 1996), 166–88, at 175 (quoting Natalie Zemon Davis).

15. Henry Expert, ed., *La Fleur des musiciens de P. de Ronsard* (Paris: Cité des Livres, 1923).

16. Roger Chartier, *The Order of Books: Readers, Authors, and Libraries in Europe between the Fourteenth and Eighteenth Centuries,* trans. Lydia G. Cochrane (Stanford, CA: Stanford University Press, 1994), viii.

17. François de la Croix du Maine, *Premier volume de la bibliotheque du sieur de la Croix du Maine. Qui est un catalogue general de toutes sortes d'Autheurs, qui ont escrit en François depuis cinq cents ans & plus, jusques à ce jourd'huy: avec trois mille qui sont compris en cet ouvre, ensemble un recit de leurs compositions, tant imprimees qu'autrement. Dedié et presenté au roy. Sur le fin de ce livre se voyent les desseins & projects dudit sieur de la CROIX, lesquels il presenta au Roy l'an 1583 pour dresser une Bibliotheque parfaite & accomplie en toutes sortes* (Paris: Abel l'Angelier, 1584); Antoine Du Verdier, *La Bibliotheque d'Antoine Du Verdier, Seigneur de Vauprivas: Contenant le Catalogue de tous ceux qui ont escrit, ou traduict en François, et autres Dialectes de ce Royaume* (Lyon: Barthélemy Honorat, 1585).

18. For the essential outlines of their biographies, see Aimé Agnel and Richard Freedman, "Certon, Pierre," in Grove Music Online, www.oxfordmusiconline.com (accessed May 3, 2012); Howard Mayer Brown and Richard Freedman, "Janequin, Clément," in Grove Music Online, www.oxfordmusiconline.com (accessed May 3, 2012); and Paul André Gaillard and Richard Freedman, "Goudimel, Claude," in Grove Music Online, www.oxfordmusiconline.com (accessed May 3, 2012).

19. On Muret's chansons, see Freedman, "Tradition and Renewal in Du Chemin's *Chansons Nouvelles.*"

20. The odes and epode set by Goudimel are from *Cinquième livre des odes*, which was published with *Les Amours* in 1552. The *Supplément* has been transcribed in its entirety by Tiersot in *Ronsard et la musique de son temps* and in partial form in Expert, *La Fleur des musiciens de P. Ronsard.* For a facsimile, see Pierre de Ronsard and Marc-Antoine de Muret, *Les Amours, leurs commentaires. Textes de 1553*, ed. Christine de Buzon and Pierre Martin, preface by Michel Simonin, postscript by Jean Céard, musical supplement of 1552 introduced by François Lesure (Paris: Didier Érudition, 1999), 294–355.

21. Pierre de Ronsard, *Abbrege de l'art poëtique françois*, facsimile edition (Geneva: Slatkine Reprints, 1962), fol. 4. ". . . plus propres à la Musicque & accord des instrumens, en faveur desquelz il semble que la Poësie soit née: car la Poësie sans les instrumens, ou sans la grace d'une seule, ou plusieurs voix n'est nullement aggreable, non plus que les instrumens sans estre animez, de la melodie d'une plaisante voix. Si de fortune tu as composé les deux premiers vers masculins, tu feras les deux autres foeminins, & paracheveras de mesme mesure le reste de ton Elegie ou chanson, afin que les Musiciens les puissent plus facilement accorder."

22. See Jeanice Brooks, "Ronsard, the Lyric Sonnet and the Late Sixteenth-Century Chanson," *Early Music History* 13 (1994): 65–84; Jean-Pierre Ouvrard, "Le sonnet ronsardien: du *Supplément* de 1552 à 1580," *Revue de musicologie* 74 (1988): 149–64; and Freedman, "Tradition and Renewal in Du Chemin's *Chansons Nouvelles.*" Also see John McClelland, "Le marriage de poésie et de musique: un projet de Pontus de Tyard," in *La chanson à la Renaissance: Actes du XXe colloque d'études humanistes du Centre d'Études Supérieures de la Renaissance de l'Université de Tours, juillet 1977*, ed. Jean-Michel Vaccaro (Tours: Éditions Van de Velde, 1981), 80–92.

23. Those eight sonnets that are not accommodated by the musical settings are ones in which the tercets begin with the same "gender" of rhyme word as the quatrains, a discrepancy that Ronsard was to correct in subsequent editions in six out of the eight instances. See Pierre de Ronsard, *Les Amours*, ed. Catherine Weber and Henri Weber (Paris: Classiques Garnier, 1963), lxiv–lxv.

24. For the quote, see Barthélemy Aneau, *Quintil Horatien*, cited in Joachim Du Bellay, *La deffence et illustration de la langue françoyse* (Paris, 1549), ed. Henri Chamard, Société des Textes Français Modernes (Paris: Didier, 1970), 115n1. For the French, see chapter 3, n. 94 above. On the rhyme schemes, see Pierre de Ronsard, *Oeuvres complètes*, ed. Paul Laumonier, 18 vols. (Paris: Société des Textes Français Modernes, 1982), 4:xvi. Du Bellay's *L'Olive*, for example, contains over sixty different combinations of rhyme schemes and patterns of masculine and feminine rhyme.

25. Here and elsewhere, I use italics to distinguish the poetic form of the *chanson* and roman characters for the music genre.

26. On the nature and persistence of Italian improvisatory practices, see James Haar, "*Improvvisatori* and Their Relationship to Sixteenth-Century Music," in *Essays on Italian Poetry and Music in the Renaissance, 1300–1600* (Berkeley and Los Angeles: University of California Press, 1986), 76–99.

27. Jean-Pierre Ouvrard argues this same point in "Le sonnet ronsardien."

28. See Daniel Heartz, "*Voix de ville:* Between Humanist Ideals and Musical Realities," in *Words and Music: The Scholar's View,* ed. Laurence Berman (Cambridge, MA: Harvard University Press, 1972), 115–35.

29. See Du Bellay, *La deffence,* 102, for one spot among many where he makes this distinction.

30. See Margaret W. Ferguson, "The Exile's Defense: Du Bellay's *La Deffence et illustration de la langue françoyse,*" *Publications of the Modern Language Association* 93 (1978): 275–89, at 279–80. On the imitative paradox, see especially Thomas M. Greene, *The Light in Troy: Imitation and Discovery in Renaissance Poetry* (New Haven, CT, and London: Yale University Press, 1982).

31. These data are compiled in Ouvrard, "Le sonnet ronsardien," 149–50.

32. Ronsard, *Oeuvres complètes,* ed. Céard, Ménager, and Simonin, 1:42–43.

33. Ouvrard, "Le sonnet ronsardien."

34. Ronsard, *Oeuvres complètes,* ed. Céard, Ménager, and Simonin, 1:171. "Or si quelqu'un apres me vient blasmer, dequoy je ne suis plus si grave en mes vers que j'estoy à mon commencement, quand l'humeur Pindarique enfloit empoulément ma bouche magnifique: dy luy que les amours ne se souspirent pas d'un vers hautement grave, ains d'un beau stile bas, populaire et plaisant, ainsi qu'a fait Tibulle, l'ingenieux Ovide, et le docte Catulle." On Ronsard's *chansons,* see Kate van Orden, "*La chanson vulgaire* and Ronsard's Poetry for Music," in *Poetry and Music in the French Renaissance: Proceedings of the Sixth Cambridge French Renaissance Colloquium, 5–7 July 1999,* ed. Jeanice Brooks, Philip Ford, and Gillian Jondorf (Cambridge: Cambridge French Colloquia, 2001), 79–109.

35. On the 1557 edition, see Jean-Paul Barbier, *Ma bibliothèque poétique. Éditions des 15e et 16e siècles des principaux poètes français,* 4 parts, part 4 in 4 vols. (Geneva: Droz, 1973), part 4, vol. 2, catalog number 21.

36. On the two editions of *Les Amours* from 1552 and 1553 (each of which survives in copies representing two impressions) and the musical supplement (which was printed only in 1552 and then appended to the 1553 edition as well), see Geneviève Thibault and Louis Perceau, *Bibliographie des poésies de P. de Ronsard mises en musique au XVIe siècle* (Paris: E. Droz, 1941), 16–19.

37. See van Orden, "*La chanson vulgaire* and Ronsard's Poetry for Music."

38. On the reception of Ronsard, see Annemarie Nilges, *Imitation als Dialog: Die europäische Rezeption Ronsards in Renaissance und Frühbarock* (Heidelberg: Carl Winter Universitätsverlag, 1988), 32–42; on his poetry in the *recueils,* see van Orden, "Vernacular Culture and the Chanson in Paris, 1570–1580" (Ph.D. diss., University of Chicago, 1996), chap. 4.

39. Ronsard, *Oeuvres complètes*, ed. Céard, Ménager, and Simonin, 1:19.

40. See Cathy M. Yandell, *Carpe Corpus: Time and Gender in Early Modern France* (Newark, DE: University of Delaware Press, and London: Associated University Presses, 2000), 51; on the Greek see Malcolm Quainton, "The Liminary Texts of Ronsard's *Amours de Cassandre* (1552): Poetics, Erotics, Semiotics," *French Studies* 53 (1999): 257–78.

41. The French inscription appears in Pierre de Ronsard, *Les Oeuvres de P. de Ronsard Gentilhomme Vandomois, revues, corrigees & augmentees par l'Autheur* (Paris: Gabriel Buon, 1584), fol. avi[v]. For a facsimile see Ronsard, *Oeuvres complètes*, ed. Céard, Ménager, and Simonin, 1:21.

42. Michel de Montaigne, *Essais*, ed. Pierre Villey and V-L Saulnier, 3 vols. (Paris: Presses universitaires de France, 1982), 1:3. Montaigne's struggles to keep his book under privilege are a testament to the limited control authors retained over their texts. In order to extend the printing privilege of the *Essais*, he was required to make extensive revisions in order to demonstrate that the new edition qualified for a new privilege. See the remarkable study by George Hoffmann, *Montaigne's Career* (Oxford: Clarendon Press, and New York: Oxford University Press, 1998). For a wonderful case of a composer inscribing his life in a book of music, see Franco Piperno, "Autobiography and Authoriality in a Madrigal Book: Leonardo Meldert's *Primo libro a cinque* (1578)," *Journal of Musicology* 30 (2013): 1–27.

43. On Ronsard and authors' portraits, see especially Marie-Madeleine Fragonard, "Ronsard en poète: portrait d'auteur, produit du texte," in *Les Figures du poète, Pierre de Ronsard*, ed. Marie-Dominique Legrand, *Littérales* 26 (2000): 15–41; and Cécile Alduy, *Politique des "amours": poétique et genèse d'un genre français nouveau (1544–1560)*, Travaux d'Humanisme et Renaissance 422 (Geneva: Droz, 2007), 317–33.

44. For a modern edition of selections from the print that includes facsimiles of the portraits, liminary verse, and preface, see Guillaume Costeley, *Guillaume Costeley, Selected Chansons*, ed. Jane A. Bernstein, The Sixteenth-Century Chanson 8 (New York: Garland, 1989).

45. Two similarly imposing prints that mixed French chansons with other genres came out the same year: *Les meslanges de maistre Pierre Certon* (Paris: Du Chemin, 1570); and the *Mellange d'Orlande de Lassus contenant plusieurs chansons, tant en vers latins qu'en ryme francoyse a quatre, cinq, six, huit, dix parties* (Paris: Le Roy & Ballard, 1570).

46. See Hoffmann, *Montaigne's Career*, 99.

47. See Irving Godt, "Guillaume Costeley, Life and Works," 2 vols. (Ph.D. diss. New York University, 1970), 1:292–320.

48. On the privilege, see Richard Freedman, "Who Owned Lasso's Chansons?" *Yearbook of the Alamire Foundation* 6 (2008): 159–76. The quote from the king comes from a letter from Adrian Le Roy to Lassus of 1574; see François Lesure and Geneviève Thibault, *Bibliographie des éditions d'Adrian Le Roy et Robert Ballard (1551–1598)* (Paris: Société Française de Musicologie, 1955), 36–37.

49. On the visit of Charles IX to Toulouse, see the preface to Guillaume Boni, *Primus liber modulorum quinis, senis, & septenis vocibus* (Paris: Le Roy & Ballard, 1573), fol. 1 verso, reproduced and translated in Guillaume Boni, *Motets (1573)*, ed. Jeanice Brooks (Tours: Centre de Musique Ancienne, 2000), xxvi–xxvii. For Boni's privilege, see E. (Eugénie) Droz, "G. Boni, musicien de Ronsard," in *Mélanges offerts à M. Abel Lefranc* (Paris: Droz, 1936), 270–81, at 275–76.

50. The preface is a revision of that fronting the 1560 *Livre de meslanges*. See van Orden, "Imitation and 'la musique des anciens' in Le Roy & Ballard's 1572 *Mellange de chansons*," *Revue de musicologie* 80 (1994): 5–37, at 8–9.

51. Modal analyses of the contents of their prints can be found in Harold S. Powers, "Tonal Types and Modal Categories in Renaissance Polyphony," *Journal of the American Musicological Society* 34 (1981): 428–70; and Howard Mayer Brown, "Theory and Practice in the Sixteenth Century: Preliminary Notes on Attaingnant's Modally Ordered Chansonniers," in *Essays in Musicology: A Tribute to Alvin Johnson*, ed. Lewis Lockwood and Edward Roesner (Philadelphia: American Musicological Society, 1990), 75–100. Many modern editions of sixteenth-century musical prints now provide tables listing the tonal configurations of each piece and the modal categories they imply.

52. This nomenclature was first developed by Harold S. Powers ("Tonal Types and Modal Categories").

53. Powers, "Tonal Types and Modal Categories." Indeed, modal theory itself originated in the eighth or ninth century not as a set of compositional paradigms but as a classification system by which to organize a large preexisting body of liturgical chants that had stabilized long before. See Harold S. Powers et. al, "Mode, §II: Medieval Modal Theory," in Grove Music Online, www.oxfordmusiconline.com (accessed May 3, 2011).

54. My characterization of the logic by which editors grouped pieces is blunt. For a fuller picture, see Powers, "Tonal Types and Modal Categories," with an analysis of a Susato chansonnier on pp. 443–45; and Brown, "Theory and Practice in the Sixteenth Century."

55. Godt, "Guillaume Costeley," 1:66–69.

56. Guillaume Costeley, "Approche toy jeune Roy debonnaire," in *Musique de Guillaume Costeley, organiste ordinaire et vallet de chambre, du treschrestien et tresinvincible roy de France, Charles IX* (Le Roy & Ballard, 1570), fols. 42r–44r.

57. In some cases where partbooks are missing from the first edition, the contents have been reconstructed based on later editions. The prints in table 4 differ from earlier ones featuring Ronsard's verse by their larger format, dedications, concentration on sonnets, and commitment to the poetry of a single poet. Nonetheless, two prints set the stage for the song cycles on *Les Amours:* Pierre Clereau, *Premier* and *Second livre d'odes de Ronsard mis en Musique à troys parties* (Paris: Le Roy & Ballard, 1566) and Nicolas de La Grotte, *Chansons de P. de Ronsard, Ph. Desportes, et autres, mises en Musique* (Paris: Le Roy & Ballard, 1569). Several other prints must also be cited as part

of the Ronsard phenomenon among chanson composers, even though not all of the settings are of Ronsard's verse, most notably François Regnard, *Poesies de P. de Ronsard & autres Poëtes mis en Musique à Quatre & Cinq parties* (Paris: Le Roy & Ballard, 1579); and Fabrice Marin Caietain, *Airs mis en musique a quatre parties par Fabrice Marin Caietain sur les poësies de P. de Ronsard & autres excelens poëtes de nostre tems* (Paris: Le Roy & Ballard, 1576). Of the forty chansons in Regnard's collection, seventeen set Ronsard's poetry; the print was a reedition of one printed in Douai in 1575: François Regnard, *Cinquante chansons à quatre et cinq parties*. For details, see François Regnard, *Chansons à quatre voix, 1579*, ed. Jeanice Brooks (Tours: Centre de Musique Ancienne, 1993). The proportion of Ronsard settings is about the same in Caietain's print (which includes eight airs by other composers). Bertrand and Maletty also followed up their books of settings from *Les Amours* with numbered volumes that include more settings of Ronsard. See Anthoine de Bertrand, *Troisiesme livre de chansons* (Paris: Le Roy & Ballard, 1578); and Jean de Maletty, [*Chansons à quatre parties . . . Second livre*] (Paris: Le Roy & Ballard, 1578). I include Castro's *Chansons, odes, et sonetz* in table 4 because it sets only the poetry of Ronsard (with the exception of one text by Du Bellay) and because half of the settings are of sonnets, a fact featured in the title.

58. For analyses of the contents and style of these collections, see Frank Dobbins, "Les madrigalistes français et la Pléiade," in *La chanson à la Renaissance: Actes du XXᵉ colloque d'études humanistes du Centre d'Études Supérieures de la Renaissance de l'Université de Tours, juillet 1977*, ed. Jean-Michel Vaccaro (Tours: Éditions Van de Velde, 1981), 157–71; Dobbins, "Ronsard et ses musiciens Toulousains," in *L'humanisme à Toulouse (1480–1596): Actes du colloque international de Toulouse, mai 2004*, ed. Nathalie Dauvois (Paris: Honoré Champion, 2006), 459–82; and Brooks, "Ronsard, the Lyric Sonnet and the Late Sixteenth-Century Chanson." For biographical information concerning the French composers see Droz, "G. Boni, musicien de Ronsard"; Geneviève Thibault, "Anthoine de Bertrand: musicien de Ronsard et ses amis toulousains," in *Mélanges offerts à M. Abel Lefranc* (Paris: Droz, 1936), 282–300; and François Lesure, "Jean de Maletty à Lyon (1583)" in *Musique et musiciens français du XVIᵉ siècle* (Geneva: Minkoff, 1976), 239–42. Also see the articles "Bertrand, Anthoine de," "Boni, Guillaume," and "Maletty, Jean de," all by Frank Dobbins in Grove Music Online, www.oxfordmusiconline.com (accessed May 27, 2011).

59. On the narrative implied by the cycle and its inconsistencies see Robert Mélançon, "Sur la structure des *Amours* de 1552 de Ronsard," *Renaissance et Réform* 1 (1977): 119–35.

60. This tension between unity and fragmentation is one hallmark of the *amours* genre described by Alduy, *Politique des "amours,"* 13–18.

61. Alduy, "Lyric Economies," 747.

62. Ibid.

63. Of Maletty's print, only the superius and contratenor partbooks survive, precluding much discussion of the music. See Geneviève Thibault, "Les

Amours de P. de Ronsard mises en musique par Jehan de Maletty (1578)," in *Mélanges de musicologie offerts à M. Lionel de la Laurencie* (Paris: Droz, 1933), 61–72.

64. "Que me servent mes vers et les sons de ma Lyre, Quand nuict et jour je change et de moeurs et de peau Pour aimer sottement un visage si beau? Que l'homme est malheureux qui pour l'amour souspire! Je pleure je me deuls je suis plein de martyre, Je fay mille Sonnets, je me romps le cerveau . . ." in Ronsard, *Oeuvres complètes*, ed. Céard, Ménager, and Simonin, 1:461.

65. For a discussion of Monte's entire print, including this striking opening, see Laura J. Brooks, "French Chanson Collections on the Texts of Ronsard" (Ph.D. diss., Catholic University of America, 1990), 110–29. I am also indebted to the research of Mark Allen Rodgers, "Monte's Sonnets of Pierre de Ronsard: the *Chanson* and the Currency of Poetic Influence" (unpublished paper, 2009); in this paper, written for a seminar at the University of California, Berkeley, Rodgers considers Monte's Ronsard settings against the backdrop of his entire career in print, especially his madrigal production.

66. It is fairly clear that the Phalèse-Bellère is a copy. It has, for instance, an error between signatures B and C of the tenor partbook, where several notes are missing from the residuum of "Hé Dieu du ciel" as it runs across pages, notes that are present in the Le Roy & Ballard edition. The Flemish edition also reproduces and compounds the errors in foliation and the table present in the Le Roy & Ballard partbook. The dedication, by Jacques Anthoine de La Chapelle, a musician in the service of d'Alençon's brother, further locates the origin of the print near the French court, where Anjou had been crowned Henry III the previous year and Alençon was under house arrest until mid-September, when he fled to Dreux. Phalèse and Bellère had a habit of reissuing music printed by Le Roy & Ballard. See Henri Vanhulst, *Catalogue des éditions de musique publiées à Louvain par Pierre Phalèse et ses fils, 1545–1578*, Mémoires de la classe des beaux-arts, 2ᵉ série, vol. 16 (Brussels: Palais des Académies, 1990), for instance, catalog nos. 152, 153, 154, and 159.

67. See Piet Nuten, "Enkele stijlkritische beschouwingen over de franse chansons van Filip de Monte," in *Renaissance-Muziek, 1400–1600, Donum Natalicium René Bernard Lenaerts*, ed. Jozef Robijns (Leuven: Katholieke Universiteit Seminarie voor Muziekwetenschap, 1969), 195–214. Monte might have planned a whole book of settings, for he chose to set the text "Que me servent mes vers, & les sons de ma lyre" in D, a standard opening tonality in modally ordered anthologies. Thus the liminary conceit of the poetry was matched with an "opening" tonality in the setting.

68. Jeanice Brooks, " 'Ses amours et les miennes tout ensemble': La structure cyclique du *Premier Livre* de Anthoine de Bertrand" *Revue de musicologie* 74 (1988): 201–20. Bertrand's *Premier* and *Second livre* have been edited by Henry Expert in Monuments de la Musique française au Temps de la Renaissance 4–5 (Paris: Senart, 1926–27).

69. Brooks, "La structure cyclique du *Premier Livre*."

70. Powers, "Tonal Types and Modal Categories." One of Powers's enduring contributions to musical studies was to establish an analytical vocabulary for describing the actual tonal configuration of polyphonic pieces; its shorthand form comprises indications of system (or signature, that is, with or without a flat), final (the bass or "root" of the final chord), and ambitus or range (observable in cleffing patterns, either *chiavette*, [high] cleffing, or "normal," low cleffing).

71. Ibid. For a reinterpretation of Powers's tonal types as subsets of modes (a view I adopt here) see Brown, "Theory and Practice in the Sixteenth Century."

72. On the local cultures of modal designations, see Powers, "Tonal Types and Modal Categories," esp. 456–59.

73. The classic study of French musical humanism at the royal court is Frances A. Yates, *The French Academies of the Sixteenth Century*, 2nd ed. (London and New York: Routledge, 1988); for just three concentrated considerations of mode and ethic effect in late sixteenth-century France, see Isabelle His, *Claude Le Jeune (v. 1530–1600): un compositeur entre Renaissance et Baroque* (Arles: Actes Sud, 2000); Jean-Pierre Ouvrard, "Modality and Text Expression in 16th-Century French Chansons: Remarks Concerning the E Mode," *Basler Jahrbuch für historische Musikpraxis* 16 (1992): 89–116; and Richard Freedman, "Le Jeune's *Dodecacorde* as a Site for Spiritual Meanings," *Revue de musicologie* 89 (2003): 297–309.

74. For the primary sources, see Pontus de Tyard, *Solitaire second* (Lyon, 1555), ed. Cathy M. Yandell (Geneva: Droz, 1980); and Pierre de Ronsard, "Préface à la musique," in *Oeuvres complètes*, ed. Céard, Ménager, and Simonin, 2:1172. On the academy of Baïf and Courville, see Yates, *The French Academies*, with the statutes of the academy given in appendix 1.

75. The prefaces to Bertrand's *Premier* and *Second livre des Amours* are reprinted in Olivier Trachier, ed., *Renaissance française: traités, méthodes, préfaces, ouvrages généraux*, 4 vols. (Courlay, France: Éditions Fuzeau Classique, [2005]), 4:104–5 and 111.

76. In the often-told story of Pythagoras and the young Tauromentian, it is a song in Hypo-Phrygian that pacifies the young man when he is on the verge of raping a neighbor girl after having been aroused by a song in the higher, anger-inducing Phrygian. The pacifying effect of the Hypo-Phrygian likewise features in the story of Alexander and Timotheus. Both are cited by Bertrand (ibid., 4:104–5). For the fascinating analysis of a chanson by Claude Le Jeune in which the calming Hypo-Phrygian is explicitly employed by a composer to negate the effects of the Phrygian, see His, *Claude Le Jeune*, 280–85, 291–95.

77. Brooks, "La structure cyclique du *Premier Livre*," 219.

78. For the study of another sonnet cycle ordered according to modal affect see James Haar, "The *Capriccio* of Giachet Berchem: A Study in Modal Organization," *Musica Disciplina* 42 (1988): 129–56.

79. See Freedman, "Who Owned Lasso's Chansons?" 171–72. For a deeper investigation of the modal organization of the books of Lassus's music printed by Le Roy & Ballard, see Freedman, *The Chansons of Orlando di Lasso and Their Protestant Listeners: Music, Piety, and Print in Sixteenth-Century France*, Eastman Studies in Music (Rochester, NY: University of Rochester Press, 2001), 136–75.

80. On the cyclic works of Lassus and Palestrina, see Powers, "Tonal Types and Modal Categories," 446–50 and 460–66. On Le Jeune, see His, *Claude Le Jeune*. Le Jeune's cycles begin on C, following Zarlino's renumbering of the modes in the revised edition of the *Istituzioni harmoniche* of 1573.

81. This is suggested by Powers, "Tonal Types and Modal Categories," 446; a similar argument is advanced in Freedman, "Le Jeune's *Dodecacorde* as a Site for Spiritual Meanings."

82. For his biography, see Thibault, "Anthoine de Bertrand."

83. On Brach, Rangouse, and Minut, see François de Gélis, *Histoire critique des jeux floraux* (Toulouse, 1912; repr. Geneva: Droz, 1981). Also see Isabelle Luciani, "Jeux Floraux et 'humanisme civique' au XVIᵉ siècle: entre enjeux de pouvoir et expérience du politique," in *L'humanisme à Toulouse (1480–1596): Actes du colloque international de Toulouse, mai 2004*, ed. Nathalie Dauvois (Paris: Honoré Champion, 2006), 301–35.

84. See Dobbins, "Ronsard et ses musiciens Toulousains," 481–82.

85. Ibid., 475–82.

86. Frédérique Lemerle, "Guillaume Philandrier et la bibliothèque du cardinal Georges d'Armagnac" in *Etudes aveyronnaises* (2003): 219–44.

87. See for instance, Nicole Lemaître, "Le Cardinal d'Armagnac et les humanistes des petites villes du Midi," in *L'humanisme à Toulouse (1480–1596): Actes du colloque international de Toulouse, mai 2004*, ed. Nathalie Dauvois (Paris: Honoré Champion, 2006), 203–21.

88. Reproduced in Lemerle, "Guillaume Philandrier et la bibliothèque du cardinal Georges d'Armagnac."

89. On the visit of Charles IX to Toulouse, see the preface to Guillaume Boni, *Primus liber modulorum*, fol. 1 verso, reproduced and translated in Guillaume Boni, *Motets (1573)*, ed. Jeanice Brooks, xxvi–xxvii.

90. See Marco Bizzarini and Massimo Privitera, "Competition, Cultural Geography, and Tonal Space in a Book of Madrigals: *L'Amorosa Ero* (1588)," *Journal of Musicology* 29 (2012): 105–43.

91. Guillaume Boni, *Sonets de P. de Ronsard*, ed. Henry Chandor (Paris: Du Chemin, 1576), chansons nos. 1–2, 9–10, 15–17, 26–27. Such pairings can be found in Boni's second book as well, in which see chansons nos. 5 and 6; 13 and 14; and 20 and 21. On these groupings and the modal implications of them see van Orden, "Vernacular Culture and the Chanson in Paris," 133–39.

92. Dedication reprinted in Guillaume Boni, *Sonetz de P. de Ronsard, mis en musique à quatre parties par Guillaume Boni*, ed. Dobbins (Paris: Éditions Salabert, 1987), 38, translation ibid., 20. In September 1576, a new royal

privilege was granted directly to Boni for the publication of his works and especially for the reprinting of his *Sonetz* by Le Roy & Ballard. It is difficult to judge whether Du Chemin's edition was full of errors, as the privilege claims—only the bassus part from Du Chemin's edition survives. The variants are given in Frank Dobbins's edition of the work. Dobbins (ibid, 19) supposes that Boni may have sought to place the first book and its sequel with Le Roy & Ballard in the wake of Du Chemin's death sometime before July 15, 1576. For the privilege, see Droz, "G. Boni, musicien de Ronsard," 275–76.

93. It is worth noting here that although Boni's *Quatrains du Sieur de Pybrac* is modally ordered, Adrian Le Roy takes credit for having devised the scheme. See the preface in Guillaume Boni, *Les quatrains du Sieur de Pybrac*, fols. Ai verso-Aii recto; a reproduction can be found in the fine recent edition, Guillaume Boni, *Les quatrains du Sieur de Pybrac (1582)*, ed. Marie-Alexis Colin (Tours: Centre de Musique Ancienne, 2000), xliv.

94. The inventory is reproduced in H. Colin Slim, "The Music Library of the Augsburg Patrician, Hans Heinrich Herwart (1520–1583)," *Annales musicologiques* 7 (1964–77): 67–109.

95. For the sonnet by Gabriel de Minut, see Trachier, *Renaissance française*, 4:115.

96. For a study of music printing and the typographical "Renaissance" in mid-century Paris, see Kate van Orden, "Robert Granjon and Music during the Golden Age of Typography," in *Music in Print and Beyond: Hildegard von Bingen to The Beatles*, a festschrift for Jane A. Bernstein, ed. Roberta M. Marvin and Craig A. Monson, Eastman Studies in Music (Rochester, NY: University of Rochester Press, 2013).

97. For an analogous argument about a set of beautifully calligraphed chansonniers from the fifteenth century, see Jane Alden, *Songs, Scribes, and Society: The History and Reception of the Loire Valley Chansonniers* (New York: Oxford University Press, 2010).

98. The single partbook from this collection, which is at the Bibliothèque nationale de France, is incomplete and lacks its title page. Of the sixteen pieces that remain, eight set texts by Ronsard, five by Desportes, and three by unidentified poets.

99. For a good analysis of tract volumes and the information they can provide about collectors, see Mary S. Lewis, "The Printed Music Book in Context: Observations on Some Sixteenth-Century Editions," *Notes* 46 (1990): 899–918. For a brief assessment of survival rates from the sixteenth century and the importance of individual collectors in shaping our historical perspective, see Kate van Orden and Alfredo Vitolo, "Padre Martini, Gaetano Gaspari, and the 'Pagliarini Collection': A Renaissance Music Library Rediscovered," *Early Music History* 29 (2010): 241–324.

100. The copies of Bertrand's *Premier-Troisiesme livre de chansons* at Harvard University and in the Rothschild collection of the Bibliothèque nationale de France may likewise have originally been bound together in the sixteenth

century—both sets are currently bound in nineteenth- or early twentieth-century bindings.

101. Marie-Madeleine Compère and Dominique Julia, *Les collèges français, 16ᵉ–18ᵉ siècles*, 3 vols. (Paris: Centre National de la Recherche Scientifique, 1984–2002), 3:174–86.

102. It is noteworthy that the other copy of Bertrand's *Les Amours de P. de Ronsard* from 1576 in a contemporary binding survives on its own, the superius part in Berkeley.

103. Antoine Furetière, *Dictionnaire universel*, 3 vols. (The Hague and Rotterdam: Arnout and Reinier Leers, 1690), fol. V3 recto, "en fait de Litterature, se dit de tous ceux qui ont mis en lumiere quelque livre. Maintenant on ne le dit que de ceux qui en ont fait imprimer." Also see Roger Chartier, "Figures of the Author," in *The Order of Books*, 25–59.

104. For an important discussion of these bibliographies, see Roger Chartier, "Libraries without Walls," in *The Order of Books*, 61–88.

105. La Croix du Maine, *Premier volume de la bibliotheque du sieur de la Croix du Maine*.

106. Anton Francesco Doni, *La libraria del Doni fiorentino. Nella quale sono scritti tutti gl'autori vulgari con cento discorsi sopra quelli. Tutte le tradutioni fatte dall'altre lingue, nella nostra & una tavola generalmente come si costuma fra librari* (Venice: Gabriel Giolito de Ferrari, 1550). Doni's *Libraria* had just been reprinted in 1580. La Croix du Maine mentions Doni in the dedication to the king.

107. Du Verdier, *La Bibliotheque d'Antoine Du Verdier*. It should be noted that the emphasis on vernacular books completely misrepresents the complexion of contemporary private collections, which included large numbers of the Latin books on theology and canon law used by churchmen and jurists, and surprisingly few recently written books of lyric poetry by comparison with chivalric romances and vernacular prayer books. See Alexander H. Schutz, *Vernacular Books in Parisian Private Libraries of the Sixteenth Century According to the Notarial Inventories* (Chapel Hill: University of North Carolina Press [1955]).

108. Du Verdier, *La Bibliotheque d'Antoine Du Verdier*, 458.

109. La Croix du Maine, *Premier volume de la bibliotheque du sieur de la Croix du Maine*, 141.

5. RESISTING THE PRESS: PERFORMANCE

1. Anthoine de Bertrand, "Au lecteur debonaire," reprinted in Olivier Trachier, ed., *Renaissance française: traités, méthodes, préfaces, ouvrages généraux*, 4 vols. (Courlay, France: Éditions Fuzeau Classique, [2005]), 4:104–5. "Voyla pourquoy en mes chansons j'ay principallement suïvy le Diatonique (as opposed to chromatic or enharmonic genres), tant pour complaire à ceux que la facilité attire & contente, que pour satisfaire à moy-mesme en cecy, qui ne prent moins de plaisir d'oüir animer par la voix mes labeurs tracez sus un

papier que ceux qui plus les desirent, ce que je ne pourrois obtenir que bien rarement la ou je rendrois mes chansons mal-aysées à les manier & chanter."

2. Elizabeth L. Eisenstein, *The Printing Revolution in Early Modern Europe* (Cambridge and New York: Cambridge University Press, 1983), chap. 4.

3. See Roger Chartier, "Libraries without Walls," in *The Order of Books: Readers, Authors, and Libraries in Europe between the Fourteenth and Eighteenth Centuries*, trans. Lydia G. Cochrane (Stanford, CA: Stanford University Press, 1994), 61–88.

4. See "La Croix du Maine (François Grudé), Sieur de," in Louis-Gabriel Michaud, *Biographie universelle ancienne et moderne*, 2nd ed., 45 vols. (Paris: Michaud, 1843–65), 22:406. Du Verdier was *conseilleur du roi* and *contrôleur-général* in Lyon, a very rich man who—like La Croix du Maine—had an extensive private library that he relied on in drawing up his bibliography.

5. Tim Carter, "Printing the 'New Music,' " in *Music and the Cultures of Print*, ed. Kate van Orden with an afterword by Roger Chartier (New York: Garland, 2000), 3–37. Also see Carter, "Artusi, Monteverdi, and the Poetics of Modern Music," in *Musical Humanism and its Legacy: Essays in Honor of Claude V. Palisca*, ed. Nancy Kovaleff Baker and Barbara Russano Hanning (Stuyvesant, NY: Pendragon Press, 1992), 171–94, at 186–88 and 191–92; Carter reconsiders the style-critical debates circa 1600 in light of print culture and the historical awareness facilitated by print.

6. On Maletty, see François Lesure, "Jean de Maletty à Lyon (1583)," in *Musique et musiciens français du XVIᵉ siècle* (Geneva: Minkoff, 1976), 239–42.

7. See Anthoine de Bertrand, *Premier [-Second] livre des Amours de Pierre de Ronsard*, ed. Henry Expert, 2 vols. Monuments de la Musique française au Temps de la Renaissance 4–5 (Paris: Senart, 1926–27). Bertrand's prefaces are reprinted in Trachier, *Renaissance française*, 4: 104–5 and 111. In addition to Expert's introduction to his Bertrand edition, the most extensive studies include Jeanice Brooks, " 'Ses amours et les miennes tout ensemble': La structure cyclique du *Premier Livre* de Anthoine de Bertrand," *Revue de musicologie* 74 (1988): 201–20; Brooks, "Ronsard, the Lyric Sonnet and the Late Sixteenth-Century Chanson," *Early Music History* 13 (1994): 65–84; and Jean-Michel Vaccaro, "Geometry and Rhetoric in Anthoine de Bertrand's *Troisiesme livre de chansons*," *Early Music History* 13 (1994): 217–48. Articles focusing on the prefaces in particular include Beverly Jean Davis, "Antoine de Bertrand: a View into the Aesthetic of Music in XVIth Century France," *Journal of Aesthetics and Art Criticism* 21 (1962–63): 189–200; and Jean-Michel Vaccaro, "Les préfaces d'Anthoine de Bertrand," *Revue de musicologie* 74 (1988): 221–36.

8. Guillaume Boni, *Sonetz de P. de Ronsard, mis en musique à quatre parties par Guillaume Boni*, ed. Frank Dobbins (Paris: Éditions Salabert, 1987); and Boni, *Les quatrains du Sieur de Pybrac (1582)*, ed. Marie-Alexis Colin (Tours: Centre de Musique Ancienne, 2000). On the spiritualized versions of Bertrand's and Boni's Ronsard settings printed in Geneva between 1578 and 1580 (all titled *Sonets chrestiens*), see Laurent Guillo, *Les éditions musicales de la renaissance lyonnaise* (Paris: Klincksieck, 1991), 99–101, and 455–56.

9. The information in this paragraph concerning royal and aristocratic musical establishments summarizes that in Jeanice Brooks, *Courtly Song in Late Sixteenth-Century France* (Chicago: University of Chicago Press, 2000), chap. 2 and appendix 1. Some musicians held two appointments simultaneously, so these numbers are approximate. For a complete account of the archives, see Isabelle Handy, *Musiciens au temps des derniers Valois (1547–1589)* (Paris: Honoré Champion, 2008).

10. On the Countess of Retz and music in her salon, see especially Jeanice Brooks, "La comtesse de Retz et l'air de cour des années 1570," in *Le concert des voix et des instruments à la Renaissance*, ed. Jean-Michel Vaccaro (Paris: Centre National de la Recherche Scientifique, 1995), 299–315. On the circle of the Guises, see Brooks, "Italy, the Ancient World and the French Musical Inheritance in the Sixteenth Century: Arcadelt and Clereau in the Service of the Guises," *Journal of the Royal Musical Association* 121 (1996): 147–90

11. On Mauduit, see Frances A. Yates, *The French Academies of the Sixteenth Century*, 2nd ed. (London and New York: Routledge, 1988), 30–31, 73–75.

12. Ibid., 251–56; Handy, *Musiciens*, 267–78.

13. On Costeley and the *puy*, see E. C. Teviotdale, "The Invitation to the Puy d'Évreux," *Current Musicology* 52 (1993): 7–26.

14. For the musicians, see Brooks, *Courtly Song*, appendices 1 and 2; and for the prints (all from Le Roy & Ballard except that from 1583), see François Lesure and Geneviève Thibault, *Bibliographie des éditions d'Adrian Le Roy et Robert Ballard (1551–1598)* (Paris: Société Française de Musicologie, 1955). A quick comparison of these two sources reveals that during the period 1569–96, Le Roy & Ballard printed only four single-composer collections by court musicians (I count first editions only, but include every polyphonic genre): Pierre Bonnet (1), Costeley (1), La Grotte (1), and Balthasar de Beaujoyeulx (1). Circling outward, the composers printed by Le Roy & Ballard who frequented the court include Fabrice Marin Caietain (in the employ of the Guise family: 4 prints), Le Jeune (member of Baïf's Academy who served a series of Huguenot nobles: 3), Adrian Le Roy (2), Jean Planson (organist at Saint-Germain-l'Auxerrois: 2), and Pietro Vecoli (whose patron was Sebastiano Zametti, an Italian financier and familiar at court: 1). Jacques Mauduit (1) is a unique case: a gentleman-composer and member of Baïf's Academy. The other living composers printed by Le Roy & Ballard in this period are: Bertrand (4), Boni (5), Jean de Castro (2), Antonio Condomirio (1), Jacob de Kerle (1), Lassus (21), Didier Le Blanc (2), Maletty (2), Philippe de Monte (1), Richard Renvoicy (1), François Regnard (1), François Roussel (1), Guillaume Thessier (1), and Regolo Vecoli (1); thanks to the phenomenal output of Lassus, 28—almost half of the 61 collections tallied here—were composed by musicians living outside of France.

15. For an overview of the complicated publication history of two such groups of poems, see Pierre de Ronsard, *Oeuvres complètes*, ed. Jean Céard, Daniel Ménager, Michel Simonin, 2 vols. (Paris Gallimard, 1993–94), 2: 1343–44 and 1373–76.

16. Handy, *Musiciens*, 321–29, 353–55.

17. See ibid., 317–21; and Jeanice Brooks, "*O quelle armonye*: Dialogue Singing in Late Renaissance France," *Early Music History* 22 (2003): 1–65.

18. See the directions to the *musique de la chambre* from 1578 in Brooks, *Courtly Song*, 93; and Handy, *Musiciens*, 39–56.

19. The La Grotte fantasy is on Rore's "Ancor che col partire"; see Frank Dobbins, "The Amateur, the Professional, and the Secret Instrumental Art: The Conflicting Evidence of Biography and Bibliography," in *Le concert des voix et des instruments à la Renaissance*, ed. Jean-Michel Vaccaro (Paris: Centre National de la Recherche Scientifique, 1995), 545–78, at 573–74. Also see Albert Cohen, "The 'Fantaisie' for Instrumental Ensemble in 17th-Century France—Its Origin and Significance," *Musical Quarterly* 48 (1962): 234–43.

20. For an analogous argument about the cultural prioritization of improvisation in the aristocratic zones inhabited by early monody, see Michael Markham, "The Heritage of Campaspe: Oral Tradition and Giulio Caccini's 'Le nuove musiche' (1602)" (Ph.D. diss., University of California, Berkeley, 2006)

21. On official readers see Roger Chartier, *Forms and Meanings: Texts, Performances, and Audiences from Codex to Computer* (Philadelphia: University of Pennsylvania Press, 1995), 40–41; William Nelson, "From 'Listen, Lordings' to 'Dear Reader,'" *University of Toronto Quarterly: A Canadian Journal of the Humanities* 46 (1976–77): 110–24; and Anthony Grafton and Lisa Jardine, " 'Studied for Action': How Gabriel Harvey Read His Livy," *Past and Present* 129 (1990): 30–78. On Louis XIV, see Henri-Jean Martin, *The French Book: Religion, Absolutism, and Readership, 1585–1715*, trans. Paul Saenger and Nadine Saenger (Baltimore and London: Johns Hopkins University Press, 1996), 49–50.

22. Brian Richardson, *Printing, Writers, and Readers in Renaissance Italy* (Cambridge and New York: Cambridge University Press, 1999), 112.

23. On Le Roy, see Yates, *The French Academies*, 49; and Handy, *Musiciens*, 44. On Beaulieu, Doria, Vaumesnil, and Courville, see Brooks, "*O quelle armonye*," esp. 10, 13, and 21–24.

24. The principal studies of the sixteenth-century *air de cour* are Brooks, *Courtly Song*; and Georgie Durosoir, *L'air de cour en France, 1571–1655* (Liège: Mardaga, 1991).

25. See the preface to Adrian Le Roy, *Livre d'airs de cour miz sur le luth* (Paris: Le Roy & Ballard, 1571), reprinted with a translation in Brooks, *Courtly Song*, 13–14. On the *voix de ville* see Daniel Heartz, "*Voix de ville*: Between Humanist Ideals and Musical Realities," in *Words and Music: The Scholar's View*, ed, Laurence Berman (Cambridge, MA: Harvard University Press, 1972), 115–35; and Jane Ozenberger Whang, "From *Voix de ville* to *Air de cour*: The Strophic Chanson c. 1545–1575" (Ph.D. diss., University of North Carolina, Chapel Hill, 1981). Jeanice Brooks unravels some of the difficulties defining the *air de cour* and gives a helpful list of prints of strophic chansons from 1559 to 1589—no matter what generic designation printers assigned to them—in *Courtly Song*, 21–22.

26. For a moving recording of "Laissez la verde couleur" made by a violin band working entirely from memory using sixteenth-century performance techniques, listen to Ellen Hargis and The King's Noyse, David Douglass, director, *Le Jardin de Mélodies: 16th-c French Dances and Songs* (Los Angeles: Harmonia Mundi, 1997) HMU 907194. Working with Hargis, Douglass, and The King's Noyse on this recording gave me an entirely new appreciation for the power of long strophic songs in performance, and I thank them for coping with extremely fragmentary musical materials—sometimes only a melody.

27. See Teviotdale, "Puy d' Évreux"; and Guillaume Boni, *Sonetz de P. de Ronsard mis en musique a quatre parties . . . Second livre* (Paris: Le Roy & Ballard, 1594), fol. Aii. "Ne penses point toy qui entens ces Chans, Que pour avoir quelque bruit en cet age Je mette' au jour ce mien petit ouvrage, Que j'ay tracé durant mes tendres ans. Car je sçay bien qu'il y a en ce temps Plusieurs Espris ayant l'art et l'usage Pour mieux escrire à qui c'est advantage Est reservé comme les plus sçavans." Quoted and translated in Boni, *Sonetz de P. de Ronsard,* ed. Dobbins, 12, 20–21.

28. For the statutes of the Académie, see Yates, *The French Academies,* appendix 1. See the classic scholarship on *musique mesurée* by Yates, *The French Academies;* and D.P. Walker, whose essays are collected in *Music, Spirit, and Language in the Renaissance,* ed. Penelope Gouk (London: Variorum Reprints, 1985).

29. On Le Blanc's print, see Durosoir, *L'air de cour en France,* esp. 34–35, 40–62; and Brooks, *Courtly Song,* esp. 299–301.

30. On Caietain, see Durosoir, *L'air de cour en France,* esp. 34, 44–61; Brooks, *Courtly Song;* the introduction to Fabrice Marin Caietain, *Airs mis en musique . . . Second livre d'airs,* The Sixteenth-Century Chanson 4, ed. Jane A. Bernstein (New York: Garland, 1995), xiii–xix; Frank Dobbins, "Les madrigalistes français et la Pléiade," in *La chanson à la Renaissance: Actes du XXe colloque d'études humanistes du Centre d'Études Supérieures de la Renaissance de l'Université de Tours, juillet 1977,* ed. Jean-Michel Vaccaro (Tours: Editions Van de Velde, 1981), 157–71, at 166–67; and Pascal Desaux, "Fabrice Marin Caietain, maître des enfants du choeur de la cathédrale Saint-Etienne de Toul et maître de musique de Henri de Lorraine, duc de Guise," in *Symphonies Lorraines,* ed. Yves Ferraton (Paris: Klinckseick, 1998), 113–50.

31. For the dedication, see Fabrice Marin Caietain, *Second livre d'airs, chansons, villanelles, napolitaines, & espagnolles mis en musique à quatre parties par Fabrice Marin Caietain* (Paris: Le Roy & Ballard, 1578), fol. Aiv-Aiir; transcribed in Lesure and Thibault, *Bibliographie des éditions d'Adrian Le Roy et Robert Ballard,* 39–40. The dedication is also reproduced in facsimile in Trachier, *Renaissance française,* 4:122–23; and Caietain, *Airs mis en musique . . . Second livre d'airs,* ed. Bernstein, plate 2. For context on the Guises as patrons of music, see Brooks, "Italy, the Ancient World and the French Musical Inheritance in the Sixteenth Century."

32. For the dedication, see Fabrice Marin Caietain, *Airs mis en musique a quatre parties par Fabrice Marin Caietain sur les poësies de P. de Ronsard &*

autres excelens poëtes de nostre tems (Paris: Le Roy & Ballard, 1576), fols. Ai^v-Aii^r; transcribed in Lesure and Thibault, *Bibliographie des éditions d'Adrian Le Roy et Robert Ballard*, 38–39. The dedication from the 1578 reprint is reproduced in facsimile in Caietain, *Airs mis en musique . . . Second livre d'airs,* ed. Bernstein, plate 1.

33. The full title of Petrucci's print is *Strambotti, Ode, Frottole, Sonetti. Et modo de cantar versi latini e capituli. Libro quarto.* [Venice: Petrucci, 1505]. Georgie Durosoir cites Caietain's "He Dieu du ciel" as a later example of the same practice evident in the 1552 *Supplément* to Ronsard's *Les Amours;* see Georgie Durosoir, "Les *Airs mis en musique à 4 parties* (1578) de Fabrice Marin Caietain sur des poésies de Ronsard," *Revue de musicologie* 74 (1988): 189–200, at 192. Jeanice Brooks interprets the song as the result of an Italian influence in France; see Brooks, "Italy, the Ancient World and the French Musical Inheritance in the Sixteenth Century," 186.

34. In 1949, Frances A. Yates cited the dedications as a central piece of evidence in her study of Baïf's Academy in *The French Academies,* 51–52, 238. A short list of subsequent discussions of them (in chronological order) includes Kenneth J. Levy, "Vaudeville, vers mesurés et airs de cours," in *Musique et poésie au XVIe siècle,* ed. Jacques Jacquot (Paris: Centre National de la Recherche Scientifique, 1954), 185–201, at 198; Whang, "From *Voix de ville* to *Air de cour*: The Strophic Chanson c. 1545–1575," 293–96; Durosoir, "Les *Airs mis en musique à 4 parties* (1578) de Fabrice Marin Caietain; Brooks, *Courtly Song,* 146–47; Brooks, "*O quelle armonye,*" 21–22; and Desaux, "Fabrice Marin Caietain," 132–34.

35. This was the subject of Kate van Orden, "Fauxbourdon, Composition, and the Chanson at Paris c. 1550" (paper presented at the Nineteenth Congress of the International Musicological Society, Rome, July 1–7, 2012).

Select Bibliography

MANUSCRIPT SOURCES

A-Wn	Mus. Hs. 18744 (Orlande de Lassus, *Sacrae lectiones ex propheta Iob* and *Prophetiae Sibyllarum*)
B-Br	MS 11239 (Chanson Album of Marguerite of Austria)
F-Pn	MS f. fr. 1584 (Machaut MS "A")
	MS f. fr. 1585 (Machaut MS "B")
	MS f. fr. 1586 (Machaut MS "C")
	MS f. fr. 9221 (Machaut MS "E")
	MS f. fr. 22545–22546 (Machaut MSS "F-G")
	MS f. fr. 25566 (La Vallière MS)
GB-Cccc	Machaut MS "Vg" (Ferrell-Vogüé MS)
I-RVat	C.S. 18 (Costanzo Festa, Hymns and Magnificats)
	C.S. 163 (Carpentras, Lamentations)

PRINTED SOURCES

Agee, Richard J. "The Venetian Privilege and Music-Printing in the Sixteenth Century." *Early Music History* 3 (1983): 1–42.

Agnel, Aimé and Richard Freedman. "Certon, Pierre." In Grove Music Online, www.oxfordmusiconline.com (accessed May 3, 2012).

Ahern, John. "Singing the Book: Orality in the Reception of Dante's *Comedy*." In *Dante: Contemporary Perspectives*. Edited by Amilcare A. Iannucci, 214–39. Toronto: University of Toronto Press, 1997.

Alden, Jane. *Songs, Scribes, and Society: The History and Reception of the Loire Valley Chansonniers*. New York: Oxford University Press, 2010.

Alduy, Cécile. "Lyric Economies: Manufacturing Values in French Petrarchan Collections (1549–1560)." *Renaissance Quarterly* 63 (2010): 721–53.

———. *Politique des "amours": poétique et genèse d'un genre français nouveau (1544–1560)*. Travaux d'Humanisme et Renaissance 422. Geneva: Droz, 2007.

Antiphonarium romanum. Venice: Luc'Antonio Giunta, 1503–4.

Arbeau, Thoinot. *Orchésographie. Et traicte en forme de dialogue, par lequel toutes personnes peuvent facilement apprendre & practiquer l'honneste exercice [des] dances*. Langres, 1589.

Arcadelt, Jacques. *Missae tres*. Paris: Le Roy & Ballard, 1557.

———. *Opera Omnia*. Edited by Albert Seay. Corpus Mensurabilis Musicae 31. 10 vols. [Rome]: American Institute of Musicology, 1965–70.

———. *Tiers livre de chansons nouvellement composé en musique a quatre parties par M. Jacques Arcadet*. Paris: Le Roy & Ballard, 1561.

Armstrong, Elizabeth. *Before Copyright: The French Book-Privilege System, 1498–1526*. Cambridge Studies in Publishing and Printing History. Cambridge: Cambridge University Press, 1990.

Atlas, Allan W. *The Cappella Giulia Chansonnier (Rome, Biblioteca Apostolica Vaticana, C.G.XIII.27)*. 2 vols. Brooklyn: Institute of Mediaeval Music, 1975–76.

Babelon, Jean-Pierre. *Paris au XVIᵉ siècle*. Paris: Hachette, 1986.

Baïf, Jean-Antoine de. *Les amours de Jan Antoine de Baif*. Paris: Veuve Maurice de la Porte, 1552.

———. *Chansonnettes*. Edited by G.C. Bird. Vancouver: University of British Columbia Press, 1964.

———. *Quatre livres de l'amour de Francine*. Paris: André Wechel, 1555.

Barbier, Jean-Paul. *Ma bibliothèque poétique. Éditions des 15e et 16e siècles des principaux poètes français*. 4 parts, part 4 in 4 vols. Geneva: Droz, 1973.

Belleau, Rémy. *Les Odes d'Anacreon Teien, traduites de Grec en François . . . par Remi Belleau ensemble quelques petites hymnes de son invention*. Paris: André Wechel, 1556.

Bent, Margaret. "The Machaut Manuscripts *Vg, B,* and *E*." *Musica Disciplina* 37 (1983): 53–82.

Berchem, Jacquet. *Madrigali a cinque voci . . . libro primo*. Venice: Gardane, 1546.

Bergquist, Peter. "The Poems of Orlando di Lasso's 'Prophetiae Sibyllarum' and Their Sources." *Journal of the American Musicological Society* 32 (1979): 516–38.

Bernstein, Jane A. "Financial Arrangements and the Role of Printer and Composer in Sixteenth-Century Italian Music Printing." *Acta Musicologica* 63 (1991): 39–56.

———, ed. *French Chansons of the Sixteenth Century*. University Park, PA: Pennsylvania State University Press, 1985.

———. "Made to Order: Choirbook Publications in Cinquecento Rome." In *Uno gentile et subtile ingenio: Studies in Renaissance Music in Honour of Bonnie J. Blackburn.* Edited by Jennifer Bloxam, Gioia Fiolcamo, and Leofranc Holford-Strevens, Collection "Épitome Musical." 669–76. Turnhout: Brepols, 2009.

———. *Music Printing in Renaissance Venice: The Scotto Press, 1539–1572.* New York: Oxford University Press, 1998.

———. *Print Culture and Music in Sixteenth-Century Venice.* Oxford: Oxford University Press, 2001.

———. "Publish or Perish? Palestrina and Print Culture in 16th-Century Italy." *Early Music* 35 (2007): 225–35.

Bernstein, Jane A., ed. *The Sixteenth-Century Chanson.* 30 vols. New York: Garland, 1987–1995.

Bernstein, Lawrence F. "The Bibliography of Music in Conrad Gesner's *Pandectae* (1548)." *Acta Musicologica* 45 (1973): 119–63.

———. "Claude Gervaise as Chanson Composer." *Journal of the American Musicological Society* 18 (1965): 359–81.

———. "The 'Parisian Chanson': Problems of Style and Terminology." *Journal of the American Musicological Society* 31 (1978): 193–240.

Bertrand, Anthoine de. *Les Amours de P. de Ronsard, mises en musique a quatre parties.* Paris: Le Roy & Ballard, 1576.

———. *Premier [-Second] livre des Amours de Pierre de Ronsard.* Edited by Henry Expert. 2 vols. Monuments de la Musique française au Temps de la Renaissance 4–5. Paris: Senart, 1926–27.

———. *Premier [-Second] livre de Sonets chrestiens mis en musique à quatre parties.* Edited by Simon Goulart. [Geneva]: [Jean Le Royer], 1580.

———. *Second livre des Amours de P. de Ronsard, mises en musique à IIII. parties.* Paris: Le Roy & Ballard, 1578.

———. *Troisiesme livre de chansons.* Paris: Le Roy & Ballard, 1578.

Bizzarini, Marco, and Massimo Privitera. "Competition, Cultural Geography, and Tonal Space in a Book of Madrigals: *L'Amorosa Ero* (1588)." *Journal of Musicology* 29 (2012): 105–43.

Blackburn, Bonnie J. "A Lost Isaac Manuscript." In *Musica Franca: Essays in Honor of Frank A. D'Accone.* Edited by Irene Alm, Alyson McLamore, and Colleen Reardon. Festschrift Series 18. 19–44. Stuyvesant, NY: Pendragon Press, 1996.

———. "Music and Festivities at the Court of Leo X: A Venetian View." *Early Music History* 11 (1992): 1–37.

———. "Petrucci's Venetian Editor: Petrus Castellanus and His Musical Garden." *Musica Disciplina* 49 (1995): 15–45.

Boetticher, Wolfgang. *Orlando di Lasso und seine Zeit, 1532–1594: Repertoire-Untersuchungen zur Musik der Spätrenaissance.* 2 vols. Quellenkataloge zur Musikgeschichte 27. Kassel: Bärenreiter, 1958. Repr. Wilhelmshaven: Florian Noetzel, Heinrichshofen, 1999.

Bonagionta, Giulio, et al, *Canzone napolitane a tre voci, secondo libro*. Venice: Scotto, 1566.

Boni, Guillaume. *Motets (1573)*. Edited by Jeanice Brooks. Tours: Centre de Musique Ancienne, 2000.

———. *Primus liber modulorum quinis, senis, & septenis vocibus*. Paris: Le Roy & Ballard, 1573.

———. *Les quatrains du Sieur de Pybrac*. Paris: Le Roy & Ballard, 1582.

———.*Les quatrains du Sieur de Pybrac (1582)*. Edited by Marie-Alexis Colin. Tours: Centre de Musique Ancienne, 2000.

———. *Sonetz chrestiens mis en musique à quatre parties par G. Boni de S. Flour en Auvergne. Premier [-Second] livre*. Edited by Simon Goulart. [Geneva]: [Jean Le Royer for Charles Pesnot in Lyon], 1578–1579.

———. *Sonets de P. de Ronsard, mis en musique à quatre parties*. Edited by Henry Chandor. Paris: Du Chemin, 1576.

———. *Sonetz de P. de Ronsard, mis en musique a quatre parties . . . Premier livre*. Paris: Le Roy & Ballard, 1576.

———. *Sonetz de P. de Ronsard mis en musique a quatre parties . . . Second livre*. Paris: Le Roy & Ballard, 1576.

———. *Sonetz de P. de Ronsard mis en musique a quatre parties . . . Second livre*. Paris: Le Roy & Ballard, 1594.

———. *Sonetz de P. de Ronsard, mis en musique a quatre parties par Guillaume Boni*. Edited by Frank Dobbins. Paris: Éditions Salabert, 1987.

Boorman, Stanley. "Early Music Printing: An Indirect Contact with the Raphael Circle." In *Renaissance Studies in Honor of Craig Hugh Smyth*. 2 vols. Edited by Andrew Morrogh, 1:533–50. Florence: Barbèra, 1985.

———. *Ottaviano Petrucci: Catalogue Raisonné*. New York: Oxford University Press, 2006.

Bossuyt, Ignace. "The Copyist Jan Pollet and the Theft in 1563 of Orlandus Lassus' 'Secret' Penitential Psalms." In *From Ciconia to Sweelinck: Donum natalicium Willem Elders*. Edited by Albert Clement and Eric Jas, 261–67. Amsterdam: Rodopi, 1994.

Boucaut-Graille, Audrey. "Les éditeurs de musique parisiens et leurs publics: 1528–1598." Ph.D. diss., Tours, Centre d'Études Supérieures de la Renaissance, 2007.

———. "L'imprimeur et son conseiller musical: les stratégies éditoriales de Nicolas du Chemin (1549–1555)." *Revue de musicologie* 91 (2005): 5–25.

Bourgain, Pascal. "L'édition des manuscrits." In *Le livre conquérant*. 49–75. Volume 1 of *Histoire de l'édition française*. Edited by Henri-Jean Martin and Roger Chartier. 4 vols. Paris: Promodis, 1982–86.

Bradshaw, Murray C. *The Falsobordone. A Study in Renaissance and Baroque Music*. Stuttgart: American Institute of Musicology, 1978.

Brauner, Mitchell P. "The Parvus Manuscripts: A Study of Vatican Polyphony, ca. 1535 to 1580." Ph.D. diss., Brandeis University, 1982.

Bridges, Thomas W. "The Publishing of Arcadelt's First Book of Madrigals." 2 vols. Ph.D. diss., Harvard University, 1982.

Brobeck, John T. "Musical Patronage in the Royal Chapel of France under Francis I (r. 1515–1547)." *Journal of the American Musicological Society* 48 (1995): 187–239.

Brooks, Jeanice. "La comtesse de Retz et l'air de cour des années 1570." In *Le concert des voix et des instruments à la Renaissance*. Edited by Jean-Michel Vaccaro, 299–315. Paris: Centre National de la Recherche Scientifique, 1995.

———. *Courtly Song in Late Sixteenth-Century France*. Chicago: University of Chicago Press, 2000.

———. "Italy, the Ancient World and the French Musical Inheritance in the Sixteenth Century: Arcadelt and Clereau in the Service of the Guises." *Journal of the Royal Musical Association* 121 (1996): 147–90.

———. "*O quelle armonye*: Dialogue Singing in Late Renaissance France." *Early Music History* 22 (2003): 1–65.

———. "Ronsard, the Lyric Sonnet and the Late Sixteenth-Century Chanson." *Early Music History* 13 (1994): 65–84.

———. "'Ses amours et les miennes tout ensemble': La structure cyclique du *Premier Livre* de Anthoine de Bertrand." *Revue de musicologie* 74 (1988): 201–20.

Brooks, Laura J. "French Chanson Collections on the Texts of Ronsard." Ph.D. diss., Catholic University of America, 1990.

Brown, Cynthia J. *Poets, Patrons, and Printers: Crisis of Authority in Late Medieval France*. Ithaca, NY, and London: Cornell University Press, 1995.

———. *The Shaping of History and Poetry in Late Medieval France: Propaganda and Artistic Expression in the Works of the Rhétoriqueurs*. Birmingham, AL: Summa, 1985.

———. "Text, Image, and Authorial Self-Consciousness in Late Medieval Paris." In *Printing the Written Word: The Social History of Books, circa 1450–1520*. Edited by Sandra L. Hindman, 103–42. Ithaca, NY, and London: Cornell University Press, 1991.

Brown, H. F. *The Venetian Printing Press 1469–1600*. London: J. C. Nimmo, 1891.

Brown, Howard Mayer. "The *Chanson rustique*: Popular Elements in the 15th- and 16th-Century Chanson." *Journal of the American Musicological Society* 12 (1959): 16–26.

———. "The Genesis of a Style: The Parisian Chanson, 1500–1530." In *Chanson and Madrigal, 1480–1530*. Edited by James Haar, 1–50. Cambridge, MA: Harvard University Press, 1964.

———. *Music in the French Secular Theater, 1400–1550*. 2 vols. Cambridge, MA: Harvard University Press, 1963.

———. "A 'New' Chansonnier of the Early Sixteenth Century in the University Library of Uppsala: A Preliminary Report." *Musica Disciplina* 37 (1983): 171–233.

———. "Theory and Practice in the Sixteenth Century: Preliminary Notes on Attaingnant's Modally Ordered Chansonniers." In *Essays in*

Musicology: A Tribute to Alvin Johnson. Edited by Lewis Lockwood and Edward Roesner, 75–100. Philadelphia: American Musicological Society, 1990.

———, ed. *A Florentine Chansonnier from the Time of Lorenzo the Magnificent: Florence, Biblioteca Nazionale Centrale, MS Banco Rari 229.* Monuments of Renaissance Music 7. 2 vols. Chicago: University of Chicago Press, 1983.

Brown, Howard Mayer, and Richard Freedman. "Chanson" §3, "1525 to the mid-16th century." In Grove Music Online. www.oxfordmusiconline.com (accessed April 28, 2011).

———. "Janequin, Clément." In Grove Music Online. www.oxfordmusiconline.com (accessed May 3, 2012).

Butt, John. "The Seventeenth-Century Musical 'Work.'" In *The Cambridge History of Seventeenth-Century Music.* Edited by Tim Carter and John Butt, 27–54. Cambridge: Cambridge University Press, 2005.

Butterfield, Ardis. "Articulating the Author: Gower and the French Vernacular Codex." *Yearbook of English Studies* 33 (2003): 80–96.

———. *Poetry and Music in Medieval France: From Jean Renart to Guillaume de Machaut.* Cambridge: Cambridge University Press, 2002.

Caietain, Fabrice Marin. *Airs mis en musique a quatre parties par Fabrice Marin Caietain sur les poësies de P. de Ronsard & autres excelens poëtes de nostre tems.* Paris: Le Roy & Ballard, 1576.

———. *Airs mis en musique . . . Second livre d'airs.* The Sixteenth-Century Chanson 4. Edited by Jane A. Bernstein. New York: Garland, 1995.

———. *Second livre d'airs, chansons, villanelles, napolitaines, & espagnolles mis en musique à quatre parties par Fabrice Marin Caietain.* Paris: Le Roy & Ballard, 1578.

Canguilhem, Philippe. "Le projet FABRICA: Oralité et écriture dans les pratiques polyphoniques du chant ecclésiastique (XVIᵉ–XXᵉ siècles)." *Journal of the Alamire Foundation* 2 (2010): 272–81.

———. "Les sources écrites du faux-bourdon au 16ᵉ siècle: un cas-limite de 'composition' à la Renaissance." Paper presented at the session "Music between *extempore* performance and *opus perfectum et absolutum.*" Nineteenth Congress of the International Musicological Society, Rome, Italy, July 2012.

Canti B. numero cinquanta B. Venice: Ottaviano Petrucci, 1502.

Canti C. No. centi cinquinta. Venice: Ottaviano Petrucci, 1504.

Canzoni, sonetti, strambotti et frottole libro quarto. Rome: Antico, 1517.

Canzoni, sonetti, strambotti e frottole libro tertio. Rome: Antico, 1513,

Cardamone, Donna G., and David L. Jackson. "Multiple Formes and Vertical Setting in Susato's First Edition of Lassus's 'Opus 1.'" *Music Library Association Notes,* 2nd Ser., 46 (1989): 7–24.

Carley, James P., ed. *The Libraries of King Henry VIII.* Corpus of British Medieval Library Catalogues 7. London: British Library and British Academy, 2000.

Carpentras (Elzéar Genet). *Liber lamentationum Hieremiae prophetae Carpentras*. Avignon: Jean de Channey, 1532.

———. *Liber primus missarum Carpentras*. Avignon: Jean de Channey, 1532.

———. *Eliziarii Geneti (Carpentras) Opera Omnia*. Edited by Albert Seay. Corpus Mensurabilis Musicae 58. 5 vols. [N.p.]: American Institute of Musicology, 1972–73.

Carter, Tim. "Artusi, Monteverdi, and the Poetics of Modern Music." In *Musical Humanism and its Legacy: Essays in Honor of Claude V. Palisca*. Edited by Nancy Kovaleff Baker and Barbara Russano Hanning, 171–94. Stuyvesant, NY: Pendragon Press, 1992.

———. "Printing the 'New Music.'" In *Music and the Cultures of Print*. Edited by Kate van Orden with an afterword by Roger Chartier, 3–37. New York: Garland, 2000.

Cartier, Alfred, and Adolphe Chenevière. "Antoine du Moulin: valet de chambre de la reine de Navarre." *Revue d'histoire littéraire de la France* 2 (1895): 469–90; and 3 (1896): 90–106.

Castiglione, Baldassare. *The Courtier*. Translated by George Bull. London: Penguin Classics, 1976.

Castro, Jean de. *Chansons, odes, et sonetz de Pierre Ronsard, mises en musique a quatre, a cinq et huit parties*. Louvain: Pierre Phalèse, and Antwerp: Jean Bellère, 1576.

Cave, Terence. *The Cornucopian Text: Problems of Writing in the French Renaissance*. Oxford: Clarendon Press, 1979.

Cazaux, Christelle. *La musique à la cour de François Ier*. Paris: École nationale des Chartes and Tours: Centre d'Études Supérieures de la Renaissance, 2002.

Cazeaux, Isabelle, and John T. Brobeck. "Sermisy, Claudin de." In Grove Music Online. www.oxfordmusiconline.com (accessed April 27, 2011).

Certon, Pierre. *Les meslanges de maistre Pierre Certon*. Paris: Nicolas Du Chemin, 1570.

———. *Premier livre de chansons en quatre parties, par M. Pierre Certon*. Paris: Le Roy & Ballard, 1552.

Chang, Leah L. *Into Print: The Production of Female Authorship in Early Modern France*. Newark, DE: University of Delaware Press, 2009.

Chapman, Catherine Weeks. "Andrea Antico." Ph.D. diss., Harvard University, 1964.

Chappuys, Claude. *Discours de la court*. Paris: Roffet, 1543.

Chardavoine, Jean. *Le recueil des plus belles et excellentes chansons en forme de voix de ville*. Paris: Claude Micard, 1576.

Chartier, Roger. *The Cultural Uses of Print in Early Modern France*. Translated by Lydia G. Cochrane. Princeton, NJ: Princeton University Press, 1987.

———. *Forms and Meanings: Texts, Performances, and Audiences from Codex to Computer*. Philadelphia: University of Pennsylvania Press, 1995.

————. *The Order of Books: Readers, Authors, and Libraries in Europe be-tween the Fourteenth and Eighteenth Centuries.* Translated by Lydia G. Cochrane. Stanford, CA: Stanford University Press, 1994.

————. "Property and Privilege in the Republic of Letters." Translated by Arthur Goldhammer. *Daedalus* 131 (2002): 60–66.

————. *Publishing Drama in Early Modern Europe.* The Panizzi Lectures 1998. London: British Library, 1999.

Christoffersen, Peter Woetmann. *French Music in the Early Sixteenth Century: Studies in the Music Collection of a Copyist of Lyons; The Manuscript 'Ny kgl. Samling 1848 2° in the Royal Library, Copenhagen.* 3 vols. Denmark: Museum Tusculanum Press, University of Copenhagen, 1994.

Clereau, Pierre. *Dixiesme livre de chansons tant Françoises qu'Italiennes nouvellement composées à quatre parties.* Paris: Le Roy & Ballard, 1559.

————. *Les odes de Pierre de Ronsard.* Edited by Jane A. Bernstein. The Sixteenth-Century Chanson 7. New York: Garland, 1988.

————. *Premier livre de chansons tant Françoises qu'Italiennes nouvellement composées à trois parties.* Paris: Le Roy & Ballard, 1559.

————. *Premier livre d'odes de Ronsard mis en Musique à troys parties.* Paris: Le Roy & Ballard, 1566.

————. *Second livre d'odes de Ronsard mis en Musique à troys parties.* Paris: Le Roy & Ballard, 1566.

Clough, Cecil H. "A Presentation Volume for Henry VIII: The Charlecote Park Copy of Erasmus's *Institutio principis Christiani.*" *Journal of the Warburg and Courtauld Institutes* 44 (1981): 199–202.

Coeurdevey, Annie. *Bibliographie des oeuvres poétiques de Clément Marot mises en musique dans les recueils profanes du XVIe siècle.* Paris: Honoré Champion, 1997.

Cohen, Albert. "The 'Fantaisie' for Instrumental Ensemble in 17th-Century France—Its Origin and Significance," *Musical Quarterly* 48 (1962): 234–43.

Colwin, Laurie. *Home Cooking: A Writer in the Kitchen.* New York: Harper, 2000.

Compère, Marie-Madeleine, and Dominique Julia. *Les collèges français, 16e–18e siècles.* 3 vols. Paris: Centre National de la Recherche Scientifique, 1984–2002.

Corteccia, Francesco. *Libro primo de madrigali a quattro voci.* Venice: Scotto, 1544.

Costeley, Guillaume. *Guillaume Costeley, Selected Chansons.* Edited by Jane A. Bernstein. The Sixteenth-Century Chanson 8. New York: Garland, 1989.

————. *Musique de Guillaume Costeley, organiste ordinaire et vallet de chambre, du treschrestien et tresinvincible roy de France, Charles IX.* Paris: Le Roy & Ballard, 1570.

Cusick, Suzanne G. *Valerio Dorico: Music Printer in Sixteenth-Century Rome*. Ann Arbor, MI: UMI Research Press, 1981.

Cy est le Romant de la roze. Edited by Clément Marot. Paris: Galliot Du Pré [1526].

Dalbanne, Claude. "Robert Granjon, imprimeur de musique." *Gutenberg Jahrbuch* 14 (1939): 226–232.

Darnton, Robert. *The Kiss of Lamourette: Reflections in Cultural History*. Rev. ed. New York: Norton, 1990.

Davis, Beverly Jean. "Antoine de Bertrand: a View into the Aesthetic of Music in XVIth Century France." *Journal of Aesthetics and Art Criticism* 21 (1962–63): 189–200.

Dean, Winton. *Handel's Operas, 1726–1741*. Woodbridge, UK, and Rochester, NY: Boydell Press, 2006.

———. and John Merrill Knapp, *Handel's Operas, 1704–1726*. Oxford and New York: Clarendon Press, 1987.

Demerson, Guy, ed. *La notion de genre à la Renaissance*. Geneva: Slatkine, 1984.

Desan, Philippe. "The Tribulations of a Young Poet: Ronsard from 1547 to 1552." In *Renaissance Rereadings: Intertext and Context*. Edited by Maryanne Cline Horowitz, Anne Cruz, and Wendy Furman, 184–202. Urbana and Chicago: University of Illinois Press, 1988.

Desan, Philippe, and Kate van Orden, "De la chanson à l'ode: musique et poésie sous le mécénat du cardinal Charles de Lorraine." In *Le mécénat et l'influence des Guises*. Edited by Yvonne Bellenger, 463–87. Paris: Honoré Champion, 1996.

Desaux, Pascal. "Fabrice Marin Caietain, maître des enfants du choeur de la cathédrale Saint-Etienne de Toul et maître de musique de Henri de Lorraine, duc de Guise." In *Symphonies Lorraines*. Edited by Yves Ferraton, 113–50. Paris: Klincksieck, 1998.

Destrez, Jean. *La "Pecia" dans les manuscrits universitaires du XIIIe et du XIVe siècle*. Paris: Éditions Jacques Vautrain, 1935.

Di Cipriano Rore et di altri eccellentissimi musici il terzo libro di madrigali a cinque voce. Venice: Scotto, 1548.

Di Constantio Festa il primo libro de madrigali a tre voci, con la gionta de quaranta madrigali di Ihan Gero . . . aggiuntovi similmente trenta canzoni francese di Janequin. Venice: Gardane, 1541.

Diderot, Denis. "Diderot's Letter on the Book Trade, Paris (1763)." In *Primary Sources on Copyright (1450–1900)*. Edited by L. Bently and M. Kretschmer, 16. www.copyrighthistory.org (accessed October 19, 2012).

Dillon, Emma. *Medieval Music-Making and the* Roman de Fauvel. Cambridge and New York: Cambridge University Press, 2002.

Dobbins, Frank. "The Amateur, the Professional, and the Secret Instrumental Art: The Conflicting Evidence of Biography and Bibliography." In *Le concert des voix et des instruments à la Renaissance*. Edited by Jean-Michel Vaccaro, 545–78. Paris: Centre National de la Recherche Scientifique, 1995.

———. "Bertrand, Anthoine de." In Grove Music Online. www.oxfordmusiconline.com (accessed May 27, 2011).

———. "Boni, Guillaume." In Grove Music Online. www.oxfordmusiconline.com (accessed May 27, 2011).

———. "Les madrigalistes français et la Pléiade." In *La chanson à la Renaissance: Actes du XXe colloque d'études humanistes du Centre d'Études Supérieures de la Renaissance de l'Université de Tours, juillet 1977*. Edited by Jean-Michel Vaccaro, 157–71. Tours: Éditions Van de Velde, 1981.

———. "Maletty, Jean de." In Grove Music Online. www.oxfordmusiconline.com (accessed May 27, 2011).

———. *Music in Renaissance Lyons*. Oxford: Clarendon Press, 1992.

———. "Ronsard, Pierre de." In Grove Music Online. www.oxfordmusiconline.com (accessed May 27, 2011).

———. "Ronsard et ses musiciens Toulousains." In *L'humanisme à Toulouse (1480–1596): Actes du colloque international de Toulouse, mai 2004*. Edited by Nathalie Dauvois, 459–82. Paris: Honoré Champion, 2006.

Doni, Anton Francesco. *Dialogo della musica*. Venice: Girolamo Scotto, 1544.

———. *La libraria del Doni fiorentino. Nella quale sono scritti tutti gl'autori vulgari con cento discorsi sopra quelli. Tutte le traditioni fatte dall'altre lingue, nella nostra & una tavola generalmente come si costuma fra librari.* Venice: Gabriel Giolito de Ferrari, 1550.

Droz, E. (Eugénie). "G. Boni, musicien de Ronsard." In *Mélanges offerts à M. Abel Lefranc*, 270–81. Paris: Droz, 1936.

Du Bellay, Joachim. *La deffence et illustration de la langue françoyse* (Paris, 1549). Edited by Henri Chamard. Société des Textes Français Modernes. Paris: Didier, 1970.

———. *Les regrets, Les antiquités de Rome*. Edited by Samuel Silvestre de Sacy. Paris: Gallimard, 1967.

———. *L'Olive et quelques autres oeuvres poeticques. Le contenu de ce livre. Cinquante sonnetz à la louange de l'olive. L'Anterotique de la vieille, & de la jeune amye. Vers lyriques. Par I.D.B.A.* Paris: pour Arnoul L'Angelier, 1549.

Ducrot, A. "Histoire de la Cappella Giulia au XVIe siècle depuis sa fondation par Jules II (1513) jusqu'à sa restauration par Grégoire XIII (1578)." *Mélanges d'archéologie et d'histoire* 75 (1963): 179–240, 467–559.

Duggan, Mary Kay. *Italian Music Incunabula: Printers and Type*. Berkeley: University of California Press, 1992.

Du Guillet, Pernette. *Louise Labé, Oeuvres poétiques, précédées des Rymes de Pernette du Guillet*. Edited by Françoise Charpentier. Paris: Gallimard, 1983.

Durosoir, Georgie. *L'air de cour en France, 1571–1655*. Liège: Mardaga, 1991.

————. "Les *Airs mis en musique à 4 parties* (1578) de Fabrice Marin Caietain sur des poésies de Ronsard." *Revue de musicologie* 74 (1988): 189–200.

Du Verdier, Antoine. *La Bibliotheque d'Antoine Du Verdier, Seigneur de Vauprivas: Contenant le Catalogue de tous ceux qui ont escrit, ou traduict en François, et autres Dialectes de ce Royaume.* Lyon: Barthélemy Honorat, 1585.

Earp, Lawrence. "Machaut's Role in the Production of Manuscripts of His Works." *Journal of the American Musicological Society* 42 (1989): 461–503.

Eisenstein, Elizabeth L. *The Printing Press as an Agent of Change: Communications and Cultural Transformations in Early Modern Europe.* 2 vols. in 1. Cambridge and New York: Cambridge University Press, 1979.

————. *The Printing Revolution in Early Modern Europe.* Cambridge and New York: Cambridge University Press, 1983.

————. "An Unacknowledged Revolution Revisited." *American Historical Review* 107 (2002): 87–105, 126–28.

Everist, Mark. "The Polyphonic *Rondeau c.* 1300, Repertory and Context." *Early Music History* 15 (1996): 59–96.

Expert, Henry, ed. *La Fleur des musiciens de P. de Ronsard.* Paris: Cité des Livres, 1923.

Fallows, David. "Henry VIII as a Composer." In *Sundry Sorts of Music Books: Essays on the British Library Collections Presented to O. W. Neighbour on His 70th Birthday.* Edited by C. Banks, A. Searle, and M. Turner, 27–39. London: British Library, 1993.

————. "Jean Molinet and the Lost Burgundian Court Chansonniers of the 1470s." In *Gestalt und Entstehung musikalischer Quellen im 15. und 16. Jahrhundert.* Edited by Martin Staehelin, 35–42. Wiesbaden: Harrassowitz Verlag, 1998.

————. *Josquin.* Collection "Épitome Musical." Turnhout: Brepols, 2009.

Farahat, Martha. "Villanescas of the Virtuosi: Lasso and the *Commedia dell'arte.*" *Performance Practice Review* 3 (1990): 121–37.

Febvre, Lucien, and Henri-Jean Martin. *The Coming of the Book: The Impact of Printing, 1450–1800.* Translated by David Gerard. 2nd edition. London and New York: Verso, 1997.

Feldman, Martha. "Authors and Anonyms: Recovering the Anonymous Subject in *Cinquecento* Vernacular Objects." In *Music and the Cultures of Print.* Edited by Kate van Orden with an afterword by Roger Chartier, 163–99. New York: Garland, 2000.

————. *City Culture and the Madrigal at Venice.* Berkeley and Los Angeles: University of California Press, 1995.

Fenlon, Iain. *Music, Print, and Culture in Early Sixteenth-Century Italy.* The Panizzi Lectures 1994. London: British Library, 1995.

Fenlon, Iain, and James Haar. *The Italian Madrigal in the Early Sixteenth Century: Sources and Interpretation.* Cambridge: Cambridge University Press, 1988.

Ferguson, Margaret W. "The Exile's Defense: Du Bellay's *La Deffence et illustration de la langue françoyse.*" *Publications of the Modern Language Association* 93 (1978): 275–89.

Fiorentino, Giuseppe. *"Folía": El origen de los esquemas armónicos entre tradición oral y transmisión escrita.* DeMusica 17. Kassel: Editions Reichenberger, 2013.

Finck, Hermann. *Practica musica* (Wittenberg, 1556). Facsimile edition. Bologna: Forni Editore, 1969.

Finkelstein, David and Alistair McCleery, eds. *The Book History Reader.* London and New York: Routledge, 2002.

Fleury, Gabriel. "Le Prieuré et l'église de Notre-Dame de Mamers." *Revue historique et archéologique du Maine* 38 (1895): 142–74.

Forney, Kristine K. "Orlando di Lasso's 'Opus 1': The Making and Marketing of a Renaissance Music Book." *Revue belge de Musicologie / Belgisch Tijdschrift voor Muziekwetenschap* 39–40 (1985–86): 33–60.

Foucault, Michel. "What Is an Author?" In *Language, Counter-Memory, Practice: Selected Essays and Interviews.* Edited by Donald F. Bouchard. Translated by Donald F. Bouchard and Sherry Simon, 113–38. Ithaca, NY: Cornell University Press, 1977.

Fragonard, Marie-Madeleine. "Ronsard en poète: portrait d'auteur, produit du texte." In *Les Figures du poète, Pierre de Ronsard.* Edited by Marie-Dominique Legrand. *Littérales* 26 (2000): 15–41.

Françon, Marcel. "Sur le premier sonnet français publié." *Bibliothèque d'Humanisme et Renaissance* 33 (1971): 365–66.

Freccero, John. "The Fig Tree and the Laurel: Petrarch's Poetics." *Diacritics* 5 (1975): 34–40.

Freedman, Richard. *The Chansons of Orlando di Lasso and Their Protestant Listeners: Music, Piety, and Print in Sixteenth-Century France.* Eastman Studies in Music. Rochester, NY: University of Rochester Press, 2001.

———. "Clément Janequin, Pierre Attaingnant, and the Changing Image of French Music, ca. 1540." In *Charting Change in France around 1540.* Edited by Marian Rothstein, 63–94. Selinsgrove: Susquehanna University Press, 2006.

———. "From Munich to Paris: Orlando di Lasso, Adrian Le Roy, and Listeners at the Royal Court of France." In *Die Münchner Hofkapelle des 16. Jahrhunderts im europäischen Kontext.* Edited by Theodor Göllner, Bernhold Schmid, and Severin Putz, 143–59. Munich: Bayerische Akademie der Wissenschaften, 2006.

———. "Le Jeune's *Dodecacorde* as a Site for Spiritual Meanings." *Revue de musicologie* 89 (2003): 297–309.

———. "Tradition and Renewal in Du Chemin's *Chansons Nouvelles.*" http://ricercar.cesr.univ-tours.fr/3-programmes/EMN/duchemin/pages/learn.asp (accessed January 23, 2013).

———. "Who Owned Lasso's Chansons?" *Yearbook of the Alamire Foundation* 6 (2008): 159–76.

Freedman, Richard, and Philippe Vendrix, directors. *Les livres de chansons nouvelles de Nicolas Duchemin, 1549–1568.* http://ricercar.cesr.univ-tours .fr/3-programmes/EMN/Duchemin/.

Frottole intabulate da sonare organi. Rome: Antico, 1517.

Furetière, Antoine. *Dictionnaire universel.* 3 vols. The Hague and Rotterdam: Arnout and Reinier Leers, 1690.

Gaillard, Paul André and Richard Freedman "Goudimel, Claude." In Grove Music Online. www.oxfordmusiconline.com (accessed May 3, 2012).

Gallagher, Sean. "The Berlin Chansonnier and French Song in Florence, 1450–1490: A New Dating and Its Implications." *Journal of Musicology* 24 (2007): 339–64.

Gélis, François de. *Histoire critique des jeux floraux.* Toulouse, 1912; repr. Geneva: Droz, 1981.

Gero, Jan. *Primo libro dei madrigali & canzoni francese a doi voci.* Venice: Gardane, 1540.

Godt, Irving. "Guillaume Costeley, Life and Works." 2 vols. Ph.D. diss. New York University, 1970.

Goehr, Lydia. *The Imaginary Museum of Musical Works: An Essay in the Philosophy of Music.* Oxford: Oxford University Press, 1994.

Gossett, Philip. *Divas and Scholars: Performing Italian Opera.* Chicago: University of Chicago Press, 2006.

Goudimel, Claude. *Les cent cinquante pseaumes de David nouvellement mis en Musique à quatre parties.* Paris: Le Roy & Ballard, 1564.

———. *Les Psalmes & Cantiques.* Paris: Le Roy & Ballard, 1583.

———. *Pseaumes de David.* Paris: Le Roy & Ballard, 1562.

Graduale romanum. Venice: Luc'Antonio Giunta, 1499–1500.

Grafton, Anthony. "How Revolutionary Was the Print Revolution?" *American Historical Review* 107 (2002): 84–86.

Grafton, Anthony, and Lisa Jardine, " 'Studied for Action': How Gabriel Harvey Read His Livy." *Past and Present* 129 (1990): 30–78.

Greene, Thomas M. *The Light in Troy: Imitation and Discovery in Renaissance Poetry.* New Haven, CT, and London: Yale University Press, 1982.

Grove's Dictionary of Music and Musicians. Edited by J.A. Fuller Maitland. 5 vols. New York and London: Macmillan, 1904.

Guilielmus Monachus, *Guilielmi Monachi De Preceptis Artis Musicae.* Edited by Albert Seay. Corpus Scriptorum de Musica 11. N.p.: American Institute of Musicology, 1965.

Guillo, Laurent. *Les éditions musicales de la renaissance lyonnaise.* Paris: Klincksieck, 1991.

Haar, James. "Arcadelt and the Frottola: The Italianate Chanson c. 1550." In *Res musicae: Essays in Honor of James Worrell Pruett.* Edited by Paul Laird and Craig Russell, 97–109. Warren, MI: Harmonie Park Press, 2001.

———. "The *Capriccio* of Giachet Berchem: A Study in Modal Organization." *Musica Disciplina* 42 (1988): 129–56.

———. "The Early Madrigals of Lassus." *Revue belge de Musicologie / Belgisch Tijdschrift voor Muziekwetenschap* 39–40 (1985–86): 17–32.

———. *Essays on Italian Poetry and Music in the Renaissance, 1300–1600.* Berkeley and Los Angeles: University of California Press, 1986.

———. "Notes on the 'Dialogo della Musica' of Antonfrancesco Doni." *Music & Letters* 47 (1966): 198–224.

———. "Orlando di Lasso, Composer and Print Entrepreneur." In *Music and the Cultures of Print.* Edited by Kate van Orden with an afterword by Roger Chartier, 125–51. New York: Garland, 2000.

Hamm, Charles. "Manuscript Structure in the Dufay Era," *Acta Musicologica* 34 (1962): 166–84.

Hampton, Timothy. " 'Trafiquer La Louange': L'économie de la poésie dans les *Regrets.*" In *Du Bellay et ses sonnets romains: études sur* Les Regrets *et* Les Antiquitez de Rome. Edited by Yvonne Bellenger and Jean Balsamo, 47–60. Paris: Honoré Champion, 1994.

Handy, Isabelle. *Musiciens au temps des derniers Valois (1547–1589).* Paris: Honoré Champion, 2008.

Harmonice Musices Odhecaton A. Venice: Ottaviano Petrucci, 1501.

Heartz, Daniel. " 'Au pres de vous': Claudin's Chanson and the Commerce of Publishers' Arrangements." *Journal of the American Musicological Society* 24 (1971): 193–225.

———. "Parisian Music Publishing under Henry II: A Propos of Four Recently Discovered Guitar Books." *Musical Quarterly* 46 (1960): 448–67.

———. *Pierre Attaingnant, Royal Printer of Music: A Historical Study and Bibliographical Catalogue.* Berkeley and Los Angeles: University of California Press, 1969.

———. "*Voix de ville*: Between Humanist Ideals and Musical Realities." In *Words and Music: The Scholar's View.* Edited by Laurence Berman, 115–35. Cambridge, MA: Harvard University Press, 1972.

His, Isabelle. *Claude Le Jeune (v. 1530–1600): un compositeur entre Renaissance et Baroque.* Arles: Actes Sud, 2000.

Hoffmann, George. *Montaigne's Career.* Oxford: Clarendon Press, and New York: Oxford University Press, 1998.

Huot, Sylvia. *From Song to Book: The Poetics of Writing in Old French Lyric and Lyrical Narrative Poetry.* Ithaca, NY: Cornell University Press, 1987.

Jeffery, Brian. *Chanson Verse of the Early Renaissance.* 2 vols. London: Tecla, 1971–76.

———. "The Idea of Music in Ronsard's Poetry." In *Ronsard the Poet.* Edited by Terence Cave, 209–39. London: Metheun, 1973.

Jeppesen, Knud. *La Frottola.* 3 vols. Aarhus: Universitetsforlaget i Aarhus, 1968–70.

———. *Die italienische Orgelmusik am Anfang des Cinquecento.* 2 vols. Copenhagen: Hansen, 1960.

Johns, Adrian. "How to Acknowledge a Revolution." *American Historical Review* 107 (2002): 106–25.

―――. *The Nature of the Book: Print and Knowledge in the Making*. Chicago: University of Chicago Press, 1998.

―――. *Piracy: The Intellectual Property Wars from Gutenberg to Gates*. Chicago: University of Chicago Press, 2009.

Josquin des Prez. *Misse Josquin*. Venice: Petrucci, 1502.

―――. *Septiesme livre contenant vingt & quatre chansons a cincq et a six parties composees par feu de bonne memoire & tresexcellent en musicque Josquin des pres*. Antwerp: Susato, 1545.

―――. *Trente sixiesme livre contenant xxx. chansons tres musicales, a quatre cinq & six parties . . . le tout de la composition de feu Josquin des Prez*. Paris: Attaingnant, 1550.

Judd, Cristle Collins. *Reading Renaissance Music Theory: Hearing with the Eyes*. Cambridge: Cambridge University Press, 2000.

Kastan, David Scott. *Shakespeare and the Book*. Cambridge: Cambridge University Press, 2001.

Kellman, Herbert. "The Origins of the Chigi Codex: The Date, Provenance, and Original Ownership of Rome, Biblioteca Vaticana, Chigiana, C. VIII. 234." *Journal of the American Musicological Society* 11 (1958): 6–19.

―――, ed. *The Treasury of Petrus Alamire: Music and Art in Flemish Court Manuscripts, 1500–1535*. Ghent and Amsterdam: Ludion, 1999.

―――, ed. *Vatican City, Biblioteca apostolica vaticana, MS Chigi C VIII 234*. Renaissance Music in Facsimile 22. New York: Garland, 1987.

King, A. Hyatt. "The Significance of John Rastell in Early Music Printing. " *Library*, 5th series, vol. 26 (1971): 197–214.

Kirkman, Andrew. "The Invention of the Cyclic Mass." *Journal of the American Musicological Society* 54 (2001): 1–47.

La Croix du Maine, François de. *Premier volume de la bibliotheque du sieur de la Croix du Maine. Qui est un catalogue general de toutes sortes d'Autheurs, qui ont escrit en François depuis cinq cents ans & plus, jusques à ce jourd'huy: avec trois mille qui sont compris en cet ouvre, ensemble un recit de leurs compositions, tant imprimees qu'autrement. Dedié et presenté au roy. Sur le fin de ce livre se voyent les desseins & projects dudit sieur de la CROIX, lesquels il presenta au Roy l'an 1583 pour dresser une Bibliotheque parfaite & accomplie en toutes sortes*. Paris: Abel l'Angelier, 1584.

La Grotte, Nicolas de. *Chansons de P. de Ronsard, Ph. Desportes, et autres, mises en Musique*. Paris: Le Roy & Ballard, 1569.

―――. *Premier livre d'airs et chansons à 3, 4, 5, 6 parties*. Paris: Leon Cavellat, 1583.

La Hèle, George de. *Octo Missae*. Antwerp: Plantin, 1578.

La journée des madrigaux. Edited by Emile Colombey. Paris: Aubry, 1856.

Lassus, Orlande de. *Magnum Opus Musicum*. Munich: Nicolai Henrici, 1604.

―――. *Mellange d'Orlande de Lassus, contenant plusieurs chansons, tant en vers latins qu'en ryme francoyse a quatre, cinq, six, huit, dix parties*. Paris: Le Roy & Ballard, 1570.

Laumonier, Paul. *Ronsard poète lyrique: étude historique et littéraire.* Geneva: Slatkine Reprints, 1972.

Le Jeune, Claude. *Airs.* Paris: Pierre Ballard, 1608.

————. *Le printans.* Paris: Veuve Robert Ballard et Pierre Ballard, 1603.

Lemaître, Nicole. "Le Cardinal d'Armagnac et les humanistes des petites villes du Midi." In *L'humanisme à Toulouse (1480–1596): Actes du colloque international de Toulouse, mai 2004.* Edited by Nathalie Dauvois, 203–21. Paris: Honoré Champion, 2006.

Lemerle, Frédérique. "Guillaume Philandrier et la bibliothèque du cardinal Georges d'Armagnac." *Études aveyronnaises* (2003): 219–44.

Le recueil de chansons nouvelles. Livre III. Paris: Bonfons, 1586.

Le Jardin de Mélodies: 16th-c French Dances and Songs. The King's Noyse, David Douglass, director. Los Angeles: Harmonia Mundi, 1997. HMU 907194.

Le Roy, Adrian. *Livre d'airs de cour miz sur le luth.* Paris: Le Roy & Ballard, 1571.

Lesure, François. "Jean de Maletty à Lyon (1583)." In *Musique et musiciens français du XVIe siècle,* 239–42. Geneva: Minkoff, 1976.

Lesure, François, and Geneviève Thibault, *Bibliographie des éditions d'Adrian Le Roy et Robert Ballard (1551–1598).* Paris: Société Française de Musicologie, 1955.

————. "Bibliographie des éditions musicales publiées par Nicolas du Chemin (1549–1576)." *Annales musicologiques* 1 (1953): 269–373.

Leuchtmann, Horst. "Ein neugefundener Lasso-Brief." In *Festschrift Rudolf Elvers zum 60. Geburtstag.* Edited by Ernst Herttrich and Hans Schneider, 349–57. Tutzing: Hans Schneider, 1985.

————. *Orlando di Lasso: sein Leben* (vol. 1), *Briefe* (vol. 2). Wiesbaden: Breitkopf und Härtel, 1976–77.

Leuchtmann, Horst, and Bernhold Schmid. *Orlando di Lasso: seine Werke in zeitgenössischen Drucken, 1555–1687.* Kassel and New York: Bärenreiter, 2001.

Levy, Kenneth J. "Vaudeville, vers mesurés et airs de cours." In *Musique et poésie au XVIe siècle.* Edited by Jacques Jacquot, 185–201. Paris: Centre National de la Recherche Scientifique, 1954.

Lewis, Mary S. *Antonio Gardano, Venetian Music Printer, 1538–1569: A Descriptive Bibliography and Historical Study.* 3 vols. New York: Garland, 1988–2005.

————. "The Printed Music Book in Context: Observations on Some Sixteenth-Century Editions." *Notes* 46 (1990): 899–918.

Liber quindecim missarum. Rome: Antico, 1516.

Liber selectarum cantionum. Augsburg: Grimm and Wirsung, 1520.

Lindell, Robert, and Brian Mann. "Monte, Philippe de." In Grove Music Online. www.oxfordmusiconline.com (accessed April 21, 2011).

Livre de meslanges, contenant six vingtz chansons, des plus rares, et plus industrieuses qui se trouvent, soit des autheurs antiques, soit des plus memo-

rables de nostre temps, composées à cinq, six, sept, & huict parties en six volumes. Paris: Le Roy & Ballard, 1560.

Longnon, Henri. "Les déboires de Ronsard à la cour." *Bibliothèque d'Humanisme et Renaissance* 12 (1950): 60–80.

Luciani, Isabelle. "Jeux Floraux et 'humanisme civique' au XVIᵉ siècle: entre enjeux de pouvoir et expérience du politique." In *L'humanisme à Toulouse (1480–1596): Actes du colloque international de Toulouse, mai 2004.* Edited by Nathalie Dauvois, 301–35. Paris: Honoré Champion, 2006.

Macé, Benedic, and Laurens Dandin. *Instruction pour apprendre a chanter a quatre parties, selon le Plainchant, les Pseaumes, & Cantiques.* Caen: Benedic Macé, 1582.

Mace, Dean. "Pietro Bembo and the Literary Origins of the Italian Madrigal." *Musical Quarterly* 55 (1969): 65–86.

Magny, Olivier de. *Les odes d'Olivier de Magny.* Edited by Prosper Blanchemain. Lyon: Scheuring, 1876.

Maletty, Jean de. *Les Amours de P. de Ronsard, mises en musique a quatre parties.* Paris: Le Roy & Ballard, 1578.

———. *[Chansons à quatre parties . . . Second livre.]* Paris: Le Roy & Ballard, 1578.

Markham, Michael. "The Heritage of Campaspe: Oral Tradition and Giulio Caccini's 'Le nuove musiche' (1602)." Ph.D. diss., University of California, Berkeley, 2006.

Marot, Clément. *L'adolescence clementine, autrement, les oeuvres de Clement Marot.* Paris: pour Pierre Roffet, par Geoffroy Tory, 1532.

———. *Les chansons nouvellement assemblées oultre les anciennes impressions.* N.p.: Marot, 1538.

———. *Les oeuvres de Clement Marot . . . Le tout songneusement par luy mesme reveu, & mieulx ordonné.* Lyon: Etienne Dolet, 1538.

Marot, Jean. *Le recueil Jehan Marot.* Printed in *L'adolescence clementine ou aultrement les oeuvres de Clement Marot.* Paris: Françoys Regnault, 1536.

Marston, John. *The Malcontent.* London: Printed by V. S. for William Aspley, 1604.

Martin, Henri-Jean. *The French Book: Religion, Absolutism, and Readership, 1585–1715.* Translated by Paul Saenger and Nadine Saenger. Baltimore and London: Johns Hopkins University Press, 1996.

Martin, Henri-Jean, and Roger Chartier, eds. *Histoire de l'édition française.* 4 vols. Paris: Promodis, 1982–86.

Mauduit, Jacques. *Chansonnettes mesurées de Jan-Antoine de Baïf.* Paris: Le Roy & Ballard, 1586.

Mayer, C. A. "Le premier sonnet français: Marot, Mellin de Saint-Gelais et J. Bouchet." *Revue d'histoire littéraire de la France* 67 (1967): 481–93.

McClelland, John. "Le marriage de poésie et de musique: un projet de Pontus de Tyard." In *La chanson à la Renaissance: Actes du XXᵉ colloque d'études humanistes du Centre d'Études Supérieures de la Renaissance de l'Université de Tours, juillet 1977.* Edited by Jean-Michel Vaccaro, 80–92. Tours: Éditions Van de Velde, 1981.

———. "La mise en musique du sonnet français avant 1552." In *Musique et humanisme à la renaissance*, 83–100. Paris: Presses de l'École normale supérieure, 1993.

———. "Sonnet ou quatorzain? Marot et le choix d'une forme poétique." *Revue d'histoire littéraire de la France* 73 (1973): 591–607.

McGowan, Margaret. *Ideal Forms in the Age of Ronsard.* Berkeley: University of California Press, 1985.

McKenzie, D. F. *Bibliography and the Sociology of Texts.* The Panizzi Lectures 1985. London: British Library, 1986.

McKitterick, David. *Print, Manuscript, and the Search for Order, 1450–1830.* Cambridge: Cambridge University Press, 2003.

Meconi, Honey. "Petrucci's Mass Prints and the Naming of Things." In *Venezia 1501: Petrucci e la stampa musicale.* Edited by Giulio Cattin and Patrizia Dalla Vecchia. 397–414. Venice: Fondazione Levi, 2005.

Meissner, Ute. *Der Antwerpener Notendrucker Tylman Susato: Eine bibliographische Studie zur niederländischen Chansonpublikation in der ersten Hälfte des 16 Jahrhunderts.* 2 vols. Berliner Studien zur Musikwissenschaft 11. Berlin: Verlag Merseburger, 1967.

Mélançon, Robert. "Sur la structure des *Amours* de 1552 de Ronsard." *Renaissance et Réform* 1 (1977): 119–35.

Mellange de chansons tant des vieux autheurs que des modernes, a cinq. six. sept. et huict parties. Paris: Le Roy & Ballard, 1572.

Menehou, Michel de. *Nouvelle instruction familiere, en laquelle sont contenus les difficultés de la Musique, avecques le nombre des concordances, & accords: ensemble la maniere d'en user, tant à deux, à trois, à quatre, qu'à cinq parties.* Paris: Nicolas Du Chemin, 1558.

Michaud, Louis-Gabriel. *Biographie universelle ancienne et moderne.* 2nd ed. 45 vols. Paris: Michaud, 1843–65.

Milsom, John. "Absorbing Lassus." *Early Music* 33 (2005): 305–20.

Minamino, Hiroyuki. "A Monkey Business: Petrucci, Antico, and the Frottola Intabulation." *Journal of the Lute Society of America* 26–27 (1993–94): 96–106.

Minnis, Alastair J. *Medieval Theory of Authorship: Scholastic Literary Attitudes in the Later Middle Ages.* London: Scolar Press, 1984.

Missarum musicalium certa vocum, varietate, secundum varios quos referunt modulos distinctarum, liber primus, ex diversis ijsdemque peritissimis auctoribus collectus. Paris: Nicolas Du Chemin, 1568.

Missarum musicalium certa vocum, varietate, secundum varios quos referunt modulos & cantiones distinctarum, liber secundus, ex diversis iisdemque peritissimis auctoribus collectus. Paris: Nicolas Du Chemin, 1568.

Montaigne, Michel de. *Essais.* Edited by Pierre Villey and V-L Saulnier. 3 vols. Paris: Presses universitaires de France, 1982.

Monte, Phillipe de. *Sonetz de P. de Ronsard, mis en Musique a 5. 6. et 7. parties.* Paris: Le Roy & Ballard, 1575.

———. *Sonetz de P. de Ronsard, mis en Musique a 5. 6. et 7. parties.* Louvain: Pierre Phalèse, and Antwerp: Jean Bellère, 1575.

Morales, Cristóbal de. *Missarum liber primus.* Rome: Dorico, 1544.

———. *Missarum liber primus.* Lyon: Moderne, 1546.

———. *Missarum liber secundus.* Rome: Dorico, 1544

Morucci, Valerio "Cardinal's Patronage and the Era of Tridentine Reforms: Giulio Feltro della Rovere as Sponsor of Sacred Music." *Journal of Musicology* 29 (2012): 262–91.

Naïs, Hélène. "La notion de genre en poésie au XVIᵉ siècle." In *La notion de genre à la Renaissance.* Edited by Guy Demerson, 103–27. Geneva: Slatkine, 1984.

Nelson, William. "From 'Listen, Lordings' to 'Dear Reader.'" *University of Toronto Quarterly: A Canadian Journal of the Humanities* 46 (1976–77): 110–24.

Newcomb, Anthony. "Carlo Gesualdo and a Musical Correspondence of 1594." *Musical Quarterly* 54 (1968): 409–36.

———. "Editions of Willaert's 'Musica Nova': New Evidence, New Speculations." *Journal of the American Musicological Society* 26 (1973): 132–45.

———. *The Madrigal at Ferrara, 1579–1597.* 2 vols. Princeton, NJ: Princeton University Press, 1980.

———. "Notions of Notation and the Concept of the Work." Paper presented at the Sixty-Ninth Annual Meeting of the American Musicological Society, Houston, Texas, November 2003.

Nilges, Annemarie. *Imitation als Dialog: Die europäische Rezeption Ronsards in Renaissance und Frühbarock.* Heidelberg: Carl Winter Universitätsverlag, 1988.

Norton, Frederick John. *Italian Printers, 1501–1520: An Annotated List with an Introduction.* Cambridge Bibliographical Society Monographs 3. Cambridge: Bowes and Bowes, 1958.

Nuten, Piet. "Enkele stijlkritische beschouwingen over de franse chansons van Filip de Monte." In *Renaissance-Muziek, 1400–1600, Donum Natalicium René Bernard Lenaerts.* Edited by Jozef Robijns, 195–214. Leuven: Katholieke Universiteit Seminarie voor Muziekwetenschap, 1969.

Oettinger, Rebecca Wagner. "Berg v. Gerlach: Printing and Lasso's Imperial Privilege of 1582." *Fontes Artis Musicae* 51(2004): 111–34.

Orgel, Stephen. "What Is an Editor?" *Shakespeare Studies* 24 (1996): 23–29.

Ouvrard, Jean-Pierre. "Modality and Text Expression in 16th-Century French Chansons: Remarks Concerning the E Mode." *Basler Jahrbuch für historische Musikpraxis* 16 (1992): 89–116.

———. "Le sonnet ronsardien en musique: du *Supplément* de 1552 à 1580." *Revue de musicologie* 74 (1988): 149–64.

Owens, Jessie Ann, ed. *Vienna Österreichisches Nationalbibliothek, Musiksammlung, Mus. Hs. 18.744,* Renaissance Music in Facsimile 25. New York and London: Garland, 1986.

Palestrina, Giovanni Pierluigi da. *Missarum liber primus: Roma 1554.* Edited by Giancarlo Rostirolla. Palestrina: Fondazione Giovanni Pierluigi da Palestrina, 1975.

Parker, Roger. *Remaking the Song: Operatic Visions and Revisions from Handel to Berio.* Berkeley and Los Angeles: University of California Press, 2006.

Patrocinium musices. 12 vols. Munich: Berg, 1573–1598.

Perkins, Leeman L. "Toward a Typology of the 'Renaissance' Chanson." *Journal of Musicology* 4 (1988): 421–47.

Petrarca, Francesco. *Petrarch's Lyric Poems: The* Rime sparse *and Other Lyrics.* Edited and translated by Robert M. Durling. Cambridge, MA: Harvard University Press, 1976.

Petrucci, Armando. *Writers and Readers in Medieval Italy: Studies in the History of Written Culture.* Edited and translated by Charles M. Radding. New Haven, CT, and London: Yale University Press, 1995.

Pettas, William. *A History & Bibliography of the Giunti (Junta) Printing Family in Spain 1514–1628.* New Castle, DE: Oak Knoll Press, 2005.

———. *A Sixteenth-Century Spanish Bookstore: The Inventory of Juan de Junta.* Philadelphia: American Philosophical Society, 1995.

Picker, Martin, ed. *The Chanson Albums of Marguerite of Austria: MSS 228 and 11239 of the Bibliothèque royale de Belgique, Brussels.* Berkeley: University of California Press, 1965.

———. "Josquin and Jean Lemaire: Four Chansons Re-examined." In *Essays Presented to Myron P. Gilmore.* Edited by Sergio Bertelli and Gloria Ramakus. 2 vols., 2: 447–56. Florence: La Nuova Italia, 1978.

———. "*Liber selectarum cantionum* (Augsburg: Grimm und Wyrsung, 1520): A Neglected Monument of Renaissance Music and Music Printing." In *Gestalt und Entstehung musikalischer Quellen im 15. und 16. Jahrhundert.* Edited by Martin Staehelin, 149–67. Wiesbaden: Harrassowitz, 1998.

Piperno, Franco. "Autobiography and Authoriality in a Madrigal Book: Leonardo Meldert's *Primo libro a cinque* (1578)." *Journal of Musicology* 30 (2013): 1–27.

Pirro, André. "Leo X and Music." *Musical Quarterly* 21 (1935): 1–16.

Pirrotta, Nino. "Music and Cultural Tendencies in 15th-Century Italy." *Journal of the American Musicological Society* 19 (1966): 127–61.

Planchart, Alejandro Enrique. "The Books that Guillaume Du Fay Left to the Chapel of Saint Stephen." In *Sine Musica Nulla Disciplina . . . Studi in Onore de Giulio Cattin.* Edited by Franco Bernabei and Antonio Lovato, 175–212. Padua: Il poligrafo, 2006.

Pogue, Samuel F. *Jacques Moderne: Lyons Music Printer of the Sixteenth Century.* Geneva: Droz, 1969.

Pohlmann, Hansjörg. *Die Frühgeschichte des musikalischen Urheberrechts (ca. 1400–1800)*. Kassel: Bärenreiter, 1962.

Powers, Harold S. "Tonal Types and Modal Categories in Renaissance Polyphony." *Journal of the American Musicological Society* 34 (1981): 428–70.

Powers, Harold S. et. al. "Mode, §II: Medieval Modal Theory." In Grove Music Online. www.oxfordmusiconline.com (accessed May 3, 2011).

Preisig, Florian. *Clément Marot et les métamorphoses de l'auteur à l'aube de la Renaissance*. Geneva: Droz, 2004.

Prizer, William F. "The Frottola and the Unwritten Tradition." *Studi musicali* 15 (1986): 3–37.

Quainton, Malcolm. "The Liminary Texts of Ronsard's *Amours de Cassandre* (1552): Poetics, Erotics, Semiotics." *French Studies* 53 (1999): 257–78.

Rabelais, François. *Pantagruel*. Edited by V. L. Saulnier. Geneva: Droz, 1965.

Regnard, François. *Chansons à quatre voix, 1579*. Edited by Jeanice Brooks. Tours: Centre de Musique Ancienne, 1993.

———. *Cinquante chansons à quatre et cinq parties*. Douai: Jean Bogard, 1575.

———. *Poesies de P. de Ronsard & autres Poëtes mis en Musique à Quatre & Cinq parties*. Paris: Le Roy & Ballard, 1579.

Reynolds, Christopher. "Musical Careers, Ecclesiastical Benefices, and the Example of Johannes Brunet." *Journal of the American Musicological Society* 37 (1984): 49–97.

Richardson, Brian. *Printing, Writers, and Readers in Renaissance Italy*. Cambridge and New York: Cambridge University Press, 1999.

RISM (*Répertoire international des sources musicales*). Series B/I *Recueils imprimés du XVIᵉ siècle*. Munich: G. Henle Verlag, 1960.

Rodgers, Mark Allen. "Monte's Sonnets of Pierre de Ronsard: the *Chanson* and the Currency of Poetic Influence." Unpublished paper, 2009.

Ronsard, Pierre de. *Abbrege de l'art poëtique françois* (Paris, 1565). Facsimile edition. Geneva: Slatkine Reprints, 1962.

———. *Les Amours*. Edited by Catherine Weber and Henri Weber. Paris: Classiques Garnier, 1963.

———. *Les Amours de P. de Ronsard, Ensemble le cinquiesme de ses Odes*. Paris: Veuve Maurice de la Porte, 1552.

———. *Les Amours de P. de Ronsard, Vandomois, nouvellement augmentées par lui, & commentées par Marc Antoine de Muret*. Paris: Veuve Maurice de la Porte, 1553.

———. *Le Bocage de P. de Ronsard, Vandomoys, dedié a P. de Paschal, du bas païs de Languedoc*. Paris: Veuve Maurice de la Porte, 1554,

———. *Les Oeuvres de P. de Ronsard Gentilhomme Vandomois, revues, corrigees & augmentees par l'Autheur*. Paris: Gabriel Buon, 1584.

———. *Oeuvres complètes*. Edited by Paul Laumonier. 18 vols. Paris: Société des Textes Français Modernes, 1982.

———. *Oeuvres complètes*. Edited by Prosper Blanchemain. Paris: P. Jannet, 1857–67.

―――. *Oeuvres complètes.* Edited by Jean Céard, Daniel Ménager, and Michel Simonin. 2 vols. Paris: Gallimard, 1993–94.

―――. *Les quatre premiers livres des Odes de Pierre de Ronsard, ... Ensemble son Bocage ... - Brève exposition de quelques passages du 1er livre des Odes de Pierre de Ronsard, par I. M. P.* Paris: G. Cavellart [sic], 1550.

Ronsard, Pierre de, and Marc-Antoine de Muret, *Les Amours, leurs commentaires. Textes de 1553.* Edited by Christine de Buzon and Pierre Martin, preface by Michel Simonin, postscript by Jean Céard, musical supplement of 1552 introduced by François Lesure. Paris: Didier Érudition, 1999.

Root, Robert K. "Publication before Printing." *Proceedings of the Modern Language Association* 28 (1913): 417–31.

Rore, Cipriano de. *Tutti i madrigali di Cipriano di Rore a quattro voci.* Venice: Gardano, 1577.

Saint-Gelais, Mellin de. *Oeuvres poétiques françaises.* Edited by Donald Stone. 2 vols. Paris: Société des Textes Français Modernes, 1993–95.

Sartori, Claudio. *Bibliografia delle opere musicali stampate da Ottaviano Petrucci.* Biblioteca di bibliografia italiana 18. Florence: L. S. Olschki, 1948.

Schlagel, Stephanie P. "A Credible (Mis)Attribution to Josquin in Hans Ott's *Novum et insigne opus musicum:* Contemporary Perceptions, Modern Conceptions, and the Case of *Veni sancte Spiritus." Tijdschrift van de Koninklijke Vereniging voor Nederlandse Muziekgeschiedenis* 56 (2006): 97–126.

Schutz, Alexander H. *Vernacular Books in Parisian Private Libraries of the Sixteenth Century According to the Notarial Inventories.* Chapel Hill: University of North Carolina Press [1955].

Sébillet, Thomas. *L'art poétique françois* (Paris, 1548). Edited by Félix Gaiffe and Francis Goyet. 3rd ed. Paris: Société des Textes Français Modernes, 1988.

Seguin, Jean-Pierre. *L'information en France avant le périodique: 517 canards imprimés entre 1529 et 1631.* Paris: G-P Maisonneuve et Larose, 1964.

Selectissimarum mutetarum ... tomus primus. Nuremberg: Petreius, 1540.

S'ensuyvent plusieurs belles chansons nouvelles nouvellement imprimees ... avec aulcunes de Clement Marot de nouveau adjoustées. Lyon: Claude Nourry, [ca. 1533–34].

Septiesme livre des chansons a quatre parties convenables tant aux instrumentz comme à la voix. Louvain: Pierre Phalèse, 1560.

Sermisy, Claudin de. *Claudii de Sermisy, Regii Sacelli Submagistri, Nova & Prima motettorum editio.* Paris: Attaingnant, 1542.

―――. *Missae tres Claudio de Sermisi.* Paris: Le Roy & Ballard, 1558.

Sherr, Richard. *Papal Music Manuscripts in the Late Fifteenth and Early Sixteenth Centuries.* Renaissance Manuscript Studies 5. N.p.: American Institute of Musicology, 1996.

Simonin, Michel. *Pierre de Ronsard*. Paris: Fayard, 1990.

———. *Vivre de sa plume au XVIᵉ siècle ou la carrière de François de Belle-forest*. Geneva: Droz, 1992.

Simpson, Christopher. *The Compendium of Practical Musick*. London: printed by William Godbid for Henry Brome, 1667.

Sixiesme livre contenant xxvij. Chansons nouvelles a quatre parties en ung volume et en deux. Paris: Attaingnant, 1539.

Slim, H. Colin. "The Music Library of the Augsburg Patrician, Hans Heinrich Herwart (1520–1583)." *Annales musicologiques* 7 (1964–77): 67–109.

Spitzer, John. "Authorship and Attribution in Western Art Music." Ph.D. diss., Cornell University, 1983.

Stellfeld, Jean-Auguste. *Bibliographie des éditions musicales plantiniennes*. Académie royale de Belgique, Classe des beaux-arts, Mémoires, Series 2, vol. 5, fasc. 3. Brussels: Palais des Académies, 1949.

Stevenson, Robert. "Francisco Guerrero (1528–1599): Seville's Sixteenth-Century Cynosure." *Inter-American Music Review* 13 (1992): 21–98.

Stone, Donald. *Mellin de Saint-Gelais and Literary History*. Lexington, KY: French Forum Press, 1983.

Stoycos, Sarah M. "Making an Initial Impression: Lassus's First Book of Five-Part Madrigals." *Music & Letters* 86 (2005): 537–59.

Strambotti, Ode, Frottole, Sonetti. Et modo de cantar versi latini e capituli. Libro quarto. [Venice: Petrucci, 1505].

Strohm, Reinhard. *The Rise of European Music, 1380–1500*. Oxford: Oxford University Press, 1993.

Teviotdale, E. C. "The Invitation to the Puy d'Évreux." *Current Musicology* 52 (1993): 7–26.

Thibault, Geneviève. "Les Amours de P. de Ronsard mises en musique par Je-han de Maletty (1578)." In *Mélanges de musicologie offerts à M. Lionel de la Laurencie*, 61–72. Paris: Droz, 1933.

———. "Anthoine de Bertrand: musicien de Ronsard et ses amis toulou-sains." In *Mélanges offerts à M. Abel Lefranc*, 282–300. Paris: Droz, 1936.

———. "De la vogue de quelques livres français à Venise." *Bibliothèque d'Humanisme et Renaissance* 2 (1935): 61–65.

Thibault, Geneviève, and Louis Perceau. *Bibliographie des poésies de P. de Ronsard mises en musique au XVIᵉ siècle*. Paris: E. Droz, 1941.

Tiersot, Julien. *Ronsard et la musique de son temps: oeuvres musicales de Certon, Goudimel, Janequin, Muret, Mauduit, etc.* Leipzig: Breitkopf und Härtel, and Paris: Fischbacher, 1903.

Tomlinson, Gary. "Musicology, Anthropology, History." In *The Cultural Study of Music: A Critical Introduction*. Edited by Martin Clayton, Trevor Herbert, and Richard Middleton, 31–44. New York and London: Routledge, 2003.

Trachier, Olivier, ed. *Renaissance française: traités, méthodes, préfaces, ouvrages généraux*. 4 vols. Courlay, France: Éditions Fuzeau Classique, [2005].

Tyard, Pontus de. *Erreurs amoureuses.* Lyon: Jean de Tournes, 1549.

———. *Solitaire premier ou prose des Muses et de la fureur poetique, plus quelques vers lyriques.* Lyon: Jean de Tournes, 1552.

———. *Solitaire second* (Lyon, 1555). Edited by Cathy M. Yandell. Geneva: Droz, 1980.

Vaccaro, Jean-Michel. "Geometry and Rhetoric in Anthoine de Bertrand's *Troisiesme livre de chansons.*" *Early Music History* 13 (1994): 217–48.

———. "Les préfaces d'Anthoine de Bertrand." *Revue de musicologie* 74 (1988): 221–36.

Vanhulst, Henri. *Catalogue des éditions de musique publiées à Louvain par Pierre Phalèse et ses fils, 1545–1578.* Mémoires de la classe des beaux-arts, 2ᵉ série, vol. 16. Brussels: Palais des Académies, 1990.

———. "Lasso et ses éditeurs: remarques à propos de deux lettres peu connues." *Revue belge de Musicologie / Belgisch Tijdschrift voor Muziekwetenschap* 39–40 (1985–86): 80–100.

———. "Un succès de l'édition musicale: le 'Septiesme livre des chansons a quatre parties' (1560–1661/3)." *Revue belge de Musicologie / Belgisch Tijdschrift voor Muziekwetenschap* 32–33 (1978–79): 97–120.

van Orden, Kate. "*La chanson vulgaire* and Ronsard's Poetry for Music." In *Poetry and Music in the French Renaissance: Proceedings of the Sixth Cambridge French Renaissance Colloquium, 5–7 July 1999.* Edited by Jeanice Brooks, Philip Ford, and Gillian Jondorf, 79–109. Cambridge: Cambridge French Colloquia, 2001.

———. "Fauxbourdon, Composition, and the Chanson at Paris c. 1550." Paper presented at the Nineteenth Congress of the International Musicological Society, Rome, July 1–7, 2012.

———. "Female Complaintes: Laments of Venus, Queens, and City Women in Late Sixteenth-Century France." *Renaissance Quarterly* 54 (2001): 801–45.

———. "Imitation and 'la musique des anciens' in Le Roy & Ballard's 1572 *Mellange de chansons.*" *Revue de musicologie* 80 (1994): 5–37.

———. "Josquin, Renaissance Historiography, and the Cultures of Print." In *The Oxford Handbook to the New Cultural History of Music.* Edited by Jane Fair Fulcher, 354–80. New York: Oxford University Press, 2011.

———. *Materialities: Books, Readers, and the Chanson in Sixteenth-Century Europe.* Forthcoming.

———. "The Parisian Chanson: Prints and Readers." *Imparare, Leggere, Comprare Musica nell'Europa del Cinquecento,* a special issue of *Il Saggiatore Musicale* 18 (2011): 191–208.

———. "Robert Granjon and Music during the Golden Age of Typography." In *Music in Print and Beyond: Hildegard von Bingen to The Beatles,* a festschrift for Jane A. Bernstein. Edited by Roberta M. Marvin and Craig A. Monson. Eastman Studies in Music. Rochester, NY: University of Rochester Press, 2013.

————. "Tielman Susato, Music, and the Cultures of Print." In *Tielman Susato and the Music of His Time*. Edited by Keith Polk, 143–63. Stuyvesant, NY: Pendragon Press, 2005.

————. "Vernacular Culture and the Chanson in Paris, 1570–1580." Ph.D. diss., University of Chicago, 1996.

van Orden, Kate, ed., with an afterword by Roger Chartier. *Music and the Cultures of Print*. New York: Garland, 2000.

van Orden, Kate, and Alfredo Vitolo, "Padre Martini, Gaetano Gaspari, and the 'Pagliarini Collection': A Renaissance Music Library Rediscovered." *Early Music History* 29 (2010): 241–324.

Vianey, Joseph. *Le pétrarquisme en France au XVIe siècle*. Geneva: Slatkine Reprints, 1969.

Vickers, Nancy J. "The Unauthored 1539 Volume in Which Is Printed the *Hectamophile, The Flowers of French Poetry*, and *Other Soothing Things*. In *Subject and Object in Renaissance Culture*. Edited by Margreta De Grazia, Maureen Quilligan, and Peter Stallybrass, 166–88. Cambridge: Cambridge University Press, 1996.

Viginti missarum musicalium. Paris: Attaingnant, 1532.

Vocabolario degli accademici della Crusca. Venice: Giovanni Alberti, 1612.

Voet, Leon. *The Golden Compasses: A History and Evaluation of the Printing and Publishing Activities of the Officina Plantiniana at Antwerp*. 2 vols. Amsterdam: Vangendt, 1972.

Walker, D. P. *Music, Spirit, and Language in the Renaissance*. Edited by Penelope Gouk. London: Variorum Reprints, 1985.

Weber, Henri. *La création poétique au XVIe siècle en France de Maurice Scève à Agrippa d'Aubigné*. Paris: Nizet, 1955.

Wegman, Rob C. " 'And Josquin Laughed . . .' Josquin and the Composer's Anecdote in the Sixteenth Century." *Journal of Musicology* 17(1999): 319–57.

————. "From Maker to Composer: Improvisation and Musical Authorship in the Low Countries, 1450–1500." *Journal of the American Musicological Society* 49 (1996): 409–79.

Whang, Jane Ozenberger. "From *Voix de ville* to *Air de cour*: The Strophic Chanson c. 1545–1575." Ph. D. diss., University of North Carolina, Chapel Hill, 1981.

Williams, Sarah Jane. "An Author's Role in Fourteenth-Century Book Production: Guillaume de Machaut's 'livre où je met toutes mes choses." *Romania* 90 (1969): 433–54.

————. "The Lady, the Lyrics, and the Letters." *Early Music* 5 (1977): 462–68.

Wistreich, Richard. "Introduction, Musical Materials and Musical Spaces." *Renaissance Studies* 26 (2012): 1–12.

————. "Music Books and Sociability." *Il Saggiatore musicale* 18 (2011): 230–44.

Yandell, Cathy M. *Carpe Corpus: Time and Gender in Early Modern France.* Newark, DE: University of Delaware Press, and London: Associated University Presses, 2000.

Yates, Frances A. *The French Academies of the Sixteenth Century.* 2nd ed. London and New York: Routledge, 1988.

Zecher, Carla. *Sounding Objects: Musical Instruments, Poetry, and Art in Renaissance France.* Toronto: University of Toronto Press, 2007.

Index

Académie des Jeux Floraux, 129
L'adolescence clementine (Marot),
    100–102
"Air pour chanter tous sonets"
    (Caietain), 154–56*fig.*, 156–58
airs de cour, 150–58
Albrecht V, Duke of Bavaria, 69–70
Alduy, Cécile, 124, 184n59
L'amorosa Ero, 131
"Amour, Amour, donne moy paix ou
    trève" (Maletty), 124
"Amour avecques Psyches" (du
    Guillet), 94
amour courtois, 113–14
Les Amours de P. de Ronsard (Ron-
    sard): chansonniers and, 122–28,
    132*t.*; formulation of authorship
    presented in, 87; overview of, 104–8;
    print and, 115–16; *Supplément
    musical* to, 109–15
Les Amours de P. de Ronsard, book 1
    (Bertrand), 123*t.*, 125–28, 130–38,
    143–44
"Amours" poetic cycles, 184n59
Aneau, Barthélemy, 94, 110
Animuccia, Giovanni, 65
anonymity: authorship and, 84–85;
    Marot and, 101; in print, 4
anonyms, 19–22
anthologies: anonyms and, 19–22;
    arrangement of chansons in,

119–21; authorship of, 15–16; editors
    and craftsmen of, 30–34, 37–38;
    organization of, 51–54, 131; Pléiade
    poets and, 95, 114–15; single-
    composer prints and, 46–47; as
    standard form for chansonniers, 21,
    74–75, 134
Antico, Andrea, 30–38, 163n1,
    168n14, 169n22. See also *Canzoni,
    sonetti, strambotti et frottole
    libro quarto* (Antico); *Frottole
    intabulate da sonare organi*
    (Antico); *Liber quindecim
    missarum* (Antico)
Antiphonarium romanum, 38
Apollo, 93, 114
Arcadelt, Jacques: in bibliographies,
    140, 141; brand-name marketing
    and, 71; knowledge concerning, 66;
    "Laissez la verde couleur," 96,
    98–99; *Missae tres*, 61*t.*, 65–66,
    117; *Primo libro di madrigali a
    quatro voci*, 23, 75; printing and
    rights to music of, 23–24
d'Armagnac, Georges, 130
"À sa lyre" (Ronsard), 72–73, 103–4
Attaingnant, Pierre: chansons printed
    by, 17, 20, 21, 22*fig.*, 75–76, 134,
    164n4; Marot and, 101–2; modal
    ordering in the chansonniers of,
    120–21; professional origins of,

Attaingnant, Pierre *(continued)*
38–39; single-impression printing
and, 19
author(s): Bertrand as, 143–44;
Costeley as, 119; defined, 6; Josquin
des Prez as, 2–3; names of, 4–5,
22–29; portraits of, 106*fig.*, 107, 116,
117*fig.*
authorship: attributing, 3–4; bibliographies and, 141–42; of chanson
composers, 139; defined, 6; as
discursive construct, 5–6; of editors
and craftsmen, 30–42; Foucault on,
4–5; and mid-century lyric
economy, 84–85; of miscellanies
and anthologies, 15–16, 20, 21;
performance and, 145, 146–58;
print and, 12, 14, 22–29, 71;
rhétoriqueurs and, 88–89; of
Ronsard, 86–88, 115; of sacred
genres, 16; of single-composer
choirbooks and Masses, 42–55

Baïf, Jean-Antoine de, 86; and the
Académie de la poésie et de la
musique, 127, 147, 151–52; *Chan-
sonettes mesurees*, 148, 152
Ballard printing dynasty, 40
Beaujoyeulx, Balthasar de, 147,
148, 152
Beaulieu, Girard de, 148–49
Belleau, Rémy, 86
Belleforest, François de, 90
Bembo, Pietro, 105, 110
benefices, 11, 76
Bent, Margaret, 48
Berchem, Jacquet, 26–27
Berg, Adam, 28, 64
Bernstein, Jane, 63
Bernstein, Lawrence, 83
Bertrand, Anthoine de: composition
and performance of works of,
143–44; critical study of, 108, 146;
culture of music books and, 129–33;
in Harcourt volumes, 138–39;
Ronsard and, 122, 125–28; survival
of prints of, 135–36; See also *Les*

Amours de P. de Ronsard, book 1
(Bertrand); *Second livre des Amours
de P. de Ronsard* (Bertrand); *Troisiesme livre de chansons* (Bertrand)
bibliographies, 108, 139–42, 144
binder's volumes, 9, 41, 43, 135–39
Blondeau, Pierre, 39
Boccaccio, Giovanni, 48
Bologna, Jacopo da, 182n46
Boni, Guillaume: *airs de cour* and,
151–52; authorial control of, 28;
Bertrand and, 130–33; critical study
of, 108, 146; fauxbourdon formula
and, 157–58; in Harcourt volumes,
138–39; Henry III and, 119, 132; in
La Croix du Maine bibliography,
140–41; privilege of, 28, 118–19,
167n37, 198–99n92; Ronsard and,
122, 125; survival of works, 136–39.
See also *Les quatrains du Sieur de
Pybrac* (Boni); *Sonetz de P. de
Ronsard . . . Premier Livre* (Boni);
*Sonetz de P. de Ronsard . . . Second
Livre* (Boni)
Boorman, Stanley, 44–45
Brooks, Jeanice, 125

Caccini, Giulio, 145
cadences, in four-voice chansons,
79–82
Caietain, Fabrice Marin, 152–58.
See also "Air pour chanter tous
sonets" (Caietain)
Canguilhem, Philippe, 181n39
*Canzoni, sonetti, strambotti et
frottole libro quarto* (Antico), 35,
36*fig.*
Canzoniere (Petrarch), 84, 86–87, 105,
122, 184n59
career musicians, 49–51
Carpentras: publications of, 55–56,
145; seeks royal privilege, 37;
tinnitus of, 55; unauthorized
publication of, 49. *See also*
"Lamentations" (Carpentras);
Manuscripts: I-Rvat C. S. 163
(Carpentras)

Carter, Tim, 145–46
Castellanus, Petrus, 171n40
Castiglione, Baldassare, 6, 23
Castro, Jean de, 123*t.*
Catherine de' Medici, 147
Cazeaux, Isabelle, 77
Certon, Pierre, 109, 136, 140; "J'espere et crains," 110*t.*, 111–112, 153; "Laissez la verde couleur," 95–96, 98–99
Chandor, Henry, 39
chansons: anthologies of, 20–21, 119–21; authority in prints of, 116–19; authorship of, 16–18, 74–84; Marot and, 100–102; and mid-century lyric economy, 84–102; Pléiade poets and, 73; single-composer prints and, 46–47
Chansons de P. de Ronsard, Ph. Desportes, et autres (La Grotte), 133, 141, 148, 151
Les chansons nouvellement assemblées oultre les anciennes impressions (Marot), 102
chapelle de musique, 147
Chardavoine, Jean, 95, 96, 97
Charles, Cardinal of Lorraine, 65–66, 98, 141
Charles IX, King of France, 27, 69, 118–19, 121–22, 131, 147, 150
Chartier, Roger, 14–15, 25, 108
Chigi Codex, 16, 46
choirbooks: authorship of, 42–55; financing of, 65–67; as luxury items, 59; organization and use of, 7–9, 41; single-composer, 55–68; of Sistine Chapel, 41; study of, 10
Clement VII, Pope, 37, 54, 56
Clereau, Pierre, 118, 188–89n4
Clermont, Catherine de, 147
collector's volumes. *See* binder's volumes
Collège d'Harcourt, 136–39
composers: authorship of, 42–55; fame of, 161n17; as lyric authors, 74–84

composers' dedications, 24, 26–27
contrafacta, 95, 111
corruption, textual, 70–72, 101–102
Corteccia, Francesco, 26, 61*t.*, 71
Costeley, Guillaume, 116–19, 121–22, 140–41, 145, 147–49, 151; portrait of, 117*fig.* See also *Musique de Guillaume Costeley* (Costeley); *Prise du Havre* (Costeley)
court musicians, 146–49, 202n14
Cousin, Jean, 116
craftsmen, authorship of, 30–42
Cramoisy, Louis, 181n31
Courville, Joachim Thibault de, 127, 150, 151–53

Dante Alighieri, 23, 47, 101; *Divine Comedy*, 45, 84
Darnton, Robert, 14
debts, 64–65
dedications, composers', 24, 26–27
La deffence et illustration de la langue françoyse (Du Bellay), 86, 93–94, 113, 115
de la Halle, Adam, 47, 49
della Rovere, Giulio Feltro, 65
Denisot, Nicolas, 116
Deploration de Venus sur la mort du bel Adonis, avec plusieurs autres compositions nouvelles (Du Moulin), 94–95
Desportes, Philippe, 148
des Prez, Josquin: authorship of, 1–3, 5–6; as career musician, 49–50; *Misse Josquin* and, 2–3, 43*fig.*, 44; print culture and, 13; scholarship on, 11–12; single-composer prints and, 42
de Wert, Giaches, 5, 64
diatonic genera, 127
Diderot, Denis, 28–29
Donato, Girolamo, 171n40
Doni, Anton Francesco, 13, 24, 140, 144
Doria, Yolande, 148–49
Dorico, Valerio, 58–60

Du Bellay, Joachim: on *chansons* of Saint-Gelais, 100; and *chanson* versus ode, 93–95; linguistic nationalism and, 113; and mid-century lyric economy, 86; on praise, 88; rhyme schemes of, 110
Du Chemin, Nicolas, 39, 41, 190n13, 199n92; *Missarum musicalium . . . liber primus* and *liber secundus*, 41
Dufay, Guillaume, 49–50, 174n75
du Guillet, Pernette, 94
Du Verdier, Antoine, 140, 144; *Bibliotheque*, 140–141

Earp, Lawrence, 48
editors, authorship of, 30–42
Eisenstein, Elizabeth, 13, 144
Expert, Henry, 146

Fabroni, Angelo, 50
Falconio, Placido, 62t., 65–66
Fallows, David, 11–12
fame: for composers, 42–55, 72, 161n17; performance and, 70, 148–49
fauxbourdon formula, 82, 156–58
Feldman, Martha, 4
Festa, Costanzo, 46, 56–57, 64
Finck, Hermann, 72
folio prints, 33–34, 41–42, 55–68, 175n89
Forster, Georg, 1, 5
Foucault, Michel, 4–5, 84–85
François Ier, King of France, 37, 77, 91, 149, 171n38
French court, 146–49, 202n14
Frottole intabulate da sonare organi (Antico), 34–35fig., 169n22

Gardane, Antonio, 19, 23–24, 39, 74
Garnier, Robert, 129
Genet, Elzéar. *See* Carpentras
Gerlach, Katharina, 28
Gervaise, Claude, 39, 76
Gesualdo, Carlo, 9
Ghiselin, Johannes, 44–45
Giunta, Antonio, 34, 38
Giunta, Jacomo di Biagio, 38

Glarean, Heinrich, 50, 120
Gombert, Nicolas, 64, 74
Goudimel, Claude, 39, 109–110
Graduale romanum, 38
Granjon, Robert, 39–40
Greek music, 93, 152
Greek modes, 127
Grévin, Jacques, 129
Gringoire, Pierre, 88–89
Guerrero, Francisco, 61–62t., 64, 65–66
Guise, Charles de. *See* Charles, Cardinal of Lorraine

Harmonice Musices Odhecaton A (Petrucci), 12, 19, 21
Handel, George Frideric, 15, 150–51
Haydn, Franz Joseph, 71–72
"He Dieu du ciel je n'eusse pas pensé" (Caietain). *See* "Air pour chanter tous sonets" (Caietain)
Henry III, King of France, 119, 147
Henry VIII, King of England, 50
Histoires tragiques (Belleforest), 90
Horace, 86–87
House of Scotto, 37–38
Hypo-Phrygian, 128, 197n76

Isaac, Heinrich, 44, 57t.

Jambe de Fer, Philibert, 71
Janequin, Clément, 75–76, 109–110, 140–141
"J'espere et crains" (Certon), 110t., 111–12, 153
Johns, Adrian, 13–14
Jonson, Ben, 25–26
Josquin. *See* des Prez, Josquin
"Jouyssance vous donneray" (Sermisy), 78–84, 111
Julius III, Pope, 58, 63

Kerle, Jacob de, 61–62t., 65, 67
King's Noyse, The, 180–81n31, 204n26

La Chapelle, Jacques Anthoine de, 123, 196n66

La Croix du Maine, François de, 139–41, 144; *Bibliotheque*, 108, 139–41

La Grotte, Nicolas de, 118, 140–41, 147–49, 152; *Chansons de P. de Ronsard, Ph. Desportes, et autres*, 133, 141, 148, 151

La Hèle, George de, 62t., 66–67

"Laissez la verde couleur" (Saint-Gelais), 93–99, 150–51, 204n26

"Lamentations" (Carpentras), 37, 46, 49, 52–53fig., 54, 57t.

La Rue, Pierre de, 30, 42; manuscripts of his music, 56, 57t.

Lassus, Orlande de: authorial control of, 27–28, 129; in bibliographies, 140; chansonniers of, 136; *Magnum Opus Musicum*, 12; Milsom on, 83; *musica reservata* of, 69–70; print and, 12, 13; printed legacy of, 145; privileges of, 66, 118, 129; *Prophetiae Sibyllarum*, 69; publication of Masses of, 64; Seven Penitential Psalms, 69–70; sonnet cycles and, 128–29; unauthorized printing and, 71; Wilhelm V and, 51

La Vigne, Andre de, 88–89

Layolle, Francesco de, 39

La légende des Vénitiens (Lemaire de Belges), 89, 90

Lemaire de Belges, Jean, 89, 90; *La légende des Vénitiens*, 89, 90; *Temple d'honneur et de vertus*, 89

Le Noir, Michel, 88

Leo X, Pope, 30–31, 32fig., 33, 34–35, 50, 56

Le Roy, Adrian, 65, 69, 95, 157; *Livre d'airs de cour miz sur le luth*, 150, 151

Le Roy, Estienne, 147, 148, 150

Le Roy & Ballard, 136–38, 190n13, 196n66, 199n92, 202n14

Leuchtmann, Horst, 64

Liber quindecim missarum (Antico), 30–34, 32fig., 37–38, 169n22

Liber vesperarum (Guerrero), 62t., 64

line openings, 82

linguistic nationalism, 113

Livre d'airs de cour miz sur le luth (Le Roy), 150, 151

Louis XIV, 51, 149

Lully, Jean-Baptiste, 51

Luther, Martin, 13, 14

lyric authors: composers as, 74–84; Pléiade poets as, 72–74; printed publications and, 69–70; textual corruption and, 70–72

lyric economy: authorship and, 84–86; Marot and, 100–102; Pléiade poets and, 86–88, 90–99; *rhétoriqueurs* and, 88–90

Macé, Benedic, 82

Machaut, Guillaume de, 47–49, 140, 173n59

madrigals: authorship of, 16–17; early prints, 23–24; Petrarch and, 105

Magnum Opus Musicum (Lassus), 12

Maletty, Jean de, 122, 123t., 124

Manuscripts: Alamire, 50, 56; I-Rvat C. S. 44, 41; I-Rvat C. S. 45, 41; I-Rvat C. S. 163 (Carpentras), 52–53fig., 54–55; I-RVat Chigi C. VIII. 234 (Chigi Codex), 16, 46; Machaut, 47–49

Marot, Clément, 73, 100–102

Marot, Jean, 89–90

Masses, authorship of, 16, 42–55

Mauduit, Jacques, 147, 148

Meconi, Honey, 160n8

Mellange de chansons, 119

Milsom, John, 83

Missae tres (Arcadelt), 65

Missarum liber primus (Morales), 57t., 60, 61t., 63

Missarum liber primus (Palestrina), 13, 57–60, 61t.

Missarum liber secundus (Morales), 57t., 58, 61t., 63

Missarum musicalium . . . liber primus (Du Chemin), 41

Missarum musicalium . . . liber secundus (Du Chemin), 41

Misse Josquin (Petrucci): authorship of, 2–3; as first single-composer print, 42; publication of, 44; title page of, 43*fig.*

modal order, 120, 125–29, 194n53

Moderne, Jacques, 39, 58

Molinet, Jean, 89

Montaigne, Michel de, 193n42

Monte, Philippe de: publications of, 176n105; Ronsard and, 122, 124–25; as self-funded author, 65–66; *Sonetz de P. de Ronsard* (Monte), 123*t.*, 124–25

Morales, Cristóbal de: duplicate editions of, 71; *Missarum liber primus*, 60, 57*t.*, 61*t.*, 63; *Missarum liber secundus*, 58, 57*t.* 61*t.*, 63; publications of, 57*t.*, 58, 60–63; as self-funded author, 65–66, 176n102

motets: anthologies of, 21–22; as preferred genre under François Ier, 171n38

Muret, Marc-Antoine de, 109, 110*t.*

musica reservata, 69–70, 152

Musique de Guillaume Costeley (Costeley), 116–19, 121–22, 137*t.*, 147–48

musique de la chambre, 147, 149, 150

musique mesurée, 151–52

names, of authors, 4–5, 22–29, 71–72

notation: and culture of writing, 54; fame and, 161n17; as revelation of composer's intent, 7

Nouvelle Continuation des Amours (Ronsard), 114

Ockeghem, Jean de, 46

"O combien est heureuse" (Saint-Gelais), 93–94

Octo Missae (La Hèle), 62*t.*, 66–67

ode, *chanson* versus, 93–95

official "readers," 149

opera, 15, 70

Orgel, Stephen, 25

Palestrina, Giovanni Pierluigi da: cyclic settings of, 129; folio publications of, 61–64; printed legacy of, 145; as self-financed author, 65–66, 176n102. See also *Missarum liber primus* (Palestrina)

paper, 33, 169n23

partbooks: as industry standard, 20, 150; organization and use of, 7–10; of Petrucci, 54

Patrocinium musices (Berg), 61–63*t.*, 64

patronage: Carpentras and, 54–55; for folio choirbooks, 64–67; of Leo X, 30–31, 33, 34–35, 50; performance and, 50–51; Pléiade poets and, 87–88, 124; *rhétoriqueurs* and, 90

pecia system, 48

performance: authorship and, 146–58; fame and, 70; patronage and, 50–51; print and, 143–46

performers: composers as, 11, 50–51, 130–131, 148–49, 152–53; at the French court, 147–57; poets as, 91–93, 103–4, 150–51

Petrarch: *Les Amours* and, 113; influence of, 86–87; madrigal culture and, 105; "Non al suo amante," 182n46; publications of, 48; sonnets of, 105, 122. See also *Canzoniere* (Petrarch)

Petrucci, Ottaviano: Andrea Antico and, 33, 34, 35, 163n1; chanson anthologies of, 19, 21; Josquin des Prez and, 2–3; publications of, 19; single-composer prints of, 42–44, 54; sources of music of, 171n40. See also *Harmonice Musices Odhecaton A* (Petrucci); *Misse Josquin* (Petrucci)

Phalèse, Pierre, and Jean Bellère, 196n66

Philip II, King of Spain, 63, 66–67

Pindaric ode, 91, 95

Pirrotta, Nino, 49–50

Pisan, Christine de, 173n61

Planson, Jean, 152

Plantin, Christopher, 65, 66–67

play scripts, 25–26
Pléiade poets: authorship and, 85–86;
    linguistic nationalism and, 113;
    and mid-century lyric economy,
    86–88, 90–99; new poetics of,
    72–73; sonnets of, 86, 124;
    visibility of, 17
Le Poème Harmonique, 180–81n31
Porta, Costanzo, 62t., 65
portraits, of authors, 106fig., 107, 116,
    117fig.
Powers, Harold S., 120, 197n70
Preisig, Florian, 100, 101
*Primo libro di madrigali a quatro
    voci* (Arcadelt), 23, 75
print and printing: anonymity in, 4;
    of anthologies, 19–21; authorship
    and, 22–29, 85; of Bertrand and
    Boni works, 133; of Bertrand
    works, 135–36; chanson and, 74;
    culture of music books and,
    134–35; cultures of, 12–15; editors
    and craftsmen and, 30–42; Lassus
    and, 128–29; Marot and, 101–2; of
    Musique de Guillaume Costeley,
    116–19; performance and, 143–58;
    Pléiade poets and, 73, 91, 94–95;
    problems engendered by, 70–72;
    rhétoriqueurs and, 88, 90;
    Ronsard and, 115–16; Saint-Gelais
    and, 92
printer's marks, 45
Prise du Havre (Costeley), 121–22
privileges: given to Antico, 33–37,
    168n14, 169n22; given to Boni,
    118–19, 198–99n92; given to
    Festa, 56; given to Lassus, 27–28,
    66, 118; given to Montaigne,
    193n42; given to Ronsard, 28;
    given to Plantin, 66; technology
    and, 40
Prophetiae Sibyllarum (Lassus), 69
Prose della volgar lingua (Bembo),
    23, 105
"Puisque vivre en servitude"
    (Sandrin), 157

Les quatrains du Sieur de Pybrac
    (Boni), 133, 146, 158
Les quatre premiers livres des Odes
    (Ronsard), 87, 91, 93, 103, 105
Quickelberg, Samuel, 69–70

Rabelais, François, 13, 130
Rangouse, Jean de, 129
recueils de chansons, 95, 97fig., 98,
    101–102
Regnard, François, 195n57
Regnes, Nicole, 39
"reserved music." See *musica
    reservata*
rhétoriqueurs, 88–90
rhyme: musical, 79; Ronsard and,
    109–10, 153
Rodgers, Mark Allen, 196n65
Ronsard, Pierre de: authorial control
    of, 17–18, 28; bibliographies and,
    141, 142; books and career of, 86;
    culture of music books and,
    129–34; debt of, to earlier French
    song, 186n87; and lyric metaphor,
    72–73; and mid-century lyric
    economy, 87–88, 91–93; modern
    reception of, 104–5; portrait of,
    106fig.; printing privilege of, 28;
    print publication and, 143; Saint-
    Gelais and, 103–4; setting and
    performance of, 150. See also *Les
    Amours de P. de Ronsard* (Ronsard);
    "À sa lyre" (Ronsard); *Nouvelle
    Continuation des Amours*
    (Ronsard); *Les quatre premiers
    livres des Odes* (Ronsard)

Saint-Gelais, Mellin de: Arcadelt's
    setting of, 96, 98–99; Certon's
    setting of, 95–96, 98–99; Char-
    davoine's setting of, 95, 96, 97; Du
    Bellay's criticism of, 93–99, 100;
    Octavien de Saint-Gelais and,
    186n86; Ronsard and, 91–93, 103–4;
    Sandrin's setting of, 157; transition
    to Ronsard from, 17. See also

Saint-Gelais, Mellin de *(continued)*
"Laissez la verde couleur" (Saint-Gelais); "O combien est heureuse" (Saint-Gelais)
Saint-Gelais, Octavien de, 92, 186n86
Salmon, Jacques, 152
Sandrin, Pierre, 157
scores, before 1600, 8–9
Scotto, Girolamo, 19, 20, 74
Scotto, Ottaviano, 23, 37–38, 45, 189–90n13
scripts, play, 25–26
Sébillet, Thomas, 94
Second livre des Amours de P. de Ronsard (Bertrand), 123t., 128, 135–39
Sermisy, Claudin de, 76–84, 140; "Jouyssance vous donneray," 78–84, 111; "Tant que vivray," 77–78
Seven Penitential Psalms (Lassus), 69–70, 128
Shakespeare, William, 25–26
Simonin, Michel, 90, 91
Simpson, Christopher, 182n42
single-composer chansonniers, 73, 75–76, 116–18
single-composer prints: choirbooks and Masses as, 42–55; of Le Roy & Ballard, 202n14; stories behind, 55–68
single-impression printing, 19–20
Sistine Chapel, choirbooks of, 41
Sonetz de P. de Ronsard . . . Premier Livre (Boni), 123t., 130–33, 138–39
Sonetz de P. de Ronsard (Monte), 123t., 124–25
Sonetz de P. de Ronsard . . . Second Livre (Boni), 123t., 151
sonnet cycles, 122–29
sonnets: *airs de cour* and, 151; chansonniers based on Ronsard's, 123t.; of Petrarch, 105, 122; of Ronsard, 18, 109–11, 113–14

stretto fugues, 83
Supplément musical to *Les Amours* (Ronsard), 107, 109–15, 110t.

"Tant que vivray" (Sermisy), 77–78
technology, publishing business's reliance on, 39–40
Temple d'honneur et de vertus (Lemaire de Belges), 89
textual corruption, 26, 28, 48–49, 70–72, 101–102
Tinctoris, Johannes, 161n17
Tomlinson, Gary, 7
tonal types, 120
Toulouse, culture of music books in, 129–31
Tournes, Jean de, 184n59
tract volumes. *See* binder's volumes
Troisiesme livre de chansons (Bertrand), 135–36, 137–38t.
Tyard, Pontus de, 86, 127

upright formats for music books: octavo, 107; quarto, 35, 189–90n13

Vaumesnil, Guillaume de, 148, 150, 152
Venice, print and authorship in, 16–17, 22–24
Verdelot, Philippe, 23
vernacular books, 22, 130, 140, 200n107
Vickers, Nancy, 107
Victoria, Tomás Luis de, 62t., 64
voix de ville, 111–13, 150

Wilhelm V, Duke of Bavaria, 51, 64
Wistreich, Richard, 26, 166n26
work: concept of, 161n17; context and significance of, 10; defined, 7

Zorzi, Marino, 50